THE
MONSTER
MAKERS

Also edited by Peter Haining

THE GENTLEWOMEN OF EVIL
THE SATANISTS
A CIRCLE OF WITCHES
THE WILD NIGHT COMPANY
THE HOLLYWOOD NIGHTMARE
THE CLANS OF DARKNESS
GOTHIC TALES OF TERROR
THE LUCIFER SOCIETY
THE MAGICIANS
NIGHTFRIGHTS

By Peter Haining

THE ANATOMY OF WITCHCRAFT

THE MONSTER MAKERS

CREATORS AND CREATIONS OF FANTASY AND HORROR

Edited by Peter Haining

ILLUSTRATIONS BY DAVID SMEE

Taplinger Publishing Company | New York

First published in the United States in 1974 by
TAPLINGER PUBLISHING CO., INC.
New York, New York

Library of Congress Catalog Card Number: 74-1961

ISBN 0-8008-5324-5

ACKNOWLEDGEMENTS

The editor is grateful to the following authors, agents, and publishers for
permission to reproduce copyright material in this collection.

"The Plague Demon" by H. P. Lovecraft. Copyright 1922 by *Weird Tales;*
copyright renewed 1948 by Arkham House. Reproduced by permission of
the Scott Meredith Literary Agency.

"The Strange Island of Dr Nork" by Robert Bloch. Copyright 1942 by *Weird
Tales;* copyright renewed 1968 by Robert Bloch. Reproduced by permission of the Scott Meredith Literary Agency.

"It" by Theodore Sturgeon. Copyright 1940 by *Unknown;* copyright renewed 1956 by Theodore Sturgeon, and reproduced with the author's
permission.

"Lazarus II" by Richard Matheson. Copyright 1952 by Richard Matheson
for "Shock 2", and reproduced with his permission.

"The Golem" by Avram Davidson. Copyright 1952 by *Magazine of Fantasy
and Science Fiction,* and reproduced with their permission.

"Men of Iron" by Guy Endore. Copyright 1948 by *Magazine of Fantasy and
Science Fiction,* and reproduced by permission of the author.

"Changeling" by Ray Bradbury. Copyright 1949 by *Super Science Stories,*
and reproduced by permission of Harold Matson Literary Agency.

"Robot AL-76 Goes Astray" by Isaac Asimov. Copyright 1941, 1967 by
Doubleday & Company, Inc., and reproduced with their permission.

"Baby" by Carol Emshwiller, Copyright © 1962 by *Fantastic,* and reproduced by permission of the authoress.

SECOND PRINTING

For
PETER CUSHING
'Monster Maker Supreme'
—with admiration and much gratitude

'I saw the pale student of unhallowed arts kneeling beside the thing he had put together. I saw the hideous phantasm of a man stretched out, and then, on the working of some powerful engine, show signs of life, and stir with an uneasy, half vital motion. Frightful must it be; for supremely frightful would be the effect of any human endeavour to mock the stupendous mechanism of the Creator of the world.'

Mary Shelley

Contents

Editor's Introduction

"Ah, welcome to my secret laboratory, dear reader! Your visit is well-timed and all stands ready. The vats are on the boil, the chemicals are mixed in their test tubes and the machinery is just warming up. Darkness will lend us privacy and the moon will give us what extra light we may require. Our monster—oh excuse me, I mean our subject—is now assembled and prepared for the experiment to begin. See, he lies there on the table awaiting our attention.

"Now, please do not be frightened! Step a little closer while I lock and bolt the door. We don't want to be disturbed, do we? And if anything should go wrong, I might have need of your services . . .

"Are you paying careful attention? I see your eyes are a little wild and you seem to be trembling. But have no fear! I have worked and planned for years for this moment. You see my creature? Oh, the toil that has gone into his making! The endless hours of study and calculation, the trials and the errors, the successes and the failures. The nights I have wandered abroad collecting my raw material while those stupid peasants were asleep. They do not understand, the fools—they only fear me and try to stop my work! But they are too late now. Too late, I tell you! I have only to throw the switch on that machine and my creature will move and breathe as we do.

"So, are you ready? Do not back away! See I turn on the machine? The energy flows—the vats bubble—the electrodes glow—the sparks fly! He stirs, he moves! My creation lives!"

THAT was how I had planned to conduct this book. I was going to embrace the role of the 'mad scientist' and conduct you through a laboratory of creations from some of the greatest horror story writers. But I have found that monsters are serious business. That despite what at first might appear to be a subject full of madcap humour and clichés, there is much that is intriguing and only too close to reality. Indeed, ever since 1816 when Mary Shelley began the tradition of the 'monster maker' in fiction with 'Frankenstein', there have been so many good and ingenious tales that to treat them all as a joke would be an insult to their creators.

What this collection sets out to do is simple. Beginning with 'Frankenstein', it follows the development of the man-made monsters, the flesh and blood of the early experimenters, through to the automatons and to the robots of today and tomorrow. It shows how some fine writers, in both Britain and America, have taken the basic concept and developed and expanded it into thought-provoking and entertaining stories. For it is the function of the horror story to be entertaining, in a world which already has too much real horror. It was Aristotle, the famous Greek philosopher, who remarked that it was the basic function of drama to 'fill an audience with terror so as to cleanse its emotions'. That is also what this book is really about.

The tradition of the 'monster makers' is a very long one. In the Greek myths, Prometheus the Titan stole heavenly fire from the gods to infuse life into the man he had created from fire, water, earth and air. (It is interesting to note, by the way, that Mary Shelley subtitled her novel, 'Frankenstein, or The Modern Prometheus'). In 'The Iliad' Thetis visits the God Hephaistos in his smithy, to find him attended by two maidens 'made of gold exactly like living girls . . . who have sense in their heads and can speak and use their muscles.' Later, the European Alchemists of the Middle Ages experimented with the creation of living beings (some of their contemporaries, the witches, said they could actually make them) and certain African legends speak of 'men who were the making of sorcerers and did their bidding'.

The time period of this collection, however, is a mere 150 years—from the creation of 'Frankenstein'. It is unfortunate that space and availability have made it impossible to include stories beyond the confines of Britain and America, for there is much of interest to be found elsewhere. In Russia, for example, apart from the tales of classic writers such as Gogol and Turgenev, modern authors like Ilya Varshavsky are keeping up the tradition; in France Jules Verne wrote of 'Master Zacharius', the maker of mechanical marvels, and the Comte de Villiers De L'Isle Adam created a masterpiece with his 'L'Eve Future'; in Germany there is the automaton woman in 'The Sandman' by E. T. W. Hoffmann; and so on through Scandinavia, the Far East and even China and Japan. But limits had to be drawn somewhere and repetition had to be avoided. I could go on at some length listing all the other stories on this theme which I read and enjoyed, but had in the end to discard, but the enthusiastic reader will doubtless search for other stories himself if he is not satiated with monsters by the end of this book.

Interest in the tradition still remains as strong as ever— one has only to turn to films, television, magazines, comics and even records, to find evidence of this—but now fact seems likely to be catching up with fiction. In the early summer of 1973 the newspapers are reporting that scientists are on the verge of perfecting a 'household robot' that will take care of all the drudgery of modern living. If that seems like the ultimate passport to happiness, defer your judgement until you have read what contributors to this collection have to say on the matter.

So there, in a nutshell, you have it: the form and purpose of the book. But, as I intimated at the begining, there will be no mad scientist to conduct you through its pages—just his sinister presence hovering over your shoulder.

Peter Haining

THE
MONSTER
MAKERS

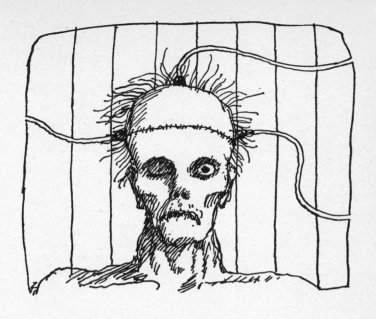

THE MONSTER LIVES!

Mary Shelley

(1797–1851)

*The story of the "Mad Scientist" and his quest to create "life" begins
with Mary Shelley's classic horror novel, "Frankenstein", first published in 1816. Although there are fables of man-made creatures
and the dead who walked again, dating back to the earliest times,
it was the beautiful teenage wife of the poet Shelley who really began
the tradition in fiction. The ghost story writer, M. K. Joseph, has
described the importance of her work succinctly: "Mary Shelley
wrote in the infancy of modern science when its enormous possibilities were just beginning to be foreseen by imaginative writers like*

Byron and Shelley. . . . At the age of nineteen she achieved the quietly astonishing feat of looking beyond them and creating a lasting symbol of the perils of scientific experiments to create life." Mary in fact wrote her masterpiece under the influence of Byron and Shelley when they were neighbours in Switzerland. The two poets and their companions decided to pass the days of a particularly wet summer by each writing a ghost or horror story. Mary was some time in finding inspiration, but after a dream in which she saw a scientist creating a monster, she put pen to paper and totally eclipsed the efforts of all the others. Her original intention had been to write a short story, but when Shelley read her work, he encouraged her to develop it into a book of several parts, including the scientist, Dr. Frankenstein, telling his side of the story, and the monster describing his experiences. The resulting volume has proved itself an enduring classic, been translated into almost every language and made into films, television plays and radio broadcasts. This collection begins, then, with the opening of Chapter 5 of Mary Shelley's book. In its completeness one can easily see why she originally believed her tale need only consist of "a few terrifying pages to haunt the midnight pillow".

IT was on a dreary night of November that I beheld the accomplishment of my toils. With an anxiety that almost amounted to agony, I collected the instruments of life around me, that I might infuse a spark of being into the lifeless thing that lay at my feet. It was already one in the morning; the rain pattered dismally against the panes, and my candle was nearly burnt out, when, by the glimmer of the half-extinguished light, I saw the dull yellow eye of the creature open; it breathed hard, and a convulsive motion agitated its limbs.

How can I describe my emotions at this catastrophe, or how delineate the wretch whom with such infinite pains and care I had endeavoured to form? His limbs were in proportion, and I had selected his features as beautiful. Beautiful!—Great God! His yellow skin scarcely covered the work of muscles and arteries beneath; his hair was of a lustrous black, and flowing; his teeth of a pearly whiteness; but these luxuriances only formed a more horrid contrast with his watery eyes, that seemed almost of the same colour as the dun white sockets in which they were set, his shrivelled complexion and straight black lips.

The different accidents of life are not so changeable as the feelings of human nature. I had worked hard for nearly two years, for the sole purpose of infusing life into an inanimate body. For this I had deprived myself of rest and health. I had desired it with an ardour that far exceeded moderation; but now that I had finished, the beauty of the dream vanished, and breathless horror and disgust filled my heart. Unable to endure the aspect of the being I had created, I rushed out of the room, and continued a long time traversing my bedchamber, unable to compose my mind to sleep. At length lassitude succeeded to the tumult I had before endured; and I threw myself on the bed in my clothes, endeavouring to seek a few moments of forgetfulness. But it was in vain: I slept, indeed, but I was disturbed by the wildest dreams. I thought I saw Elizabeth, in the bloom of health, walking in the streets of Ingolstadt. Delighted and surprised, I embraced her; but as I imprinted the first kiss on her lips, they became livid with the hue of death; her features appeared to change, and I thought that I held the corpse of my dead mother in my arms; a shroud enveloped her form, and I saw the grave-worms crawling in the folds of the flannel. I started from my sleep with horror; a cold dew covered my forehead, my teeth chattered, and every limb became convulsed: when, by the dim and yellow light of the moon, as it forced its way through the window shutters, I beheld the wretch—the miserable monster whom I had created. He held up the curtain of the bed; and his eyes, if eyes they may be called, were fixed on me. His jaws opened, and he muttered some inarticulate sounds, while a grin wrinkled his cheeks. He might have spoken, but I did not hear; one hand was stretched out, seemingly to detain me, but I escaped, and rushed down the stairs. I took refuge in the courtyard belonging to the house which I inhabited; where I remained during the rest of the night, walking up and down in the greatest agitation, listening attentively, catching and fearing each sound as if it were to announce the approach of the demoniacal corpse to which I had so miserably given life.

Oh! no mortal could support the horror of that countenance. A mummy again endued with animation could not be so hideous as that wretch. I had gazed on him while unfinished; he was ugly then; but when those muscles and joints were rendered capable of motion, it became a thing such as even Dante could not have conceived.

I passed the night wretchedly. Sometimes my pulse beat so quickly and hardly that I felt the palpitation of every artery; at others, I nearly sank to the ground through languor and extreme weakness. Mingled with this horror, I felt the bitterness of disappointment; dreams that had been my food and pleasant rest for so long a space were now become a hell to me; and the change was so rapid, the overthrow so complete!

Morning, dismal and wet, at length dawned, and discovered to my sleepless and aching eyes the church of Ingolstadt, its white steeple and clock, which indicated the sixth hour. The porter opened the gates of the court, which had that night been my asylum, and I issued into the streets, pacing them with quick steps, as if I sought to avoid the wretch whom I feared every turning of the street would present to my view. I did not dare return to the apartment which I inhabited, but felt impelled to hurry on, although drenched by the rain which poured from a black and comfortless sky.

I continued walking in this manner for some time, endeavouring, by bodily exercise, to ease the load that weighed upon my mind. I traversed the streets, without any clear

conception of where I was, or what I was doing. My heart
palpitated in the sickness of fear; and I hurried on with
irregular steps, not daring to look about me :—

> *"Like one who, on a lonely road,*
> *Doth walk in fear and dread,*
> *And, having once turned round, walks on,*
> *And turns no more his head ;*
> *Because he knows a frightful fiend*
> *Doth close behind him tread."*[1]

Continuing thus, I came at length opposite to the inn at
which the various diligences and carriages usually stopped.
Here I paused, I knew not why; but I remained some
minutes with my eyes fixed on a coach that was coming
towards me from the other end of the street. As it drew
nearer, I observed that it was the Swiss diligence : it stopped
just where I was standing, and, on the door being opened,
I perceived Henry Clerval, who, on seeing me, instantly
sprung out. 'My dear Frankenstein,' exclaimed he, 'how
glad I am to see you ! how fortunate that you should be here
at the very moment of my alighting !'

Nothing could equal my delight on seeing Clerval; his
presence brought back to my thoughts my father, Elizabeth,
and all those scenes of home so dear to my recollection. I
grasped his hand, and in a moment forgot my horror and
misfortune; I felt suddenly, and for the first time during
many months, calm and serene joy. I welcomed my friend,
therefore, in the most cordial manner, and we walked towards my college. Clerval continued talking for some time
about our mutual friends, and his own good fortune in being
permitted to come to Ingolstadt. 'You may easily believe,'
said he, 'how great was the difficulty to persuade my father
that all necessary knowledge was not compromised in the
noble art of book-keeping; and, indeed, I believe I left him

---

[1] Coleridge's *Ancient Mariner*.

incredulous to the last, for his constant answer to my un-
wearied entreaties was the same as that of the Dutch schoolmaster in the *Vicar of Wakefield*:—"I have ten thousand
florins a year without Greek, I eat heartily without Greek."
But his affection for me at length overcame his dislike of
learning, and he has permitted me to undertake a voyage
of discovery to the land of knowledge.'

'It gives me the greatest delight to see you; but tell me
how you left my father, brothers, and Elizabeth.'

'Very well, and very happy, only a little uneasy that they
hear from you so seldom. By the by, I mean to lecture you a
little upon their account myself.—But, my dear Frankenstein,' continued he, stopping short, and gazing full in my
face, 'I did not before remark how very ill you appear; so
thin and pale; you look as if you had been watching for
several nights.'

'You have guessed right; I have lately been so deeply
engaged in one occupation that I have not allowed myself
sufficient rest, as you see: but I hope, I sincerely hope, that
all these employments are now at an end, and that I am
at length free.'

I trembled excessively; I could not endure to think of,
and far less to allude to, the occurrences of the preceding
night. I walked with a quick pace, and we soon arrived at
my college. I then reflected, and the thought made me
shiver, that the creature whom I had left in my apartment
might still be there, alive, and walking about. I dreaded to
behold this monster; but I feared still more that Henry
should see him. Entreating him, therefore, to remain a few
minutes at the bottom of the stairs, I darted up towards my
own room. My hand was already on the lock of the door
before I recollected myself. I then paused; and a cold shivering came over me. I threw the door forcibly open, as children
are accustomed to do when they expect a spectre to stand
in waiting for them on the other side; but nothing appeared.
I stepped fearfully in: the apartment was empty; and my

bedroom was also freed from its hideous guest. I could hardly believe that so great a good fortune could have befallen me; but when I became assured that my enemy had indeed fled, I clapped my hands for joy, and ran down to Clerval.

We ascended into my room, and the servant presently brought breakfast; but I was unable to contain myself. It was not joy only that possessed me; I felt my flesh tingle with excess of sensitiveness, and my pulse beat rapidly. I was unable to remain for a single instant in the same place; I jumped over the chairs, clapped my hands, and laughed aloud. Clerval at first attributed my unusual spirits to joy on his arrival; but when he observed me more attentively he saw a wildness in my eyes for which he could not account; and my loud, unrestrained, heartless laughter, frightened and astonished him.

'My dear Victor,' cried he, 'what, for God's sake, is the matter? Do not laugh in that manner. How ill you are! What is the cause of all this?'

'Do not ask me,' cried I, putting my hands before my eyes, for I thought I saw the dreaded spectre glide into the room; '*he* can tell.—Oh, save me! save me!' I imagined that the monster seized me; I struggled furiously, and fell down in a fit.

Poor Clerval! what must have been his feelings? A meeting, which he anticipated with such joy, so strangely turned to bitterness. But I was not the witness of his grief; for I was lifeless, and did not recover my senses for a long, long time.

This was the commencement of a nervous fever, which confined me for several months. During all that time Henry was my only nurse. I afterwards learned that, knowing my father's advanced age, and unfitness for so long a journey, and how wretched my sickness would make Elizabeth, he spared them this grief by concealing the extent of my disorder. He knew that I could not have a more kind and attentive nurse than himself; and, firm in the hope he felt of my recovery, he did not doubt that, instead of doing harm, he performed the kindest action that he could towards them.

But I was in reality very ill; and surely nothing but the unbounded and unremitting attentions of my friend could have restored me to life. The form of the monster on whom I had bestowed existence was for ever before my eyes, and I raved incessantly concerning him. Doubtless my words surprised Henry: he at first believed them to be the wanderings of my disturbed imagination; but the pertinacity with which I continually recurred to the same subject, persuaded him that my disorder indeed owed its origin to some uncommon and terrible event.

By very slow degrees, and with frequent relapses that alarmed and grieved my friend, I recovered. I remember the first time I became capable of observing outward objects with any kind of pleasure, I perceived that the fallen leaves had disappeared, and that the young buds were shooting forth from the trees that shaded my window. It was a divine spring; and the season contributed greatly to my convalescence. I felt also sentiments of joy and affection revive in my bosom. But still, on the occasion, thoughts of the monster returned to me and I knew that soon I must set out to find what had become of the terrible creation of my hands. . . .

THE FACTS OF M. VALDEMAR'S CASE

Edgar Allan Poe

(1809–1849)

Perhaps only the complete works of Edgar Allan Poe can be said to equal Mary Shelley's masterpiece. Like her, his stories have endured the passing years and he is still just as eagerly received and enjoyed by each new generation. He, too, was much intrigued by scientific discoveries and from his American viewpoint he released the horror story from many of the restrictions and conventions of the Gothic period which was just ending. Poe can definitely be said to have created the Detective Story as we know it today, and in his handling of the macabre tale he created a style which subsequently became the pattern for all such tales. A strange recluse, drawn to the dreary and the dismal by his own sad life, he wrote several stories dealing with unholy experimentation. "The Facts of M. Valdemar's Case" is one of the best of these. It was published in New York in 1846 and is clearly in the tradition of "Frankenstein". Poe had been studying the art of mesmerism for some years (he had written an article "Mesmeric Revelation" in 1844) and in the story he describes how a dying man is hypnotised and then questioned about life after death. From here the plot builds to a horrifying climax. It is interesting to note that when the story was republished in England as a threepenny pamphlet, its scientific approach and convincing reality made many people believe it was completely true!

OF course I shall not pretend to consider it any matter for wonder that the extraordinary case of M. Valdemar has excited discussion. It would have been a miracle had it not—especially under the circumstances. Through the desire of all parties concerned to keep the affair from the public, at least for the present, or until we had further opportunities for investigation—through our endeavours to effect this—a garbled or exaggerated account made its way into society and became the source of many unpleasant misrepresentations; and, very naturally, of a great deal of disbelief.

It is now rendered necessary that I give the *facts*—as far as I comprehend them myself. They are, succinctly, these:

My attention for the last three years had been repeatedly drawn to the subject of Mesmerism; and about nine months ago it occurred to me, quite suddenly, that in the series of experiments made hitherto there had been a very remarkable and most unaccountable omission:—no person had as yet been mesmerised *in articulo mortis*. It remained to be seen, first, whether, in such condition, there existed in the patient any susceptibility to the magnetic influence: secondly, whether, if any existed, it was impaired or increased by the condition; thirdly, to what extent, or for how long a period, the encroachments of Death might be arrested by the process. There were other points to be ascertained, but these most excited my curiosity—the last in especial, from the immensely important character of its consequences.

In looking around me for some subject by whose means I might test these particulars, I was brought to think of my friend, M. Ernest Valdemar, the well-known compiler of the 'Bibliotheca Forensica', and author (under the *nom de plume* of 'Issachar Marx') of the Polish versions of 'Wallenstein' and 'Gargantua'. M. Valdemar, who has resided principally at Harlem, N.Y., since the year 1839, is (or was) particularly noticeable for the extreme spareness of his person—his lower limbs much resembling those of John Randolph; and also for the whiteness of his whiskers, in violent contrast to the blackness of his hair—the latter, in consequence, being very generally mistaken for a wig. His temperament was markedly nervous, and rendered him a good subject for mesmeric experiment. On two or three occasions I had put him to sleep with little difficulty, but was disappointed in other results which his peculiar constitution had naturally led me to anticipate. His will was at no period positively or thoroughly under my control, and in regard to *clairvoyance*, I could accomplish with him nothing to be relied upon. I always attributed my failure at these points to the disordered state of his health. For some months previous to my becoming acquainted with him his physicians had declared him in a confirmed phthisis. It was his custom, indeed, to speak calmly of his approaching dissolution as of a matter neither to be avoided nor regretted.

When the ideas to which I have alluded first occurred to me, it was of course very natural that I should think of M. Valdemar. I knew the steady philosophy of the man too well to apprehend any scruples from *him*; and he had no relatives in America who would be likely to interfere. I spoke to him frankly upon the subject, and to my surprise his interest seemed vividly excited. I say to my surprise; for, although he had always yielded his person freely to my experiments, he had never before given me any tokens of sympathy with what I did. His disease was of that character which would admit of exact calculation in respect to the epoch of its termination in death; and it was finally arranged between us that he would send for me about twenty-four hours before the period announced by his physicians as that of his decease.

It is now rather more than seven months since I received, from M. Valdemar himself, the subjoined note:

'My Dear P—,

'You may as well come *now*. D— and F— are agreed that I cannot hold out beyond tomorrow midnight; and I think they have hit the time very nearly.

Valdemar.'

I received this note within half-an-hour after it was written, and in fifteen minutes more I was in the dying man's chamber. I had not seen him for ten days, and was appalled by the fearful alteration which the brief interval had wrought in him. His face wore a leaden hue; the eyes were utterly lustreless; and the emaciation was so extreme that the skin had been broken through by the cheek-bones. His expectoration was excessive. The pulse was barely perceptible. He retained, nevertheless, in a very remarkable manner, both his mental power and a certain degree of physical strength. He spoke with distinctness—took some palliative medicines without aid—and, when I entered the room, was occupied in pencilling memoranda in a pocket-book. He was propped up in the bed by pillows. Doctors D— and F— were in attendance.

After pressing Valdemar's hand, I took these gentlemen aside, and obtained from them a minute account of the patient's condition. The left lung had been for eighteen months in a semiosseous or cartilaginous state, and was of course entirely useless for all purposes of vitality. The right, in its upper portion, was also partially if not thoroughly ossified, while the lower region was merely a mass of purulent

tubercles running one into another. Several extensive per-
forations existed, and at one point permanent adhesion to
the ribs had taken place. These appearances in the right lobe
were of comparatively recent date. The ossification had proceeded with very unusual rapidity; no sign of it had been
discovered a month before, and the adhesion had only been
observed during the three previous days. Independently of
the phthisis, the patient was suspected of aneurism of the
aorta; but on this point the osseous symptoms rendered an
exact diagnosis impossible. It was the opinion of both
physicians that M. Valdemar would die about midnight on
the morrow (Sunday). It was then seven o'clock on Saturday
evening.

On quitting the invalid's bedside to hold conversation
with myself, Doctors D— and F— had bidden him a final
farewell. It had not been their intention to return; but, at
my request, they agreed to look in upon the patient about
ten the next night.

When they had gone, I spoke freely with M. Valdemar
on the subject of his approaching dissolution, as well as,
more particularly, of the experiment proposed. He still
professed himself quite willing and even anxious to have it
made, and urged me to commence it at once. A male and a
female nurse were in attendance; but I did not feel myself
altogether at liberty to engage in a task of this character
with no more reliable witnesses than these people, in case
of sudden accident, might prove. I therefore postponed
operations until about eight the next night, when the arrival
of a medical student, with whom I had some acquaintance,
(Mr. Theodore L—l), relieved me from further embarrass-
ment. It had been my design, originally, to wait for the
physicians; but I was induced to proceed, first, by the urgent
entreaties of M. Valdemar, and secondly, by my conviction
that I had not a moment to lose, as he was evidently sinking
fast.

Mr. L—l was so kind as to accede to my desire that he

would take notes of all that occurred: and it is from his memoranda that what I now have to relate is, for the most part, either condensed or copied *verbatim*.

It wanted about five minutes of eight when, taking the patient's hand, I begged him to state, as distinctly as he could, to Mr. L—l, whether he (M. Valdemar) was entirely willing that I should make the experiment of mesmerising him in his then condition.

He replied feebly, yet quite audibly, 'Yes, I wish to be mesmerised'—adding immediately afterwards, 'I fear you have deferred it too long.'

While he spoke thus, I commenced the passes which I had already found most effectual in subduing him. He was evidently influenced with the first lateral stroke of my hand across his forehead; but although I exerted all my powers, no further perceptible effect was induced until some minutes after ten o'clock, when Doctors D— and F— called, according to appointment. I explained to them in a few words what I designed, and as they opposed no objection, saying that the patient was already in the death agony, I proceeded without hesitation—exchanging, however, the lateral passes for downward ones, and directing my gaze entirely into the right eye of the sufferer.

By this time his pulse was imperceptible and his breathing was stertorous, and at intervals of half-a-minute.

This condition was nearly unaltered for a quarter of an hour. At the expiration of this period, however, a natural although a very deep sigh escaped the bosom of the dying man, and the stertorous breathing ceased—that is to say, its stertorousness was no longer apparent; the intervals were undiminished. The patient's extremities were of an icy coldness.

At five minutes before eleven I perceived unequivocal signs of the mesmeric influence. The glassy roll of the eye was changed for that expression of uneasy *inward* examination which is never seen except in cases of sleep-waking, and which it is quite impossible to mistake. With a few rapid lateral passes I made the lids quiver, as in incipient sleep, and with a few more I closed them altogether. I was not satisfied, however, with this, but continued the manipulations vigorously, and with the fullest exertion of the will, until I had completely stiffened the limbs of the slumberer, after placing them in a seemingly easy position. The legs were at full length; the arms were nearly so, and reposed on the bed at a moderate distance from the loins. The head was very slightly elevated.

When I had accomplished this it was fully midnight, and I requested the gentlemen present to examine M. Valdemar's condition. After a few experiments, they admitted him to be in an unusually perfect state of mesmeric trance. The curiosity of both the physicians was greatly excited. Dr. D— resolved at once to remain with the patient all night, while Dr. F— took leave with a promise to return at daybreak. Mr. L—l and the nurses remained.

We left M. Valdemar entirely undisturbed until about three o'clock in the morning, when I approached him and found him in precisely the same condition as when Dr. F— went away—that is to say, he lay in the same position; the pulse was imperceptible; the breathing was gentle (scarcely noticeable, unless through the application of a mirror to the lips); the eyes were closed naturally; and the limbs were as rigid and as cold as marble. Still, the general appearance was certainly not that of death.

As I approached M. Valdemar I made a kind of half-effort to influence his right arm into pursuit of my own, as I passed the latter gently to and fro above his person. In such experiments with this patient, I had never perfectly succeeded before, and assuredly I had little thought of succeeding now; but, to my astonishment, his arm very readily, although feebly, followed every direction I assigned it with mine. I determined to hazard a few words of conversation.

'M. Valdemar,' I said, 'are you asleep?' He made no

answer, but I perceived a tremor about the lips, and was thus induced to repeat the question, again and again. At this third repetition, his whole frame was agitated by a very slight shivering: the eyelids unclosed themselves so far as to display a white line of a ball; the lips moved sluggishly, and from between them, in a barely audible whisper, issued the words:

'Yes;—asleep now. Do not wake me!—let me die so!'

I here felt the limbs, and found them as rigid as ever. The right arm, as before, obeyed the direction of my hand. I questioned the sleep-waker again:

'Do you still feel pain in the breast, M. Valdemar?'

The answer now was immediate, but even less audible than before:

'No pain—I am dying.'

I did not think it advisable to disturb him further just then, and nothing more was said or done until the arrival of Dr. F—, who came a little before sunrise, and expressed unbounded astonishment at finding the patient still alive. After feeling the pulse and applying a mirror to the lips he requested me to speak to the sleep-waker again. I did so, saying:

'M. Valdemar, do you still sleep?'

As before, some minutes elapsed ere a reply was made; and during the interval the dying man seemed to be collecting his energies to speak. At my fourth repetition of the question, he said very faintly, almost inaudibly:

'Yes, still asleep—dying.'

It was now the opinion, or rather the wish, of the physicians, that M. Valdemar should be suffered to remain undisturbed in his present apparently tranquil condition until death should supervene; and this, it was generally agreed, must now take place within a few minutes. I concluded, however, to speak to him once more, and merely repeated my previous question.

While I spoke, there came a marked change over the

countenance of the sleep-waker. The eyes rolled themselves slowly open, the pupils disappearing upwardly; the skin generally assumed a cadaverous hue, resembling not so much parchment as white paper: and the circular hectic spots, which hitherto had been strongly defined in the centre of each cheek, *went out* at once. I use this expression, because the suddenness of their departure put me in mind of nothing so much as the extinguishment of a candle by a puff of the breath. The upper lip, at the same time, writhed itself away from the teeth, which it had previously covered completely; while the lower jaw fell with an audible jerk, leaving the mouth widely extended, and disclosing in full view the swollen and blackened tongue. I presume that no member of the party then present had been unaccustomed to death-bed horrors; but so hideous beyond conception was the appearance of M. Valdemar at this moment, that there was a general shrinking back from the region of the bed.

I now feel that I have reached a point of this narrative at which every reader will be startled into positive disbelief. It is my business, however, simply to proceed.

There was no longer the faintest sign of vitality in M. Valdemar; and, concluding him to be dead, we were con-signing him to the charge of the nurses, when a strong vibra-tory motion was observable in the tongue. This continued for perhaps a minute. At the expiration of this period, there issued from the distended and motionless jaws a voice— such as it would be madness in me to attempt describing. There are, indeed, two or three epithets which might be considered as applicable to it in part; I might say, for example, that the sound was harsh, and broken and hollow; but the hideous whole is indescribable, for the simple reason that no similar sounds have ever jarred upon the ear of humanity. There were two particulars, nevertheless, which I thought then, and still think, might fairly be stated as characteristic of the intonation—as well adapted to convey some idea of its unearthly peculiarity. In the first place, the voice seemed to reach our ears—at least mine—from a vast distance, or from some deep cavern within the earth. In the second place, it impressed me (I fear, indeed, that it will be impossible to make myself comprehended) as gelatinous or glutinous matters impress the sense of touch.

I have spoken both of 'sound' and of 'voice'. I mean to say that the sound was one of distinct—of even wonderfully thrillingly distinct syllabification. M. Valdemar spoke— obviously in reply to the question I had propounded to him a few minutes before. I had asked him, it will be remembered, if he still slept. He now said:

'Yes;—no;—I *have been* sleeping—and now—now—I *am dead.*'

No person present even affected to deny, or attempted to repress, the unutterable, shuddering horror which these few words, thus uttered, were so well calculated to convey. Mr. L—l (the student) swooned. The nurses immediately left the chamber, and could not be induced to return. My own impressions I would not pretend to render intelligible to the reader. For nearly an hour we busied ourselves, silently —without the utterance of a word—in endeavours to revive Mr. L—l. When he came to himself we addressed ourselves again to an investigation of M. Valdermar's condition.

It remained in all respects as I have last described it, with the exception that the mirror no longer afforded evidence of respiration. An attempt to draw blood from the arm failed. I should mention, too, that this limb was no further subject to my will. I endeavoured in vain to make it follow the direction of my hand. The only real indication, indeed, of the mesmeric influence was now found in the vibratory movement of the tongue, whenever I addressed M. Valdemar a question. He seemed to be making an effort to reply, but had no longer sufficient volition. To queries put to him by any other person than myself he seemed utterly insensible— although I endeavoured to place each member of the company in mesmeric *rapport* with him. I believe that I have now related all that is necessary to an understanding of the sleep-waker's state at this epoch. Other nurses were procured; and at ten o'clock I left the house in company with the two physicians and Mr. L—l.

In the afternoon we all called again to see the patient. His condition remained precisely the same. We had now some discussion as to the propriety and feasibility of awakening him; but we had little difficulty in agreeing that no good purpose would be served by so doing. It was evident that, so far, death (or what is usually termed death) had been arrested by the mesmeric process. It seemed clear to us all that to awaken M. Valdemar would be merely to insure his instant, or at least his speedy dissolution.

From this period until the close of last week—*an interval of nearly seven months*—we continued to make daily calls at M. Valdemar's house, accompanied now and then by medical and other friends. All this time the sleep-waker remained *exactly* as I have last described him. The nurses' attentions were continual.

It was on Friday last that we finally resolved to make the experiment of awakening, or attempting to awaken him; and it is the (perhaps) unfortunate result of this latter experiment which has given rise to so much discussion in private circles—to so much of what I cannot help thinking unwarranted popular feeling.

For the purpose of relieving M. Valdemar from the mesmeric trance, I made use of the customary passes. These, for a time, were unsuccessful. The first indication of revival was afforded by a partial descent of the iris. It was observed, as especially remarkable, that this lowering of the pupil was accompanied by the profuse out-flowing of a yellowish ichor (from beneath the lids) of a pungent and highly offensive odour.

It was now suggested that I should attempt to influence the patient's arm, as heretofore. I made the attempt and failed. Dr. F— then intimated a desire to have me put a question. I did so, as follows:

'M. Valdemar, can you explain to us what are your feelings or wishes now?'

There was an instant return of the hectic circles on the cheeks: the tongue quivered, or rather rolled violently in the mouth (although the jaws and lips remained rigid as before); and at length the same hideous voice which I have already described, broke forth:

'For God's sake!—quick!—quick!—put me to sleep—or, quick!—waken me!—quick—*I say to you that I am dead!*'

I was thoroughly unnerved, and for an instant remained undecided what to do. At first I made an endeavour to recompose the patient; but, failing in this through total abeyance of the will, I retraced my steps and as earnestly struggled to awaken him. In this attempt I soon saw that I should be successful—or at least I soon fancied that my success would be complete; and I am sure that all in the room were prepared to see the patient awaken.

For what really occurred, however, it is quite impossible that any human being could have been prepared.

As I rapidly made the mesmeric passes, amid ejaculations of 'dead! dead!' absolutely *bursting* from the tongue and not from the lips of the sufferer, his whole frame at once—within the space of a single minute, or even less, shrunk—crumbled—absolutely *rotted* away beneath my hands. Upon the bed, before that whole company, there lay a nearly liquid mass of loathsome—of detestable putrescence.

THE DANCING PARTNER

Jerome K. Jerome

(1859—1927)

One of the first modern writers to develop the theme of robots was, rather surprisingly, the English humorist, Jerome K. Jerome. Famous throughout the world for his great comic novel, "Three Men In A Boat" (1889), Jerome claimed that "The Dancing Partner" was nothing more than a piece of sheer inspiration. However, it showed how this new "monster" could be adapted for man's pleasure, or at least harnessed for his pleasure; the sting is in the tail. Jerome had various occupations, including schoolmaster, clerk and actor, before turning to journalism; he was first joint editor of the popular humorist magazine "The Idler" (in which "The Dancing Partner" first appeared in 1893) and then started his own journal "To-day".

Apart from his classic novel of the boat cruise, he also wrote "The Idle Thoughts of an Idle Fellow" (1889), several plays, and some short stories—of which this must be accounted one of the best.

'THIS story,' commenced MacShaugnassy, 'comes from Furtwangen, a small town in the Black Forest. There lived there a very wonderful old fellow named Nicholaus Geibel. His business was the making of mechanical toys, at which work he had acquired an almost European reputation. He made rabbits that would emerge from the heart of a cabbage, flop their ears, smooth their whiskers, and disappear again; cats that would wash their faces, and mew so naturally that dogs would mistake them for real cats, and fly at them; dolls, with phonographs concealed within them, that would raise their hats and say, "Good morning; how do you do?" and some that would even sing a song.

'But he was something more than a mere mechanic; he was an artist. His work was with him a hobby, almost a passion. His shop was filled with all manner of strange things that never would, or could, be sold—things he had made for the pure love of making them. He had contrived a mechanical donkey that would trot for two hours by means of stored electricity, and trot, too, much faster than the live article, and with less need for exertion on the part of the driver; a bird that would shoot up into the air, fly round and round in a circle, and drop to earth at the exact spot from where it started; a skeleton that, supported by an upright iron bar, would dance a hornpipe; a life-size lady doll that could play the fiddle; and a gentleman with a hollow inside who could smoke a pipe and drink more lager beer than any three average German students put together, which is saying much.

'Indeed, it was the belief of the town that old Geibel could make a man capable of doing everything that a respectable man need want to do. One day he made a man who did too much, and it came about in this way:

'Young Doctor Follen had a baby, and the baby had a birthday. Its first birthday put Doctor Follen's household into somewhat of a flurry, but on the occasion of its second birthday, Mrs. Doctor Follen gave a ball in honour of the event. Old Geibel and his daughter Olga were among the guests.

'During the afternoon of the next day some three or four of Olga's bosom friends, who had also been present at the ball, dropped in to have a chat about it. They naturally fell to discussing the men, and to criticising their dancing. Old Geibel was in the room, but he appeared to be absorbed in his newspaper, and the girls took no notice of him.

' "There seem to be fewer men who can dance at every ball you go to," said one of the girls.

' "Yes, and don't the ones who can give themselves airs," said another; "they make quite a favour of asking you."

' "And how stupidly they talk," added a third. "They always say exactly the same things: 'How charming you are looking to-night.' 'Do you often go to Vienna? Oh, you should, it's delightful.' 'What a charming dress you have on.' 'What a warm day it has been.' 'Do you like Wagner?' I do wish they'd think of something new."

' "Oh, I never mind how they talk," said a fourth. "If a man dances well he may be a fool for all I care."

' "He generally is," slipped in a thin girl, rather spitefully.

' "I go to a ball to dance," continued the previous speaker, not noticing the interruption. "All I ask of a partner is that he shall hold me firmly, take me round steadily, and not get tired before I do."

' "A clockwork figure would be the thing for you," said the girl who had interrupted.

' "Bravo!" cried one of the others, clapping her hands, "what a capital idea!"

' "What's a capital idea?" they asked.

' "Why, a clockwork dancer, or, better still, one that would go by electricity and never run down."

' The girls took up the idea with enthusiasm.

' "Oh, what a lovely partner he would make," said one; "he would never kick you, or tread on your toes."

'Or tear your dress," said another.

' "Or get out of step."

' "Or get giddy and lean on you."

' "And he would never want to mop his face with his handkerchief. I do hate to see a man do that after every dance."

' "And wouldn't want to spend the whole evening in the supper room."

' "Why, with a phonograph inside him to grind out all the stock remarks, you would not be able to tell him from a real man," said the girl who had first suggested the idea.

' "Oh, yes, you would," said the thin girl, "he would be so much nicer."

'Old Geibel had laid down his paper, and was listening with both his ears. On one of the girls glancing in his direction, however, he hurriedly hid himself again behind it.

'After the girls were gone, he went into his workshop, where Olga heard him walking up and down, and every now and then chuckling to himself; and that night he talked to her a good deal about dancing and dancing men—asked what they usually said and did—what dances were most popular—what steps were gone through, with many other questions bearing on the subject.

'Then for a couple of weeks he kept much to his factory, and was very thoughtful and busy, though prone at unexpected moments to break into a quiet low laugh, as if enjoying a joke that nobody else knew of.

'A month later another ball took place in Furtwangen. On this occasion it was given by old Wenzel, the wealthy timber merchant, to celebrate his niece's betrothal, and Geibel and his daughter were again among the invited.

'When the hour arrived to set out, Olga sought her father. Not finding him in the house, she tapped at the door of his workshop. He appeared in his shirt-sleeves, looking hot but radiant.

' "Don't wait for me," he said, "you go on, I'll follow you. I've got something to finish."

'As she turned to obey he called after her, "Tell them I'm going to bring a young man with me—such a nice young man, and an excellent dancer. All the girls will like him." Then he laughed and closed the door.

'Her father generally kept his doings secret from everybody, but she had a pretty shrewd suspicion of what he had been planning, and so, to a certain extent, was able to prepare the guests for what was coming. Anticipation ran high, and the arrival of the famous mechanist was eagerly awaited.

'At length the sound of wheels was heard outside, followed by a great commotion in the passage, and old Wenzel himself, his jolly face red with excitement and suppressed laughter, burst into the room and announced in stentorian tones:

' "Herr Geibel—and a friend."

'Herr Geibel and his "friend" entered, greeted with shouts of laughter and applause, and advanced to the centre of the room.

' "Allow me, ladies and gentlemen," said Herr Geibel, "to introduce you to my friend, Lieutenant Fritz. My dear fellow, bow to the ladies and gentlemen."

'Geibel placed his hand encouragingly on Fritz's shoulder, and the lieutenant bowed low, accompanying the action with a harsh clicking noise in his throat, unpleasantly suggestive of a death rattle. But that was only a detail.

' "He walks a little stiffly" (old Geibel took his arm and walked him forward a few steps. He certainly did walk stiffly), "but then walking is not his forte. He is essentially a dancing man. I have only been able to teach him the waltz as yet, but at that he is faultless. Come, which of you ladies may I introduce him to as a partner? He keeps perfect time; he never gets tired; he won't kick you or tread on your dress;

he will hold you as firmly as you like, and go as quickly or as slowly as you please; he never gets giddy; and he is full of conversation. Come, speak up for yourself, my boy."

'The old gentleman twisted one of the buttons at the back of his coat, and immediately Fritz opened his mouth, and in thin tones that appeared to proceed from the back of his head, remarked suddenly, "May I have the pleasure?" and then shut his mouth again with a snap.

'That Lieutenant Fritz had made a strong impression on the company was undoubted, yet none of the girls seemed inclined to dance with him. They looked askance at his waxen face, with its staring eyes and fixed smile, and shuddered. At last old Geibel came to the girl who had conceived the idea.

' "It is your own suggestion, carried out to the letter," said Geibel, "an electric dancer. You owe it to the gentleman to give him a trial."

'She was a bright, saucy little girl, fond of a frolic. Her host added his entreaties, and she consented.

'Herr Geibel fixed the figure to her. Its right arm was screwed round her waist, and held her firmly; its delicately jointed left hand was made to fasten itself upon her right. The old toymaker showed her how to regulate its speed, and how to stop it, and release herself.

' "It will take you round in a complete circle," he explained; "be careful that no one knocks against you, and alters its course."

'The music struck up. Old Geibel put the current in motion, and Annette and her strange partner began to dance.

'For a while everyone stood watching them. The figure performed its purpose admirably. Keeping perfect time and step, and holding its little partner tight clasped in an unyielding embrace, it revolved steadily, pouring forth at the same time a constant flow of squeaky conversation, broken by brief intervals of grinding silence.

' "How charming you are looking to-night," it remarked

in its thin, far-away voice. "What a lovely day it has been. Do you like dancing? How well our steps agree. You will give me another, won't you? Oh, don't be so cruel. What a charming gown you have on. Isn't waltzing delightful? I could go on dancing for ever—with you. Have you had supper?"

'As she grew more familiar with the uncanny creature, the girl's nervousness wore off, and she entered into the fun of the thing.

' "Oh, he's just lovely," she cried, laughing, "I could go on dancing with him all my life."

'Couple after couple now joined them, and soon all the dancers in the room were whirling round behind them. Nicholaus Geibel stood looking on, beaming with childish delight at his success.

'Old Wenzel approached him, and whispered something in his ear. Geibel laughed and nodded, and the two worked their way quietly towards the door.

' "This is the young people's house to-night," said Wenzel, so soon as they were outside; "you and I will have a quiet pipe and a glass of hock, over in the counting-house."

'Meanwhile the dancing grew more fast and furious. Little Annette loosened the screw regulating her partner's rate of progress, and the figure flew round with her swifter and swifter. Couple after couple dropped out exhausted, but they only went the faster, till at length they remained dancing alone.

'Madder and madder became the waltz. The music lagged behind: the musicians, unable to keep pace, ceased, and sat staring. The younger guests applauded, but the older faces began to grow anxious.

' "Hadn't you better stop, dear," said one of the women, "you'll make yourself so tired."

'But Annette did not answer.

' "I believe she's fainted," cried out a girl who had caught sight of her face as it was swept by.

'One of the men sprang forward and clutched at the figure, but its impetus threw him down on to the floor, where its steel-cased feet laid bare his cheek. The thing evidently did not intend to part with its prize easily.

'Had anyone retained a cool head, the figure, one cannot help thinking, might easily have been stopped. Two or three men acting in concert might have lifted it bodily off the floor, or have jammed it into a corner. But few human heads are capable of remaining cool under excitement. Those who are not present think how stupid must have been those who were; those who are reflect afterwards how simple it would have been to do this, that, or the other, if only they had thought of it at the time.

'The women grew hysterical. The men shouted contradictory directions to one another. Two of them made a bungling rush at the figure, which had the result of forcing it out of its orbit in the centre of the room, and sending it crashing against the walls and furniture. A stream of blood showed itself down the girl's white frock, and followed her along the floor. The affair was becoming horrible. The women rushed screaming from the room. The men followed them.

'One sensible suggestion was made: "Find Geibel—fetch Geibel."

'No one had noticed him leave the room, no one knew where he was. A party went in search of him. The others, too unnerved to go back into the ball-room, crowded outside the door and listened. They could hear the steady whir of the wheels upon the polished floor as the thing spun round and round; the dull thud as every now and again it dashed itself and its burden against some opposing object and ricocheted off in a new direction.

'And everlastingly it talked in that thin ghostly voice, repeating over and over the same formula: "How charming you are looking to-night. What a lovely day it has been. Oh, don't be so cruel. I could go on dancing for ever—with you. Have you had supper?"

'Of course they sought for Geibel everywhere but where he was. They looked in every room in the house, then they rushed off in a body to his own place, and spent precious minutes in waking up his deaf old housekeeper. At last it occurred to one of the party that Wenzel was missing also, and then the idea of the counting-house across the yard presented itself to them, and there they found him.

'He rose up, very pale, and followed them; and he and old Wenzel forced their way through the crowd of guests gathered outside, and entered the room, and locked the door behind them.

'From within there came the muffled sound of low voices and quick steps, followed by a confused scuffling noise, then silence, then the low voices again.

'After a time the door opened, and those near it pressed forward to enter, but old Wenzel's broad shoulders barred the way.

' "I want you—and you, Bekler," he said, addressing a couple of the elder men. His voice was calm, but his face was deadly white. "The rest of you, please go—get the women away as quickly as you can."

'From that day old Nicholaus Geibel confined himself to the making of mechanical rabbits, and cats that mewed and washed their faces.'

MOXON'S MASTER

Ambrose Bierce

(1842–1914)

"Automatons" are defined in the Oxford English Dictionary as "pieces of mechanism having their motive power so concealed as to appear to move spontaneously". Their origins are known to be in the ancient temples of Greece and the experiments of mediaeval sorcerers. Not surprisingly they have intrigued writers for a great many years and there have been some interesting books on their history. Edgar Allan Poe was a fascinated onlooker whenever one of these pieces of machinery was on show, and indeed was responsible for exposing one particularly cunning fraud, a chess-playing automaton, in his essay "Maelzel's Chess-Player". (He proved that, far

from it being a highly sophisticated machine which took on all comers and beat them, it was merely the hiding place of a human chess player who operated the controls!) Ambrose Bierce, the author of this next story, was also a journalist like his fellow-countryman Poe, and an enquirer into all things strange. His many weird and macabre short stories and essays have earned him a position of pre-eminence in the horror story genre, and his talent is rarely shown to better effect than in this story of a scientist-mechanic who tries to combine the attributes of man with the special abilities of a machine, in order to create a unique kind of automaton. Despite his fame, Bierce is still a figure of mystery, his sardonic and wicked prose earning him the title "Bitter Bierce". Always a restless and inquisitive person, he left his American haunts in 1913 to observe at first hand the civil war which had just broken out in Mexico, and he was never heard of again.

'ARE you serious? Do you really believe that a machine thinks?'

I got no immediate reply; Moxon was apparently intent upon the coals in the grate, touching them deftly here and there with the fire-poker till they signified a sense of his attention by a brighter glow. For several weeks I had been observing in him a growing habit of delay in answering even the most trivial of commonplace questions. His air, however, was that of preoccupation rather than deliberation: one might have said that he had 'something on his mind'.

Presently he said:

'What is a "machine"? The word has been variously defined. Here is one definition from a popular dictionary: "Any instrument or organization by which power is applied and made effective, or a desired effect produced." Well, then, is not a man a machine? And you will admit that he thinks —or thinks he thinks.'

'If you do not wish to answer my question,' I said, rather testily, 'why not say so? All that you say is mere evasion. You know well enough that when I say "machine" I do not mean a man, but something that man has madeand controls.'

'When it does not control him,' he said rising abruptly and looking out of a window, whence nothing was visible in the blackness of a stormy night. A moment later he turned about and with a smile said: 'I beg your pardon; I had no thought of evasion. I considered the dictionary man's unconscious testimony suggestive and worth something in the discussion. I can give your question a direct answer easily enough: I do believe that a machine thinks about the work that it is doing.'

That was direct enough, certainly. It was not altogether pleasing for it tended to confirm a sad suspicion that Moxon's devotion to study and work in his machine-shop had not been good for him. I knew, for one thing, that he suffered from insomnia, and that is no light affliction. Had it affected his mind? His reply to my question seemed to me then evidence that it had; perhaps I should think differently about it now. I was younger then, and among the blessings that are not denied to youth is ignorance. Incited by that great stimulant to controversy, I said:

'And what, pray, does it think with—in the absence of a brain?'

The reply, coming with less than his customary delay, took his favourite form of counter-interrogation:

'With what does a plant think—in the absence of a brain?'

'Ah, plants also belong to the philosopher class! I should be pleased to know some of their conclusions; you may omit the premises.'

'Perhaps,' he replied apparently unaffected by my foolish irony, 'you may be able to infer their convictions from their acts. I will spare you the familiar examples of the sensitive mimosa, the several insectivorous flowers and those whose stamens bend down and shake their pollen upon the entering bee in order that he may fertilize their distant mates. But observe this. In an open spot in my garden I planted a climbing vine. When it was barely above the surface I set a stake into the soil a yard away. The vine at once made for

it, but as it was about to reach it after several days I removed
it a few feet. The vine at once altered its course, making an
acute angle, and again made for the stake. This manoeuvre
was repeated several times, but finally, as if discouraged, the
vine abandoned the pursuit and ignoring further attempts
to divert it, travelled to a small tree, farther away, which it
climbed.

'Roots of the eucalyptus will prolong themselves incredibly
in search of moisture. A well-known horticulturist relates
that one entered an old drain pipe and followed it until it
came to a break, where a section of the pipe had been removed to make way for a stone wall that had been built
across its course. The root left the drain and followed the
wall until it found an opening where a stone had fallen out.
It crept through, and following the other side of the wall
back to the drain, entered the unexplored part and resumed
its journey.'

'And all this?'

'Can you miss the significance of it? It shows the consciousness of plants. It proves that they think.'

'Even if it did—what then? We were speaking, not of
plants, but of machines. They may be composed partly of
wood—wood that has no longer vitality—or wholly of metal.
Is thought an attribute also of the mineral kingdom?'

'How else do you explain the phenomena, for example,
of crystallization?'

'I do not explain them.'

'Because you cannot without affirming what you wish to
deny, namely, intelligent co-operation among the constituent
elements of the crystals. When soldiers form lines, or hollow
squares, you call it reason. When wild geese in flight take
the form of a letter V you say instinct. When the homo-
geneous atoms of a mineral, moving freely in solution, arrange
themselves into shapes mathematically perfect, or particles
of frozen moisture into the symmetrical and beautiful forms
of snowflakes, you have nothing to say. You have not

even invented a name to conceal your heroic unreason.'

Moxon was speaking with unusual animation and earnestness. As he paused I heard in an adjoining room known to me as his 'machine-shop', which no one but himself was permitted to enter, a singular thumping sound, as of someone pounding upon a table with an open hand. Moxon heard it at the same moment and, visibly agitated, rose and hurriedly passed into the room whence it came. I thought it odd that anyone else should be in there, and my interest in my friend—with doubtless a touch of unwarrantable curiosity —led me to listen intently, though, I am happy to say, not at the keyhole. There were confused sounds, as of a struggle or scuffle; the floor shook. I distinctly heard hard breathing and a hoarse whisper which said, 'Damn you!' Then all was silent, and presently Moxon reappeared and said, with a rather sorry smile:

'Pardon me for leaving you so abruptly. I have a machine in there that lost its temper and cut up rough.'

Fixing my eyes steadily upon his left cheek, which was traversed by four parallel excoriations showing blood, I said:

'How would it do to trim its nails?'

I could have spared myself the jest; he gave it no attention, but seated himself in the chair that he had left and resumed the interrupted monologue as if nothing had occurred:

'Doubtless you do not hold with those (I need not name them to a man of your reading) who have taught that all matter is sentient, that every atom is a living, feeling, conscious being. *I* do. There is no such thing as dead, inert matter: it is all alive; all instinct with force, actual and potential; all sensitive to the same forces in its environment, and susceptible to the contagion of higher and subtler ones residing in such superior organisms as it may be brought into relation with, as those of man when he is fashioning it into an instrument of his will. It absorbs something of his intelligence and purpose—more of them in proportion to the complexity of the resulting machine and that of its work.

'Do you happen to recall Herbert Spencer's definition of Life'? I read it thirty years ago. He may have altered it afterward, for anything I know, but in all that time I have been unable to think of a single word that could profitably be changed or added or removed. It seems to me not only the best definition, but the only possible one.

' "Life," he says, "is a definite combination of heterogeneous changes, both simultaneous and successive, in correspondence with external coexistences and sequences." '

'That defines the phenomenon,' I said, 'but gives no hint of its cause.'

'That,' he replied, 'is all that any definition can do. As Mill points out, we know nothing of cause except as an antecedent—nothing of effect except as a consequent. Of certain phenomena one never occurs without another, which is dissimilar: the first in point of time we call cause, the second, effect. One who had many times seen a rabbit pursued by a dog, and had never seen rabbits and dogs otherwise, would think the rabbit the cause of the dog.

'But I fear,' he added, laughing naturally enough, 'that my rabbit is leading me a long way from the track of my legitimate quarry: I'm indulging in the pleasure of the chase for its own sake. What I want you to observe is that in Herbert Spencer's definition of "life" the activity of a machine is included—there is nothing in the definition that is not applicable to it. According to this sharpest of observers and deepest of thinkers, if a man during his period of activity is alive, so is a machine when in operation. As an inventor and constructor of machines I know that to be true.'

Moxon was silent for a long time, gazing absently into the fire. It was growing late and I thought it time to be going, but somehow I did not like the notion of leaving him in that isolated house, all alone except for the presence of some person of whose nature my conjectures could go no further than that it was unfriendly, perhaps malign. Leaning toward him and looking earnestly into his eyes while making

a motion with my hand through the door of his workshop,
I said:

'Moxon, whom have you in there?'

Somewhat to my surprise he laughed lightly and answered
without hesitation:

'Nobody; the incident that you have in mind was caused
by my folly in leaving a machine in action with nothing to
act upon, while I undertook the interminable task of en-
lightening your understanding. Do you happen to know
that Consciousness is the creature of Rhythm?'

'O bother them both!' I replied, rising and laying hold
of my overcoat. 'I'm going to wish you good night; and I'll
add the hope that the machine which you inadvertently left
in action will have her gloves on the next time you think it
needful to stop her.'

Without waiting to observe the effect of my shot I left
the house.

Rain was falling, and the darkness was intense. In the sky
beyond the crest of a hill towards which I groped my way
along precarious plank sidewalks and across miry, unpaved
streets I could see the faint glow of the city's lights, but behind me nothing was visible but a single window of Moxon's
house. It glowed with what seemed to me a mysterious and
fateful meaning. I knew it was an uncurtained aperture in
my friend's 'machine-shop,' and I had little doubt that he
had resumed the studies interrupted by his duties as my
instructor in mechanical consciousness and the fatherhood
of Rhythm. Odd, and in some degree humorous, as his
convictions seemed to me at that time, I could not wholly
divest myself of the feeling that they had some tragic relation
to his life and character—perhaps to his destiny—although
I no longer entertained the notion that they were the vagaries
of a disordered mind. Whatever might be thought of his
views, his exposition of them was too logical for that. Over
and over, his last words came back to me: 'Consciousness is
the creature of Rhythm.' Bald and terse as the statement

was, I now found it infinitely alluring. At each recurrence it broadened in meaning and deepened in suggestion. Why, here (I thought) is something upon which to found a philosophy. If Consciousness is the product of Rhythm all things *are* conscious, for all have motion, and all motion is rhythmic. I wondered if Moxon knew the significance and breadth of his thought—the scope of this momentous generalization; or had he arrived at his philosophic faith by the tortuous and uncertain road of observation?

That faith was then new to me, and all Moxon's expounding had failed to make me a convert; but now it seemed as if a great light shone about me, like that which fell upon Saul of Tarsus; and out there in the storm and darkness and solitude I experienced what Lewes calls 'The endless variety and excitement of philosophic thought'. I exulted in a new sense of knowledge, a new pride of reason. My feet seemed hardly to touch the earth; it was as if I were uplifted and borne through the air by invisible wings.

Yielding to an impulse to seek further light from him whom I now recognised as my master and guide, I had unconsciously turned about, and almost before I was aware of having done so, found myself again at Moxon's door. I was drenched with rain, but felt no discomfort. Unable in my excitement to find the door-bell I instinctively tried the knob. It turned and, entering, I mounted the stairs to the room that I had so recently left. All was dark and silent; Moxon, as I had supposed, was in the adjoining room—the 'machine-shop'. Groping along the wall until I found the communicating door, I knocked loudly several times, but got no response, which I attributed to the uproar outside, for the wind was blowing a gale and dashing the rain against the thin walls in sheets. The drumming upon the shingle roof spanning the unceiled room was loud and incessant.

I had never been invited into the machine-shop—had, indeed, been denied admittance, as had all others, with one exception, a skilled metal worker, of whom no one knew anything except that his name was Haley and his habit silence. But in my spiritual exaltation, discretion and civility were alike forgotten, and I opened the door. What I saw took all philosophical speculation out of me in short order.

Moxon sat facing me at the farther side of a small table upon which a single candle made all the light that was in the room. Opposite him, his back toward me, sat another person. On the table between the two was a chess-board; the men were playing. I knew little of chess, but as only a few pieces were on the board it was obvious that the game was near its close. Moxon was intensely interested—not so much, it seemed to me, in the game as in his antagonist, upon whom he had fixed so intent a look that, standing though I did directly in the line of his vision, I was altogether unobserved. His face was ghastly white, and his eyes glittered like diamonds. Of his antagonist I had only a back view, but that was sufficient; I should not have cared to see his face.

He was apparently not more than five feet in height, with proportions suggesting those of a gorilla—a tremendous breadth of shoulders, thick, short neck and broad, squat head, which had a tangled growth of black hair and was topped with a crimson fez. A tunic of the same colour, belted tightly to the waist, reached the seat—apparently a box— upon which he sat; his legs and feet were not seen. His left forearm appeared to rest in his lap; he moved his pieces with his right hand, which seemed disproportionately long.

I had shrunk back and now stood a little to one side of the doorway and in shadow. If Moxon had looked farther than the face of his opponent he could have observed nothing now, except that the door was open. Something forbade me either to enter or to retire, a feeling—I know not how it came— that I was in the presence of an imminent tragedy and might serve my friend by remaining. With a scarcely conscious rebellion against the indelicacy of the act, I remained.

The play was rapid. Moxon hardly glanced at the board

before making his moves, and to my unskilled eye seemed to move the piece most convenient to his hand, his motions in doing so being quick, nervous and lacking in precision. The response of his antagonist, while equally prompt in the inception, was made with a slow, uniform, mechanical and, I thought, somewhat theatrical movement of the arm, that was a sore trial to my patience. There was something unearthly about it all, and I caught myself shuddering. But I was wet and cold.

Two or three times after moving a piece the stranger slightly inclined his head, and each time I observed that Moxon shifted his king. All at once the thought came to me that the man was dumb. And then that he was a machine—an automaton chess-player! Then I remembered that Moxon had once spoken to me of having invented such a piece of mechanism, though I did not understand that it had actually been constructed. Was all this talk about the consciousness and intelligence of machines merely a prelude to eventual exhibition of this device—only a trick to intensify the effect of its mechanical action upon me in my ignorance of its secret?

A fine end this, of all my intellectual transports—my 'endless variety and excitement of philosophic thought'! I was about to retire in disgust when something occurred to hold my curiosity. I observed a shrug of the thing's great shoulders, as if it were irritated: and so natural was this—so entirely human—that in my new view of the matter it startled me. Nor was that all, for a moment later it struck the table sharply with its clenched hand. At that gesture Moxon seemed even more startled than I: he pushed his chair a little backward, as in alarm.

Presently Moxon, whose play it was, raised his hand high above the board, pounced upon one of his pieces like a sparrow-hawk, and with the exclamation 'checkmate!' rose quickly to his feet and stepped behind his chair. The automaton sat motionless.

The wind had now gone down, but I heard, at lessening intervals and progressively louder, the rumble and roll of thunder. In the pauses between I now became conscious of a low humming or buzzing which, like the thunder, grew momentarily louder and more distinct. It seemed to come from the body of the automaton, and was unmistakably a whirring of wheels. It gave me the impression of a disordered mechanism which had escaped the repressive and regulating action of some controlling part—an effect such as might be expected if a pawl should be jostled from the teeth of a ratchet-wheel. But before I had time for much conjecture as to its nature my attention was taken by the strange motions of the automaton itself. A slight but continuous convulsion appeared to have possession of it. In body and head, it shook like a man with palsy or an ague chill, and the motion augmented every moment until the entire figure was in violent agitation. Suddenly it sprang to its feet and with a movement almost too quick for the eye to follow shot forward across table and chair, with both arms thrust forth to their full length—the posture and lunge of a diver. Moxon tried to throw himself backward out of reach, but he was too late: I saw the horrible thing's hands close upon his throat, his own clutch its wrists. Then the table was overturned, the candle thrown to the floor and extinguished, and all was black dark. But the noise of the struggle was dreadfully distinct, and most terrible of all were the raucous, squawking sounds made by the strangled man's efforts to breathe. Guided by the infernal hubbub, I sprang to the rescue of my friend, but had hardly taken a stride in the darkness when the whole room blazed with a blinding white light that burned into my brain and heart and memory a vivid picture of the combatants on the floor, Moxon underneath, his throat still in the clutch of those iron hands, his head forced backward, his eyes protruding, his mouth wide open and his tongue thrust out; and—horrible contrast!—upon the painted face of his assassin an expression of tranquil and profound thought, as in the solution of a problem in chess! This I observed, tenh all was blackness and silence.

Three days later I recovered consciousness in a hospital. As the memory of that tragic night slowly evolved in my ailing brain I recognised in my attendant Moxon's confidential workman, Haley. Responding to a look he approached, smiling.

'Tell me about it,' I managed to say, faintly—'all about it.'

'Certainly,' he said; 'you were carried unconscious from a burning house—Moxon's. Nobody knows how you came to be there. You may have to do a little explaining. The origin of the fire is a bit mysterious, too. My own notion is that the house was struck by lightning.'

'And Moxon?'

'Buried yesterday—what was left of him.'

Apparently this reticent person could unfold himself on occasion. When imparting shocking intelligence to the sick he was affable enough. After some moments of the keenest mental suffering I ventured to ask another question:

'Who rescued me?'

'Well, if that interests you—I did.'

'Thank you, Mr. Haley, and may God bless you for it. Did you rescue, also, that charming product of your skill, the automaton chess-player that murdered its inventor?'

The man was silent a long time, looking away from me. Presently he turned and gravely said:

'Do you know that?'

'I do,' I replied; 'I saw it done.'

That was many years ago. If asked today I should answer less confidently.

THE MONSTER MAKER

William C. Morrow

(1858–1920)

After two stories about mechanical monsters, it is time to return to the flesh and blood variety. For this kind of experimentation the "mad scientists" needed a ready supply of corpses and not infrequently they had to call on the services of the notorious Resurrectionists or "Body Snatchers". Several classic short stories about these people exist (the most famous being Robert Louis Stevenson's "The Body Snatcher"), but in every case the men were performing their nefarious trade for the benefit of surgeons and medical students, and so there is no suitable example for this collection. Bodies were procured either from the graveyard or the charnel house—although rarely in the method demonstrated in this next story, where the corpse-to-be presents itself to the scientist and offers itself for whatever purpose the man may have in mind! The author, William C. Morrow, was an American horror story writer in the gruesome and imaginative tradition of Poe and Ambrose Bierce and was one of the nation's most popular contributors

*to the genre at the turn of the century. While his compatriots could
fairly be called prolific writers, William Morrow has left only a
scattering of short stories and one collection, "The Ape, The Idiot
and Other People" (1897). He was, however, a master of mounting
suspense and this story contains many of the devices so successfully
employed by the makers of modern horror films and television plays.*

A YOUNG man of refined appearance, but evidently suffering
great mental distress, presented himself one morning at the
residence of a singular old man, who was known as a surgeon
of remarkable skill. The house was a queer and primitive
brick affair, entirely out of date, and tolerable only in the
decayed part of the city in which it stood. It was large,
gloomy, and dark, and had long corridors and dismal
rooms; and it was absurdly large for the small family—man
and wife—that occupied it. The house described, the man
is portrayed—but not the woman. He could be agreeable
on occasion, but, for all that, he was but animated mystery.
His wife was weak, wan, reticent, evidently miserable, and
possibly living a life of dread or horror—perhaps witness
of repulsive things, subject of anxieties, and victim of fear
and tyranny; but there is a great deal of guessing in these
assumptions. He was about sixty-five years of age and she
about forty. He was lean, tall, and bald, with thin, smooth-
shaven face, and very keen eyes; she kept always at home, and
was slovenly. The man was strong, the woman weak; he
dominated, she suffered.

Although he was a surgeon of rare skill, his practice was
almost nothing, for it was a rare occurrence that the few
who knew of his great ability were brave enough to penetrate
the gloom of his house, and when they did so it was with a
deaf ear turned to sundry ghoulish stories that were whispered concerning him. These were, in great part, but exag-
gerations of his experiments in vivisection; he was devoted
to the science of surgery.

The young man who presented himself on the morning

just mentioned was a handsome fellow, yet of evident weak character and unhealthy temperament—sensitive, and easily exalted or depressed. A single glance convinced the surgeon that his visitor was seriously affected in mind, for there was never a bolder skull-grin of melancholia, fixed and irremediable.

A stranger would not have suspected any occupancy of the house. The street door—old, warped, and blistered by the sun—was locked, and the small, faded-green window-blinds were closed. The young man rapped at the door. No answer. He rapped again. Still no sign. He examined a slip of paper, glanced at the number on the house, and then, with the impatience of a child, he furiously kicked the door. There were signs of numerous other such kicks. A response came in the shape of a shuffling footstep in the hall, a turning of the rusty key, and a sharp face that peered through a cautious opening in the door.

'Are you the doctor?' asked the young man.

'Yes, yes! Come in,' briskly replied the master of the house. The young man entered. The old surgeon closed the door and carefully locked it. 'This way,' he said, advancing to a rickety flight of stairs. The young man followed. The surgeon led the way up the stairs, turned into a narrow, musty-smelling corridor at the left, traversed it, rattling the loose boards under his feet, at the farther end opened a door at the right, and beckoned his visitor to enter. The young man found himself in a pleasant room, furnished in antique fashion and with hard simplicity.

'Sit down,' said the old man, placing a chair so that its occupant should face a window that looked out upon a dead wall about six feet from the house. He threw open the blind, and a pale light entered. He then seated himself near his visitor and directly facing him, and with a searching look, that had all the power of a microscope, he proceeded to diagnosticate the case.

'Well?' he presently asked.

The young man shifted uneasily in his seat.

'I—I have come to see you,' he finally stammered, 'because I'm in trouble.'

'Ah!'

'Yes; you see, I—that is—I have given it up.'

'Ah!' There was pity added to sympathy in the ejaculation.

'That's it. Given it up,' added the visitor. He took from his pocket a roll of banknotes, and with the utmost deliberation he counted them out upon his knee. 'Five thousand dollars,' he calmly remarked. 'That is for you. It's all I have; but I presume—I imagine—no; that is not the word—*assume*—yes; that's the word—assume that five thousand —is it really that much? Let me count.' He counted again. 'That five thousand dollars is a sufficient fee for what I want you to do.'

The surgeon's lips curled pityingly—perhaps disdainfully also. 'What do you want me to do?' he carelessly inquired.

The young man rose, looked around with a mysterious air, approached the surgeon, and laid the money across his knee. Then he stooped and whispered two words in the surgeon's ear.

These words produced an electric effect. The old man started violently; then, springing to his feet, he caught his visitor angrily, and transfixed him with a look that was as sharp as a knife. His eyes flashed, and he opened his mouth to give utterance to some harsh imprecation, when he suddenly checked himself. The anger left his face, and only pity remained. He relinquished his grasp, picked up the scattered notes, and offering them to the visitor, slowly said:

'I do not want your money. You are simply foolish. You think you are in trouble. Well, you do not know what trouble is. Your only trouble is that you have not a trace of manhood in your nature. You are merely insane—I shall not say pusillanimous. You should surrender yourself to the authorities, and be sent to a lunatic asylum for proper treatment.'

The young man keenly felt the intended insult, and his eyes flashed dangerously.

'You old dog—you insult me thus!' he cried. 'Grand airs, these, you give yourself! Virtuously indignant, old murderer, you! Don't want my money, eh? When a man comes to you himself and wants it done, you fly into a passion and spurn his money; but let an enemy of his come and pay you, and you are only too willing. How many such jobs have you done in this miserable old hole? It is a good thing for you that the police have not run you down, and brought spade and shovel with them. Do you know what is said of you? Do you think you have kept your windows so closely shut that no sound has ever penetrated beyond them? Where do you keep your infernal implements?'

He had worked himself into a high passion. His voice was hoarse, loud, and rasping. His eyes, bloodshot, started from their sockets. His whole frame twitched, and his fingers writhed. But he was in the presence of a man infinitely his superior. Two eyes, like those of a snake, burned two holes through him. An overmastering, inflexible presence confronted one weak and passionate. The result came.

'Sit down,' commanded the stern voice of the surgeon.

It was the voice of father to child, of master to slave. The fury left the visitor, who, weak and overcome, fell upon a chair.

Meanwhile, a peculiar light had appeared in the old surgeon's face, the dawn of a strange idea; a gloomy ray, strayed from the fires of the bottomless pit; the baleful light that illumines the way of the enthusiast. The old man remained a moment in profound abstraction, gleams of eager intelligence bursting momentarily through the cloud of sombre meditation that covered his face. Then broke the broad light of a deep, impenetrable determination. There was something sinister in it, suggesting the sacrifice of something held sacred. After a struggle, mind had vanquished conscience.

Taking a piece of paper and a pencil, the surgeon carefully wrote answers to questions which he peremptorily addressed to his visitor, such as his name, age, place of residence, occupation, and the like, and the same inquiries concerning his parents, together with other particular matters.

'Does anyone know you came to this house?' he asked.

'No.'

'You swear it?'

'Yes.'

'But your prolonged absence will cause alarm and lead to search.'

'I have provided against that.'

'How?'

'By depositing a note in the post, as I came along, announcing my intention to drown myself.'

'The river will be dragged.'

'What then?' asked the young man, shrugging his shoulders with careless indifference. 'Rapid undercurrent, you know. A good many are never found.'

There was a pause.

'Are you ready?' finally asked the surgeon.

'Perfectly.' The answer was cool and determined.

The manner of the surgeon, however, showed much perturbation. The pallor that had come into his face at the moment his decision was formed became intense. A nervous tremulousness came over his frame. Above it all shone the light of enthusiasm.

'Have you a choice in the method?' he asked.

'Yes; extreme anæsthesia.'

'With what agent?'

'The surest and quickest.'

'Do you desire any—any subsequent disposition?'

'No; only nullification; simply a blowing out, as of a candle in the wind; a puff—then darkness, without a trace. A sense of your own safety may suggest the method. I leave it to you.'

'No delivery to your friends?'

'None whatever.'

Another pause.

'Did you say you are quite ready?' asked the surgeon.

'Quite ready.'

'And perfectly willing?'

'Anxious.'

'Then wait a moment.'

With this request the old surgeon rose to his feet and stretched himself. Then with the stealthiness of a cat he opened the door and peered into the hall, listening intently. There was no sound. He softly closed the door and locked it. Then he closed the window-blinds and locked them. This done, he opened a door leading into an adjoining room, which, though it had no window, was lighted by means of a small skylight. The young man watched closely. A strange change had come over him. While his determination had not one whit lessened, a look of great relief came into his face, displacing the haggard, despairing look of a half-hour before. Melancholic then, he was ecstatic now.

The opening of the second door disclosed a curious sight. In the centre of the room, directly under the skylight, was an operating-table, such as is used by demonstrators of anatomy. A glass case against the wall held surgical instruments of every kind. Hanging in another case were human skeletons of various sizes. In sealed jars, arranged on shelves, were monstrosities of divers kinds preserved in alcohol. There were also, among innumerable other articles scattered about the room, a manikin, a stuffed cat, a desiccated human heart, plaster casts of various parts of the body, numerous charts, and a large assortment of drugs and chemicals. There was also a lounge, which could be opened to form a couch. The surgeon opened it and moved the operating-table aside, giving its place to the lounge.

'Come in,' he called to his visitor.

The young man obeyed without the least hesitation.

'Take off your coat.'

He complied.

'Lie down on that lounge.'

In a moment the young man was stretched at full length, eyeing the surgeon. The latter undoubtedly was suffering under great excitement, but he did not waver; his movements were sure and quick. Selecting a bottle containing a liquid, he carefully measured out a certain quantity. While doing this he asked: 'Have you ever had any irregularity of the heart?'

'No.'

The answer was prompt, but it was immediately followed by a quizzical look in the speaker's face.

'I presume,' he added, 'you mean by your question that it might be dangerous to give me a certain drug. Under the circumstances, however, I fail to see any relevancy in your question.'

This took the surgeon aback; but he hastened to explain that he did not wish to inflict unnecessary pain, and hence his question.

He placed the glass on a stand, approached his visitor, and carefully examined his pulse.

'Wonderful!' he exclaimed.

'Why?'

'It is perfectly normal.'

'Because I am wholly resigned. Indeed, it has been long since I knew such happiness. It is not active, but infinitely sweet.'

'You have no lingering desire to retract?'

'None whatever.'

The surgeon went to the stand and returned with the draught.

'Take this,' he said, kindly.

The young man partially raised himself and took the glass in his hand. He did not show the vibration of a single nerve. He drank the liquid, draining the last drop. Then he returned the glass with a smile.

'Thank you,' he said; 'you are the noblest man that lives. May you always prosper and be happy! You are my benefactor, my liberator. Bless you, bless you! You reach down from your seat with the gods and lift me up into glorious peace and rest. I love you—I love you with all my heart!'

These words, spoken earnestly in a musical, low voice, and accompanied with a smile of ineffable tenderness, pierced the old man's heart. A suppressed convulsion swept over him; intense anguish wrung his vitals; perspiration trickled down his face. The young man continued to smile.

'Ah, it does me good!' said he.

The surgeon, with a strong effort to control himself, sat down upon the edge of the lounge and took his visitor's wrist, counting the pulse.

'How long will it take?' the young man asked.

'Ten minutes. Two have passed.' The voice was hoarse.

'Ah, only eight minutes more! . . . Delicious, delicious! I feel it coming. . . . What was that? . . . Ah, I understand. Music. . . . Beautiful! . . . Coming, coming. . . . Is that—that—water? . . . Trickling? Dripping? Doctor!'

'Well?'

'Thank you, . . . thank you. . . . Noble man, . . . my saviour, . . . my bene . . . bene . . . factor. . . . Trickling, . . . trickling. . . . Dripping, dripping. . . . Doctor!'

'Well?'

'Doctor!'

'Past hearing,' muttered the surgeon.

'Doctor!'

'And blind.'

Response was made by a firm grasp of the hand.

'Doctor!'

'And numb.'

'Doctor!'

The old man watched and waited.

'Dripping, . . . dripping.'

The last drop had run. There was a sigh, and nothing more.

The surgeon laid down the hand.

'The first step,' he groaned, rising to his feet; then his whole frame dilated. 'The first step—the most difficult, yet the simplest. A providential delivery into my hands of that for which I have hungered for forty years. No withdrawal now! It is possible, because scientific; rational, but perilous. If I succeed—*if*? I *shall* succeed. I *will* succeed. . . . And after success—what? . . . Yes; what? Publish the plan and the result? The gallows. . . . So long as *it* shall exist, . . . and *I exist*, the gallows. That much. . . . But how account for its presence? Ah, that pinches hard! I must trust to the future.'

He tore himself from the reverie and started.

'I wonder if *she* heard or saw anything.'

With that reflection he cast a glance upon the form on the lounge, and then left the room, locked the door, locked also the door of the outer room, walked down two or three corridors, penetrated to a remote part of the house, and rapped at a door. It was opened by his wife. He, by this time, had regained complete mastery over himself.

'I thought I heard someone in the house just now,' he said, 'but I can find no one.'

'I heard nothing.'

He was greatly relieved.

'I did hear someone knock at the door less than an hour ago,' she resumed, 'and heard you speak, I think. Did he come in?'

'No.'

The woman glanced at his feet and seemed perplexed.

'I am almost certain,' she said, 'that I heard foot-falls in the house, and yet I see that you are wearing slippers.'

'Oh, I had on my shoes then!'

'That explains it,' said the woman, satisfied; 'I think the sound you heard must have been caused by rats.'

'Ah, that was it!' exclaimed the surgeon. Leaving, he

closed the door, reopened it, and said, 'I do not wish to be disturbed today.' He said to himself, as he went down the hall, 'All is clear there.'

He returned to the room in which his visitor lay, and made a careful examination.

'Splendid specimen!' he softly exclaimed; 'every organ sound, every function perfect; fine, large frame; well-shaped muscles, strong and sinewy; capable of wonderful development—if given opportunity. . . . I have no doubt it can be done. Already I have succeeded with a dog,—a task less difficult than this, for in a man the cerebrum overlaps the cerebellum, which is not the case with a dog. This gives a wide range for accident, with but one opportunity in a lifetime! In the cerebrum, the intellect and the affections; in the cerebellum, the senses and the motor forces; in the medulla oblongata, control of the diaphragm. In these two latter lie all the essentials of simple existence. The cerebrum is merely an adornment; that is to say, reason and the affections are almost purely ornamental. I have already proved it. My dog, with its cerebrum removed, was idiotic, but it retained its physical senses to a certain degree.'

While thus ruminating he made careful preparations. He moved the couch, replaced the operating-table under the skylight, selected a number of surgical instruments, prepared certain drug-mixtures, and arranged water, towels, and all the accessories of a tedious surgical operation. Suddenly he burst into laughter.

'Poor fool!' he exclaimed. 'Paid me five thousand dollars to kill him! Didn't have the courage to snuff his own candle! Singular, singular, the queer freaks these madmen have! You thought you were dying, poor idiot! Allow me to inform you, sir, that you are as much alive at this moment as ever you were in your life. But it will be all the same to you. You shall never be more conscious than you are now; and for all practical purposes, so far as they concern you, you are dead henceforth, though you shall live. By the way, how should you feel *without a head*? Ha, ha, ha!... But that's a sorry joke.'

He lifted the unconscious form from the lounge and laid it upon the operating-table.

About three years afterwards the following conversation was held between a captain of police and a detective:

'She may be insane,' suggested the captain.

'I think she is.'

'And yet you credit her story!'

'I do.'

'Singular!'

'Not at all. I myself have learned something.'

'What!'

'Much, in one sense; little, in another. You have heard those queer stories of her husband. Well, they are all non-sensical—probably with one exception. He is generally a harmless old fellow, but peculiar. He has performed some wonderful surgical operations. The people in his neighbour-hood are ignorant, and they fear him and wish to be rid of him; hence they tell a great many lies about him, and they come to believe their own stories. The one important thing that I have learned is that he is almost insanely enthusiastic on the subject of surgery—especially experimental surgery; and with an enthusiast there is hardly such a thing as a scruple. It is this that gives me confidence in the woman's story.'

'You say she appeared to be frightened?'

'Doubly so—first, she feared that her husband would learn of her betrayal of him; second, the discovery itself had ter-rified her.'

'But her report of this discovery is very vague,' argued the captain. 'He conceals everything from her. She is merely guessing.'

'In part—yes; in other part—no. She heard the sounds distinctly, though she did not see clearly. Horror closed her eyes. What she thinks she saw is, I admit, preposterous; but she undoubtedly saw something extremely frightful. There are many peculiar little circumstances. He has eaten with her but few times during the last three years, and nearly always carries his food to his private rooms. She says that he either consumes an enormous quantity, throws much away, or is feeding something that eats prodigiously. He explains this to her by saying that he has animals with which he experiments. This is not true. Again, he always keeps the door to these rooms carefully locked; and not only that, but he has had the doors doubled and otherwise strengthened, and has heavily barred a window that looks from one of the rooms upon a dead wall a few feet distant.'

'What does it mean?' asked the captain.

'A prison.'

'For animals, perhaps.'

'Certainly not.'

'Why!'

'Because, in the first place, cages would have been better; in the second place, the security that he has provided is infinitely greater than that required for the confinement of ordinary animals.'

'All this is easily explained: he has a violent lunatic under treatment.'

'I had thought of that, but such is not the fact.'

'How do you know?'

'By reasoning thus: He has always refused to treat cases of lunacy; he confines himself to surgery; the walls are not padded, for the woman has heard sharp blows upon them; no human strength, however morbid, could possibly require such resisting strength as has been provided; he would not be likely to conceal a lunatic's confinement from the woman; no lunatic could consume all the food that he provides; so extremely violent mania as these precautions indicate could not continue three years; if there is a lunatic in the case it is very probable that there should have been communication with someone outside concerning the patient, and there has been none; the woman has listened at the keyhole and has heard no human voice within; and last, we have heard the woman's vague description of what she saw.'

'You have destroyed every possible theory,' said the captain, deeply interested, 'and have suggested nothing new.'

'Unfortunately, I cannot; but the truth may be very simple, after all. The old surgeon is so peculiar that I am prepared to discover something remarkable.'

'Have you suspicions?'

'I have.'

'Of what?'

'A crime. The woman suspects it.'

'And betrays it?'

'Certainly, because it is so horrible that her humanity revolts; so terrible that her whole nature demands of her that she hand over the criminal to the law; so frightful that she is in mortal terror; so awful that it has shaken her mind.'

'What do you propose to do?' asked the captain.

'Secure evidence. I may need help.'

'You shall have all the men you require. Go ahead, but be careful. You are on dangerous ground. You would be a mere plaything in the hands of that man.'

Two days afterwards the detective again sought the captain.

'I have a queer document,' he said, exhibiting torn fragments of paper, on which there was writing. 'The woman stole it and brought it to me. She snatched a handful out of a book, getting only a part of each of a few leaves.'

These fragments, which the men arranged as best they could, were (the detective explained) torn by the surgeon's wife from the first volume of a number of manuscript books which her husband had written on one subject,—the very one that was the cause of her excitement. 'About the time that he began a certain experiment three years ago,' continued the detective, 'he removed everything from the suite of two rooms containing his study and his operating-room. In one of the bookcases that he removed to a room across the passage was a drawer, which he kept locked, but which he opened from time to time. As is quite common with such pieces of furniture, the lock of the drawer is a very poor one; and so the woman, while making a thorough search yesterday, found a key on her bunch that fitted this lock. She opened the drawer, drew out the bottom book of a pile (so that its mutilation would more likely escape discovery), saw that it might contain a clue, and tore out a handful of the leaves. She had barely replaced the book, locked the drawer, and made her escape when her husband appeared. He hardly ever allows her to be out of his sight when she is in that part of the house.'

The fragments read as follows: '. . . the motory nerves. I had hardly dared to hope for such a result, although inductive reasoning had convinced me of its possibility, my only doubt having been on the score of my lack of skill. Their operation has been only slightly impaired, and even this would not have been the case had the operation been performed in infancy, before the intellect had sought and obtained recognition as an essential part of the whole. Therefore I state, as a proved fact, that the cells of the motory nerves have inherent forces sufficient to the purposes of those nerves. But hardly so with the sensory nerves. These latter are, in fact, an offshoot of the former, evolved from them by natural (though not essential) heterogeneity, and to a certain extent are dependent on the evolution and expansion of a contemporaneous tendency, that developed into mentality, or mental function. Both of these latter tendencies, these evolvements, are merely refinements of the motory system, and not independent entities; that is to say, they are the blossoms of a plant that propagates from its roots. The motory system is the first . . . nor am I surprised that such prodigious muscular energy is developing. It promises yet to surpass the wildest dreams of human strength. I account for it thus: The powers of assimilation had reached their full development. They had formed the habit of doing a certain amount of work. They sent their products to all parts of the system. As a result of my operation the consumption of these products was reduced fully one-half; that is to say, about one-half of the demand for them was withdrawn. But force of habit required the production to proceed. This production was strength, vitality, energy. Thus double the usual quantity of this strength, this energy, was stored in the remaining . . . developed a tendency that did surprise me. Nature, no longer suffering the distraction of extraneous interferences, and at the same time being cut in two (as it were), with reference to this case, did not fully adjust herself to the new situation, as does a magnet, which, when divided at the point of equilibrium, renews itself in its two fragments by investing each with opposite poles; but, on the contrary, being severed from laws that theretofore had controlled her, and possessing still that mysterious tendency to develop into something more potential and complex, she blindly (having lost her lantern) pushed her demands for material that would secure this development, and as blindly used it when it was given her. Hence this marvellous voracity, this insatiable hunger, this wonderful ravenousness; and hence also (there being nothing but the physical part to receive this vast storing of energy) this strength that is becoming almost hourly herculean, almost daily appalling. It is becoming a serious . . . narrow escape today. By some means, while I was absent, it unscrewed the stopper of the silver feeding-pipe (which I have already herein termed "the artificial mouth"), and, in one of its curious antics, allowed all the chyle to escape from its stomach through the tube. Its hunger then became intense—I may say furious. I placed my hands upon it to push it into a chair, when, feeling my touch, it caught me, clasped me around the neck, and would have crushed me to death instantly had I not slipped from its powerful grasp. Thus I always had to be on my guard. I have provided the screw stopper with a spring catch, and . . . usually docile when not hungry; slow and heavy in its movements, which are, of course, purely unconscious; any apparent excitement in movement being due to local irregularities in the blood-supply of the cerebellum, which, if I did not have it enclosed in a silver case that is immovable, I should expose and . . .'

The captain looked at the detective with a puzzled air.

'I don't understand it at all,' said he.

'Nor I,' agreed the detective.

'What do you propose to do?'

'Make a raid.'

'Do you want a man?'

'Three. The strongest men in your district.'

'Why, the surgeon is old and weak!'

'Nevertheless, I want three strong men; and for that matter, prudence really advises me to take twenty.'

At one o'clock the next morning a cautious, scratching sound might have been heard in the ceiling of the surgeon's operating-room. Shortly afterwards the skylight sash was carefully raised and laid aside. A man peered into the opening. Nothing could be heard.

'That is singular,' thought the detective.

He cautiously lowered himself to the floor by a rope, and then stood for some moments listening intently. There was a dead silence. He shot the slide of a dark-lantern, and rapidly swept the room with the light. It was bare, with the exception of a strong iron staple and ring, screwed to the floor in the centre of the room, with a heavy chain attached. The detective then turned his attention to the outer room; it was perfectly bare. He was deeply perplexed. Returning to the inner room, he called softly to the men to descend. While they were thus occupied he re-entered the outer room and examined the door. A glance sufficed. It was kept closed by a spring attachment, and was locked with a strong spring-lock that could be drawn from the inside.

'The bird has just flown,' mused the detective. 'A singular accident! The discovery and proper use of this thumb-bolt might not have happened once in fifty years, if my theory is correct.'

By this time the men were behind him. He noiselessly drew the spring-bolt, opened the door, and looked out into the hall. He heard a peculiar sound. It was as though a gigantic lobster was floundering and scrambling in some distant part of the old house. Accompanying this sound was a loud, whistling breathing, and frequent rasping gasps.

These sounds were heard by still another person—the surgeon's wife; for they originated very near her rooms, which were a considerable distance from her husband's. She had been sleeping lightly, tortured by fear and harassed by frightful dreams. The conspiracy into which she had recently entered, for the destruction of her husband, was a source of great anxiety. She constantly suffered from the most gloomy forebodings, and lived in an atmosphere of terror. Added to the natural horror of her situation were those countless sources of fear which a fright-shaken mind creates and then magnifies. She was, indeed, in a pitiable state, having been driven first by terror to desperation, and then to madness.

Startled thus out of fitful slumber by the noise at her door, she sprang from her bed to the floor, every terror that lurked in her acutely tense mind and diseased imagination starting up and almost overwhelming her. The idea of flight—one of the strongest of all instincts—seized upon her, and she ran to the door, beyond all control of reason. She drew the bolt and flung the door wide open, and then fled wildly down the passage, the appalling hissing and rasping gurgle ringing in her ears apparently with a thousandfold intensity. But the passage was in absolute darkness, and she had not taken a half-dozen steps when she tripped upon an unseen object on the floor. She fell headlong upon it, encountering in it a

large, soft, warm substance that writhed and squirmed, and
from which came the sounds that had awakened her. Instantly realising her situation, she uttered a shriek such as
only an unnamable terror can inspire. But hardly had her cry
started the echoes in the empty corridor when it was suddenly stifled. Two prodigious arms had closed upon her and
crushed the life out of her.

The cry performed the office of directing the detective
and his assistants, and it also aroused the old surgeon, who
occupied rooms between the officers and the object of their
search. The cry of agony pierced him to the marrow, and a
realization of the cause of it burst upon him with frightful
force.

'It has come at last!' he gasped, springing from his bed.

Snatching from a table a dimly-burning lamp and a long
knife which he had kept at hand for three years, he dashed
into the corridor. The four officers had already started forward, but when they saw him emerge they halted in silence.
In that moment of stillness the surgeon paused to listen. He
heard the hissing sound and the clumsy floundering of a
bulky, living object in the direction of his wife's apartments.
It evidently was advancing towards him. A turn in the corridor shut out the view. He turned up the light, which revealed
a ghastly pallor in his face.

'Wife!' he called.

There was no response. He hurriedly advanced, the four
men following quietly. He turned the angle of the corridor,
and ran so rapidly that by the time the officers had come
in sight of him again he was twenty steps away. He ran past
a huge, shapeless object, sprawling, crawling, and floundering along, and arrived at the body of his wife.

He gave one horrified glance at her face, and staggered
away. Then a fury seized him. Clutching the knife firmly,
and holding the lamp aloft, he sprang towards the ungainly
object in the corridor. It was then that the officers, still advancing cautiously, saw a little more clearly, though still in-

distinctly, the object of the surgeon's fury, and the cause of the look of unutterable anguish in his face. The hideous sight caused them to pause. They saw what appeared to be a man, yet evidently was not a man; huge, awkward, shapeless; a squirming, lurching, stumbling mass, completely naked. It raised its broad shoulders. *It had no head*, but instead of it a small metallic ball surmounting its massive neck.

'Devil!' exclaimed the surgeon, raising the knife.

'Hold, there!' commanded a stern voice.

The surgeon quickly raised his eyes and saw the four officers, and for a moment fear paralysed his arm.

'The police!' he gasped.

Then, with a look of redoubled fury, he sent the knife to the hilt into the squirming mass before him. The wounded monster sprang to its feet and wildly threw its arms about, meanwhile emitting fearful sounds from a silver tube through which it breathed. The surgeon aimed another blow, but never gave it. In his blind fury he lost his caution, and was caught in an iron grasp. The struggle threw the lamp some feet towards the officers, and it fell to the floor, shattered to pieces. Simultaneously with the crash the oil took fire, and the corridor was filled with flame. The officers could not approach. Before them was the spreading blaze, and secure behind it were two forms struggling in a fearful embrace. They heard cries and gasps, and saw the gleaming of a knife.

The wood in the house was old and dry. It took fire at once, and the flames spread with great rapidity. The four officers turned and fled, barely escaping with their lives. In an hour nothing remained of the mysterious old house and its inmates but a blackened ruin.

AND THE DEAD SPAKE—

E. F. Benson

(1867–1940)

In the years between the First and Second World Wars, stories of "mad scientists" and their bizarre creations enjoyed a tremendous vogue on both sides of the Atlantic—a vogue perhaps not equalled since Mary Shelley's time. The stories varied from those concerned with creating life to those who sought to travel in space and time, or to wreak terrible vengeance on mankind. In England, a notable contributor to this school was E. F. Benson. Edward Frederic Benson was one of three remarkable English brothers who wrote some of the most ingenious and spine-chilling ghost and horror stories of the first quarter of this century. All were literary men, the sons of a one-time Archbishop of Canterbury, and all were fascinated by history and archaeology. Of the three, E. F. Benson has achieved the most enduring reputation and many of his short stories still find a place in anthologies and collections. A story which everyone seems to have missed and which fits well into this collection is "And The Dead Spake—" which he wrote in 1923. The author was a keen student of scientific developments and doubtless followed the progress of John Logie Baird as he made his final preparations for television transmissions in the early 1920s. (The first practical demonstration was actually given in January 1926). This probably inspired E. F. Benson to create this story of an inventor who devises a machine to speak to the dead! As with all experiments which interfere with the laws of nature, the results prove most unexpected.

THERE is not in all London a quieter spot, or one, apparently, more withdrawn from the heat and bustle of life than New-some Terrace. It is a cul-de-sac, for at the upper end the roadway between its two lines of square, compact little residences is brought to an end by a high brick wall, while at the lower end, the only access to it is through Newsome Square, that small discreet oblong of Georgian houses, a relic of the time when Kensington was a suburban village sundered from the metropolis by a stretch of pastures stretching to the river. Both square and terrace are most inconveniently situated for those whose ideal environment includes a rank of taxicabs immediately opposite their door, a spate of buses roaring down the street, and a procession of underground trains, accessible by a station a few yards away, shaking and rattling the cutlery and silver on their dining tables. In consequence Newsome Terrace had come, two years ago, to be inhabited by leisurely and retired folk or by those who wished to pursue their work in quiet and tranquillity. Children with hoops and scooters are phenomena rarely encountered in the Terrace and dogs are equally uncommon.

In front of each of the couple of dozen houses of which

the Terrace is composed lies a little square of railinged garden, in which you may often see the middle-aged or elderly mistress of the residence horticulturally employed. By five o'clock of a winter's evening the pavements will generally be empty of all passengers except the policeman, who with felted step, at intervals throughout the night, peers with his bull's-eye into these small front gardens, and never finds anything more suspicious there than an early crocus or an aconite. For by the time it is dark the inhabitants of the Terrace have got themselves home, where behind drawn curtains and bolted shutters they will pass a domestic and uninterrupted evening. No funeral (up to the time I speak of) had I ever seen leave the Terrace, no marriage party had strewed its pavements with confetti, and perambulators were unknown. It and its inhabitants seemed to be quietly mellowing like bottles of sound wine. No doubt there was stored within them the sunshine and summer of youth long past, and now, dozing in a cool place, they waited for the turn of the key in the cellar door, and the entry of one who would draw them forth and see what they were worth.

Yet, after the time of which I shall now speak, I have never passed down its pavement without wondering whether each house, so seemingly-tranquil, is not, like some dynamo, softly and smoothly bringing into being vast and terrible forces, such as those I once saw at work in the last house at the upper end of the Terrace, the quietest, you would have said, of all the row. Had you observed it with continuous scrutiny, for all the length of a summer day, it is quite possible that you might have only seen issue from it in the morning an elderly woman whom you would have rightly conjectured to be the housekeeper, with her basket for marketing on her arm, who returned an hour later. Except for her the entire day might often pass without there being either ingress or egress from the door. Occasionally a middle-aged man, lean and wiry, came swiftly down the pavement, but his exit was by no means a daily occurrence, and indeed when he did emerge, he broke the almost universal usage of the Terrace, for his appearances took place, when such there were, between nine and ten in the evening. At that hour sometimes he would come round to my house in Newsome Square to see if I was at home and inclined for a talk a little later on. For the sake of air and exercise he would then have an hour's tramp through the lit and noisy streets, and return about ten, still pale and unflushed, for one of those talks which grew to have an absorbing fascination for me. More rarely through the telephone I proposed that I should drop in on him: this I did not often do, since I found that if he did not come out himself, it implied that he was busy with some investigation, and though he made me welcome, I could easily see that he burned for my departure, so that he might get busy with his batteries and pieces of tissue, hot on the track of discoveries that never yet had presented themselves to the mind of man as coming within the horizon of possibility.

My last sentence may have led the reader to guess that I am indeed speaking of none other than that recluse and mysterious physicist Sir James Horton, with whose death a hundred half-hewn avenues into the dark forest from which life comes must wait completion till another pioneer as bold as he takes up the axe which hitherto none but himself has been able to wield. Probably there was never a man to whom humanity owed more, and of whom humanity knew less. He seemed utterly independent of the race to whom (though indeed with no service of love) he devoted himself: for years he lived aloof and apart in his house at the end of the Terrace. Men and women were to him like fossils to the geologist, things to be tapped and hammered and dissected and studied with a view not only to the reconstruction of past ages, but to construction in the future. It is known, for instance, that he made an artificial being formed of the tissue, still living, of animals lately killed, with the brain of an ape and the heart of a bullock, and a sheep's thyroid, and so forth. Of that I can give no first-hand account; Horton, it is true, told me something about it, and in his will directed that certain memoranda on the subject should on his death be sent to me. But on the bulky envelope there is the direction, 'Not to be opened till January, 1925.' He spoke with some reserve and, so I think, with slight horror at the strange things which had happened on the completion of this creature. It evidently made him uncomfortable to talk about it, and for that reason I fancy he put what was then a rather remote date to the day when his record should reach my eye. Finally, in these preliminaries, for the last five years before the war, he had scarcely entered, for the sake of companionship, any house other than his own and mine. Ours was a friendship dating from school-days, which he had never suffered to drop entirely, but I doubt if in those years he spoke except on matters of business to half a dozen other people. He had already retired from surgical practice in which his skill was unapproached, and most completely now did he avoid the slightest intercourse with his colleagues, whom he regarded as ignorant pedants without courage or the rudiments of knowledge. Now and then he would write an epoch-making little monograph, which he flung to them like a bone to a starving dog, but for the most part, utterly absorbed in his own investigations, he left them to grope along unaided. He frankly told me that he enjoyed talking to me about such subjects, since I was utterly unacquainted with them. It clarified his mind to be obliged to put his theories and guesses and confirmations with such simplicity that anyone could understand them.

I well remember his coming in to see me on the evening of the 4th of August, 1914.

'So the war has broken out,' he said, 'and the streets are impassable with excited crowds. Odd, isn't it? Just as if each of us already was not a far more murderous battlefield than any which can be conceived between warring nations.'

'How's that?' said I.

'Let me try to put it plainly, though it isn't that I want to talk about. Your blood is one eternal battlefield. It is full of armies eternally marching and counter-marching. As long as the armies friendly to you are in a superior position, you remain in good health; if a detachment of microbes that, if suffered to establish themselves, would give you a cold in the head, entrench themselves in your mucous membrane, the commander-in-chief sends a regiment down and drives them out. He doesn't give his orders from your brain, mind you—those aren't his headquarters, for your brain knows nothing about the landing of the enemy till they have made good their position and given you a cold.'

He paused a moment.

'There isn't one headquarters inside you,' he said, 'there are many. For instance, I killed a frog this morning; at least most people would say I killed it. But had I killed it, though its head lay in one place and its severed body in another? Not a bit: I had only killed a piece of it. For I opened the body afterwards and took out the heart, which I put in a sterilised chamber of suitable temperature, so that it wouldn't get cold or be infected by any microbe. That was about twelve o'clock today. And when I came out just now, the heart was beating still. It was alive, in fact. That's full of suggestions, you know. Come and see it.'

The Terrace had been stirred into volcanic activity by the news of war: the vendor of some late edition had penetrated into its quietude, and there were half a dozen parlourmaids fluttering about like black and white moths. But once inside Horton's door isolation as of an Arctic night seemed to close round me. He had forgotten his latch-key, but his housekeeper, then newly come to him, who became so regular and familiar a figure in the Terrace, must have heard his step, for before he rang the bell she had opened the door, and stood with his forgotten latch-key in her hand.

'Thanks, Mrs. Gabriel,' said he, and without a sound the door shut behind us. Both her name and face, as reproduced in some illustrated daily paper, seemed familiar, rather terribly familiar, but before I had time to grope for the association, Horton supplied it.

'Tried for the murder of her husband six months ago,' he said. 'Odd case. The point is that she is the one and perfect housekeeper. I once had four servants, and everything was all mucky, as we used to say at school. Now I live in amazing comfort and propriety with one. She does everything. She is cook, valet, housemaid, butler, and won't have anyone to help her. No doubt she killed her husband, but she planned it so well that she could not be convicted. She told me quite frankly who she was when I engaged her.'

Of course I remembered the whole trial vividly now. Her husband, a morose, quarrelsome fellow, tipsy as often as sober, had, according to the defence cut his own throat while shaving; according to the prosecution, she had done that for him. There was the usual discrepancy of evidence as to whether the wound could have been self-inflicted, and the prosecution tried to prove that the face had been lathered after his throat had been cut. So singular an exhibition of forethought and nerve had hurt rather than helped their case, and after prolonged deliberation on the part of the jury, she had been acquitted. Yet not less singular was Horton's selection of a probable murderess, however efficient, as housekeeper.

He anticipated this reflection.

'Apart from the wonderful comfort of having a perfectly appointed and absolutely silent house,' he said, 'I regard Mrs. Gabriel as a sort of insurance against my being murdered. If you had been tried for your life, you would take very especial care not to find yourself in suspicious proximity to a murdered body again: no more deaths in your house, if you could help it. Come through to my laboratory, and look at my little instance of life after death.'

Certainly it was amazing to see that little piece of tissue still pulsating with what must be called life; it contracted and expanded faintly indeed but perceptibly, though for nine hours now it had been severed from the rest of the organisation. All by itself it went on living, and if the heart could go on living with nothing, you would say, to feed and stimulate its energy, there must also, so reasoned Horton, reside in all the other vital organs of the body other independent focuses of life.

'Of course a severed organ like that,' he said, 'will run down quicker than if it had the co-operation of the others, and presently I shall apply a gentle electric stimulus to it. If I can keep that glass bowl under which it beats at the temperature of a frog's body, in sterilised air, I don't see why it should not go on living. Food—of course there's the question of feeding it. Do you see what that opens up in the way of surgery? Imagine a shop with glass cases containing healthy organs taken from the dead. Say a man dies of pneumonia. He should, as soon as ever the breath is out of his body, be dissected, and though they would, of course, destroy his lungs, as they will be full of pneumococci, his liver and digestive organs are probably healthy. Take them out, keep them in a sterilised atmosphere with the temperature at 98·4, and sell the liver, let us say, to another poor devil who has cancer there. Fit him with a new healthy liver, eh?'

'And insert the brain of someone who has died of heart disease into the skull of a congenital idiot?' I asked.

'Yes, perhaps; but the brain's tiresomely complicated in its connections and the joining up of the nerves, you know. Surgery will have to learn a lot before it fits new brains in. And the brain has got such a lot of functions. All thinking, all inventing seem to belong to it, though, as you have seen, the heart can get on quite well without it. But there are other functions of the brain I want to study first. I've been trying some experiments already.'

He made some little readjustment to the flame of the spirit lamp which kept at the right temperature the water that surrounded the sterilised receptacle in which the frog's heart was beating.

'Start with the more simple and mechanical uses of the brain,' he said. 'Primarily it is a sort of record office, a diary. Say that I rap your knuckles with that ruler. What happens? The nerves there send a message to the brain, of course, saying—how can I put it most simply—saying, "Somebody is hurting me." And the eye sends another, saying "I perceive a ruler hitting my knuckles," and the ear sends another, saying "I hear the rap of it." But leaving all that alone, what else happens? Why, the brain records it. It makes a note of your knuckles having been hit.'

He had been moving about the room as he spoke, taking off his coat and waistcoat and putting on in their place a thin black dressing-gown, and by now he was seated in his favourite attitude cross-legged on the hearth-rug, looking like some magician or perhaps the afrit which a magician of black arts had caused to appear. He was thinking intently now, passing through his fingers his string of amber beads, and talking more to himself than to me.

'And how does it make that note?' he went on. 'Why, in the manner in which phonograph records are made. There are millions of minute dots, depressions, pockmarks on your brain which certainly record what you remember, what you have enjoyed or disliked, or done or said. The surface of the brain anyhow is large enough to furnish writing-paper for the record of all these things, of all your memories. If the impression of an experience has not been acute, the dot is not sharply impressed, and the record fades: in other words, you come to forget it. But if it has been vividly impressed, the record is never obliterated. Mrs. Gabriel, for instance, won't lose the impression of how she lathered her husband's face after she had cut his throat. That's to say, if she did it.'

'Now do you see what I'm driving at? Of course you do. There is stored within a man's head the complete record of all the memorable things he has done and said: there are all his thoughts there, and all his speeches, and, most well-marked of all, his habitual thoughts and the things he has often said; for habit, there is reason to believe, wears a sort of rut in the brain, so that the life-principle, whatever it is, as it gropes and steals about the brain, is continually stumbling into it. There's your record, your gramophone plate all ready. What we want, and what I'm trying to arrive at, is a needle which, as it traces its minute way over these dots, will come across words or sentences which the dead have uttered, and will reproduce them. My word, what Judgment Books! What a resurrection!'

Here in this withdrawn situation no remotest echo of the excitement which was seething through the streets penetrated; through the open window there came in only the tide of the midnight silence. But from somewhere closer at hand, through the wall surely of the laboratory, there came a low, somewhat persistent murmur.

'Perhaps our needle—unhappily not yet invented—as it passed over the record of speech in the brain, might induce even facial expression,' he said. 'Enjoyment or horror might even pass over dead features. There might be gestures and movements even, as the words were reproduced in our gramophone of the dead. Some people when they want to think intensely walk about: some, there's an instance of it audible now, talk to themselves aloud.'

He held up his finger for silence.

'Yes, that's Mrs. Gabriel,' he said. 'She talks to herself by the hour together. She's always done that, she tells me. I shouldn't wonder if she has plenty to talk about.'

It was that night when, first of all, the notion of intense activity going on below the placid house-fronts of the Terrace occurred to me. None looked more quiet than this, and yet there was seething here a volcanic activity and intensity of living, both in the man who sat cross-legged on the floor and behind that voice just audible through the partition wall.

But I thought of that no more, for Horton began speaking of the brain-gramophone again. . . . Were it possible to trace those infinitesimal dots and pockmarks in the brain by some needle exquisitely fine, it might follow that by the aid of some such contrivance as translated the pock-marks on a gramophone record into sound, some audible rendering of speech might be recovered from the brain of a dead man. It was necessary, so he pointed out to me, that this strange gramophone record should be new; it must be that of one lately dead, for corruption and decay would soon obliterate these infinitesimal markings. He was not of opinion that unspoken thought could be thus recovered: the utmost he hoped for from his pioneering work was to be able to recapture actual speech, especially when such speech had habitually dwelt on one subject, and thus had worn a rut on that part of the brain known as the speech-centre.

'Let me get, for instance,' he said, 'the brain of a railway porter, newly dead, who has been accustomed for years to call out the name of a station, and I do not despair of hearing his voice through my gramophone trumpet. Or again, given that Mrs. Gabriel, in all her interminable conversations with herself, talks about one subject, I might, in similar circumstances, recapture what she had been constantly saying. Of course my instrument must be of a power and delicacy still unknown, one of which the needle can trace the minutest irregularities of surface, and of which the trumpet must be of immense magnifying power, able to translate the smallest whisper into a shout. But just as a microscope will show you the details of an object invisible to the eye, so there are instruments which act in the same way on sound. Here, for instance, is one of remarkable magnifying power. Try it if you like.'

He took me over to a table on which was standing an electric battery connected with a round steel globe, out of the side of which sprang a gramophone trumpet of curious construction. He adjusted the battery, and directed me to

click my fingers quite gently opposite an aperture in the
globe, and the noise, ordinarily scarcely audible, resounded
through the room like a thunderclap.

'Something of that sort might permit us to hear the record
on a brain,' he said.

After this night my visits to Horton became far more common than they had hitherto been. Having once admitted me
into the region of his strange explorations, he seemed to
welcome me there. Partly, as he had said, it clarified his
own thought to put it into simple language, partly, as he
subsequently admitted, he was beginning to penetrate into
such lonely fields of knowledge by paths so utterly untrodden,
that even he, the most aloof and independent of mankind,
wanted some human presence near him. Despite his utter
indifference to the issues of the war—for, in his regard, issues
far more crucial demanded his energies—he offered himself
as surgeon to a London hospital for operations on the brain,
and his services, naturally, were welcomed, for none brought
knowledge or skill like his to such work. Occupied all day,
he performed miracles of healing, with bold and dexterous
excisions which none but he would have dared to attempt.
He would operate, often successfully, for lesions that seemed
certainly fatal, and all the time he was learning. He refused
to accept any salary; he only asked, in cases where he had
removed pieces of brain matter, to take these away, in order
by further examination and dissection, to add to the knowledge and manipulative skill which he devoted to the
wounded. He wrapped these morsels in sterilised lint, and
took them back to the Terrace in a box, electrically heated
to maintain the normal temperature of a man's blood. His
fragment might then, so he reasoned, keep some sort of independent life of its own, even as the severed heart of a frog
had continued to beat for hours without connection with
the rest of the body. Then for half the night he would continue to work on these sundered pieces of tissue scarcely

dead, which his operations during the day had given him. Simultaneously, he was busy over the needle that must be of such infinite delicacy.

One evening, fatigued with a long day's work, I had just heard with a certain tremor of uneasy anticipation the whistles of warning which heralded an air-raid, when my telephone bell rang. My servants, according to custom, had already betaken themselves to the cellar, and I went to see what the summons was, determined in any case not to go out into the streets. I recognised Horton's voice. 'I want you at once,' he said.

'But the warning whistles have gone,' said I. 'And I don't like showers of shrapnel.'

'Oh, never mind that,' said he. 'You must come. I'm so excited that I distrust the evidence of my own ears. I want a witness. Just come.'

He did not pause for my reply, for I heard the click of his receiver going back into its place. Clearly he assumed that I was coming, and that I suppose had the effect of suggestion on my mind. I told myself that I would not go, but in a couple of minutes his certainty that I was coming, coupled with the prospect of being interested in something else than air-raids, made me fidget in my chair and eventually go to the street door and look out. The moon was brilliantly bright, the square quite empty, and far away the coughings of very distant guns. Next moment, almost against my will, I was running down the deserted pavements of Newsome Terrace. My ring at his bell was answered by Horton, before Mrs. Gabriel could come to the door, and he positively dragged me in.

'I shan't tell you a word of what I am doing,' he said. 'I want you to tell me what you hear. Come into the laboratory.'

The remote guns were silent again as I sat myself, as directed, in a chair close to the gramophone trumpet, but suddenly through the wall I heard the familiar mutter of

Mrs. Gabriel's voice. Horton, already busy with his battery, sprang to his feet.

'That won't do,' he said. 'I want absolute silence.'

He went out of the room, and I heard him calling to her. While he was gone I observed more closely what was on the table. Battery, round steel globe, and gramophone trumpet were there, and some sort of a needle on a spiral steel spring linked up with the battery and the glass vessel, in which I had seen the frog's heart beat. In it now there lay a fragment of grey matter.

Horton came back in a minute or two, and stood in the middle of the room listening.

'That's better,' he said. 'Now I want you to listen at the mouth of the trumpet. I'll answer any questions afterwards.'

With my ear turned to the trumpet, I could see nothing of what he was doing, and I listened till the silence became a rustling in my ears. Then suddenly that rustling ceased, for it was overscored by a whisper which undoubtedly came from the aperture on which my aural attention was fixed. It was no more than the faintest murmur, and though no words were audible, it had the timbre of a human voice.

'Well, do you hear anything?' asked Horton.

'Yes, something very faint, scarcely audible.'

'Describe it,' said he.

'Somebody whispering.'

'I'll try a fresh place,' said he.

The silence descended again; the mutter of the distant guns was still mute, and some slight creaking from my shirt front, as I breathed, alone broke it. And then the whispering from the gramophone trumpet began again, this time much louder than it had been before—it was as if the speaker (still whispering) had advanced a dozen yards—but still blurred and indistinct. More unmistakable, too, was it that the whisper was that of a human voice, and every now and then, whether fancifully or not, I thought I caught a word or two. For a moment it was silent altogether, and then with a

sudden inkling of what I was listening to I heard something
begin to sing. Though the words were still inaudible there
was melody, and the tune was 'Tipperary'. From that
convolvulus-shaped trumpet there came two bars of it.

'And what do you hear now?' cried Horton with a crack
of exultation in his voice. 'Singing, singing! That's the tune
they all sang. Fine music that from a dead man. Encore!
you say? Yes, wait a second, and he'll sing it again for you.
Confound it, I can't get on to the place. Ah! I've got it:
listen again.'

Surely that was the strangest manner of song ever yet
heard on the earth, this melody from the brain of the dead.
Horror and fascination strove within me, and I suppose the
first for the moment prevailed, for with a shudder I jumped
up.

'Stop it!' I said. 'It's terrible.'

His face, thin and eager, gleamed in the strong ray of the
lamp which he had placed close to him. His hand was on
the metal rod from which depended the spiral spring and
the needle, which just rested on that fragment of grey stuff
which I had seen in the glass vessel.

'Yes, I'm going to stop it now,' he said, 'or the germs will
be getting at my gramophone record, or the record will get
cold. See, I spray it with carbolic vapour, I put it back into
its nice warm bed. It will sing to us again. But terrible? What
do you mean by terrible?'

Indeed, when he asked that I scarcely knew myself what
I meant. I had been witness to a new marvel of science as
wonderful perhaps as any that had ever astounded the be-
holder, and my nerves—these childish whimperers—had
cried out at the darkness and the profundity. But the horror
diminished, the fascination increased as he quite shortly
told me the history of this phenomenon. He had attended
that day and operated upon a young soldier in whose brain
was embedded a piece of shrapnel. The boy was *in extremis*,
but Horton had hoped for the possibility of saving him. To

extract the shrapnel was the only chance, and this involved the cutting away of a piece of brain known as the speech-centre, and taking from it what was embedded there. But the hope was not realised, and two hours later the boy died. It was to this fragment of brain that, when Horton returned home, he had applied the needle of his gramophone, and had obtained the faint whisperings which had caused him to ring me up, so that he might have a witness of this wonder. Witness I had been, not to these whisperings alone, but to the fragment of singing.

'And this is but the first step on the new road,' said he. 'Who knows where it may lead, or to what new temple of knowledge it may not be the avenue? Well, it is late: I shall do no more tonight. What about the raid, by the way?'

To my amazement I saw that the time was verging on midnight. Two hours had elapsed since he let me in at his door; they had passed like a couple of minutes. Next morning some neighbours spoke of the prolonged firing that had gone on, of which I had been wholly unconscious.

Week after week Horton worked on this new road of research, perfecting the sensitiveness and subtlety of the needle, and, by vastly increasing the power of his batteries, enlarging the magnifying power of his trumpet. Many and many an evening during the next year did I listen to voices that were dumb in death, and the sounds which had been blurred and unintelligible mutterings in the earlier experiments, developed, as the delicacy of his mechanical devices increased, into coherence and clear articulation. It was no longer necessary to impose silence on Mrs. Gabriel when the gramophone was at work, for now the voice we listened to had risen to the pitch of ordinary human utterance, while as for the faithfulness and individuality of these records, striking testimony was given more than once by some living friend of the dead, who, without knowing what he was about to hear, recognised the tones of the speaker. More than once also, Mrs. Gabriel, bringing in syphons and whisky, provided us with three glasses, for she had heard, so she told us, three different voices in talk. But for the present no fresh phenomenon occurred: Horton was but perfecting the mechanism of his previous discovery and, rather grudging the time, was scribbling at a monograph, which presently he would toss to his colleagues, concerning the results he had already obtained. And then, even while Horton was on the threshold of new wonders, which he had already foreseen and spoken of as theoretically possible, there came an evening of marvel and of swift catastrophe.

I had dined with him that day, Mrs. Gabriel deftly serving the meal that she had so daintily prepared, and towards the end, as she was clearing the table for our dessert, she stumbled, I supposed, on a loose edge of carpet, quickly recovering herself. But instantly Horton checked some half-finished sentence, and turned to her.

'You're all right, Mrs. Gabriel?' he asked quickly.

'Yes, sir, thank you,' said she, and went on with her serving.

'As I was saying,' began Horton again, but his attention clearly wandered, and without concluding his narrative, he relapsed into silence, till Mrs. Gabriel had given us our coffee and left the room.

'I'm sadly afraid my domestic felicity may be disturbed,' he said. 'Mrs. Gabriel had an epileptic fit yesterday, and she confessed when she recovered that she had been subject to them when a child, and since then had occasionally experienced them.'

'Dangerous, then?' I asked.

'In themselves not in the least,' said he. 'If she was sitting in her chair or lying in bed when one occurred, there would be nothing to trouble about. But if one occurred while she was cooking my dinner or beginning to come downstairs, she might fall into the fire or tumble down the whole flight. We'll hope no such deplorable calamity will happen. Now, if you've finished your coffee, let us go into the laboratory.

Not that I've got anything very interesting in the way of new records. But I've introduced a second battery with a very strong induction coil into my apparatus. I find that if I link it up with my record, given that the record is a—a fresh one, it stimulates certain nerve centres. It's odd, isn't it, that the same forces which so encourage the dead to live would certainly encourage the living to die, if a man received the full current. One has to be careful in handling it. Yes, and what then? you ask.'

The night was very hot, and he threw the windows wide before he settled himself cross-legged on the floor.

'I'll answer your question for you,' he said, 'though I believe we've talked of it before. Supposing I had not a fragment of brain-tissue only, but a whole head, let us say, or best of all, a complete corpse, I think I could expect to produce more than mere speech through the gramophone. The dead lips themselves perhaps might utter—God! what's that?'

From close outside, at the bottom of the stairs leading from the dining room which we had just quitted to the laboratory where we now sat, there came a crash of glass followed by the fall as of something heavy which bumped from step to step, and was finally flung on the threshold against the door with the sound as of knuckles rapping at it, and demanding admittance. Horton sprang up and threw the door open, and there lay, half inside the room and half on the landing outside, the body of Mrs. Gabriel. Round her were splinters of broken bottles and glasses, and from a cut in her forehead, as she lay ghastly with face upturned, the blood trickled into her thick grey hair.

Horton was on his knees beside her, dabbing his handkerchief on her forehead.

'Ah! that's not serious,' he said; 'there's neither vein nor artery cut. I'll just bind that up first.'

He tore his handkerchief into strips which he tied together, and made a dexterous bandage covering the lower part of her forehead, but leaving her eyes unobscured. They stared with a fixed meaningless steadiness, and he scrutinised them closely.

'But there's worse yet,' he said. 'There's been some severe blow on the head. Help me to carry her into the laboratory. Get round to her feet and lift underneath the knees when I am ready. There! Now put your arm right under her and carry her.'

Her head swung limply back as he lifted her shoulders, and he propped it up against his knee, where it mutely nodded and bowed, as his leg moved, as if in silent assent to what we were doing, and the mouth, at the extremity of which there had gathered a little lather, lolled open. He still supported her shoulders as I fetched a cushion on which to place her head, and presently she was lying close to the low table on which stood the gramophone of the dead. Then with light deft fingers he passed his hands over her skull, pausing as he came to the spot just above and behind her right ear. Twice and again his fingers groped and lightly pressed, while with shut eyes and concentrated attention he interpreted what his trained touch revealed.

'Her skull is broken to fragments just here,' he said. 'In the middle there is a piece completely severed from the rest, and the edges of the cracked pieces must be pressing on her brain.'

Her right arm was lying palm upwards on the floor, and with one hand he felt her wrist with finger-tips.

'Not a sign of pulse,' he said. 'She's dead in the ordinary sense of the word. But life persists in an extraordinary manner, you may remember. She can't be wholly dead: no one is wholly dead in a moment, unless every organ is blown to bits. But she soon will be dead, if we don't relieve the pressure on the brain. That's the first thing to be done. While I'm busy at that, shut the window, will you, and make up the fire. In this sort of case the vital heat, whatever that is, leaves the body very quickly. Make the room as hot as you can—fetch an oil-stove, and turn on the electric radiator, and stoke up a roaring fire. The hotter the room is the more slowly will the heat of life leave her.'

Already he had opened his cabinet of surgical instruments, and taken out of it two drawers full of bright steel which he laid on the floor beside her. I heard the grating chink of scissors severing her long grey hair, and as I busied myself with laying and lighting the fire in the hearth, and kindling the oil-stove, which I found, by Horton's directions, in the pantry, I saw that his lancet was busy on the exposed skin. He had placed some vaporising spray, heated by a spirit lamp close to her head, and as he worked its fizzing nozzle filled the air with some clean and aromatic odour. Now and then he threw out an order.

'Bring me that electric lamp on the long cord,' he said. 'I haven't got enough light. Don't look at what I'm doing if you're squeamish, for if it makes you feel faint, I shan't be able to attend to you.'

I suppose that violent interest in what he was doing overcame any qualm that I might have had, for I looked quite unflinching over his shoulder as I moved the lamp about till it was in such a place that it threw its beam directly into a dark hole at the edge of which depended a flap of skin. Into this he put his forceps, and as he withdrew them they grasped a piece of blood-stained bone.

'That's better,' he said, 'and the room's warming up well. But there's no sign of pulse yet. Go on stoking, will you, till the thermometer on the wall there registers a hundred degrees.'

When next, on my journey from the coal-cellar, I looked, two more pieces of bone lay beside the one I had seen extracted, and presently referring to the thermometer, I saw that between the oil-stove and the roaring fire and the electric radiator, I had raised the room to the temperature he wanted. Soon, peering fixedly at the seat of his operation, he felt for her pulse again.

'Not a sign of returning vitality,' he said, 'and I've done all I can. There's nothing more possible that can be devised to restore her.'

As he spoke the zeal of the unrivalled surgeon relaxed, and with a sigh and a shrug he rose to his feet and mopped his face. Then suddenly the fire and eagerness blazed there again. 'The gramophone!' he said. 'The speech centre is close to where I've been working, and it is quite uninjured. Good heavens, what a wonderful opportunity. She served me well living, and she shall serve me dead. And I can stimulate the motor nerve-centre, too, with the second battery. We may see a new wonder tonight.'

Some qualm of horror shook me.

'No, don't!' I said. 'It's terrible: she's just dead. I shall go if you do.'

'But I've got exactly all the conditions I have long been wanting,' said he. 'And I simply can't spare you. You must be witness: I must have a witness. Why, man, there's not a surgeon or a physiologist in the kingdom who would not give an eye or an ear to be in your place now. She's dead. I pledge you my honour on that, and it's grand to be dead if you can help the living.'

Once again, in a far fiercer struggle, horror and the intensest curiosity strove together in me.

'Be quick, then,' said I.

'Ha! That's right,' exclaimed Horton. 'Help me to lift her on to the table by the gramophone. The cushion too; I can get at the place more easily with her head a little raised.'

He turned on the battery and with the movable light close beside him, brilliantly illuminating what he sought, he inserted the needle of the gramophone into the jagged aperture in her skull. For a few minutes, as he groped and explored there, there was silence, and then quite suddenly Mrs. Gabriel's voice, clear and unmistakable and of the normal loudness of human speech, issued from the trumpet.

'Yes, I always said that I'd be even with him,' came the

articulated syllables. 'He used to knock me about, he did, when he came home drunk, and often I was black and blue with bruises. But I'll give him a redness for the black and blue.'

The record grew blurred; instead of articulate words there came from it a gobbling noise. By degrees that cleared, and we were listening to some dreadful suppressed sort of laughter, hideous to hear. On and on it went.

'I've got into some sort of rut,' said Horton. 'She must have laughed a lot to herself.'

For a long time we got nothing more except the repetition of the words we had already heard and the sound of that suppressed laughter. Then Horton drew towards him the second battery.

'I'll try a stimulation of the motor nerve-centres,' he said. 'Watch her face.'

He propped the gramophone needle in position, and inserted into the fractured skull the two poles of the second battery, moving them about there very carefully. And as I watched her face, I saw with a freezing horror that her lips were beginning to move.

'Her mouth's moving,' I cried. 'She can't be dead.'

He peered into her face.

'Nonsense,' he said. 'That's only the stimulus from the current. She's been dead half an hour. Ah! what's coming now?'

The lips lengthened into a smile, the lower jaw dropped, and from her mouth came the laughter we had heard just now through the gramophone. And then the dead mouth spoke, with a mumble of unintelligible words, a bubbling torrent of incoherent syllables.

'I'll turn the full current on,' he said.

The head jerked and raised itself, the lips struggled for utterance, and suddenly she spoke swiftly and distinctly.

'Just when he'd got his razor out,' she said, 'I came up behind him, and put my hand over his face and bent his neck back over his chair with all my strength. And I picked up his razor and with one slit—ha, ha, that was the way to pay him out. And I didn't lose my head, but I lathered his chin well, and put the razor in his hand, and left him there, and went downstairs and cooked his dinner for him, and then an hour afterwards, as he didn't come down, up I went to see what kept him. It was a nasty cut in his neck that had kept him——'

Horton suddenly withdrew the two poles of the battery from her head, and even in the middle of her word the mouth ceased working, and lay rigid and open.

'By God!' he said. 'There's a tale for dead lips to tell. But we'll get more yet.'

Exactly what happened then I never knew. It appeared to me that as he still leaned over the table with the two poles of the battery in his hand, his foot slipped, and he fell forward across it. There came a sharp crack, and a flash of blue dazzling light, and there he lay face downwards, with arms that just stirred and quivered. With his fall the two poles that must momentarily have come into contact with his hand were jerked away again, and I lifted him and laid him on the floor. But his lips as well as those of the dead woman had spoken for the last time.

THE STOLEN BODY

H. G. Wells

(1866–1946)

The high-point of Science Fiction and Fantasy writing this century was undoubtedly reached by the remarkable H. G. Wells whose span of storytelling covered nearly fifty years. Apart from his many stories of space exploration and creatures from other planets, it is certainly no surprise to find that he was a distinguished writer of "monster maker" stories. When I was young I can remember being spellbound by his "Island of Doctor Moreau"—the story of a once-famous London scientist who is trying to mould animals into the likeness of humans. The adventures of the young man who is shipwrecked on Dr. Moreau's island and encounters the "Beast Men" are memorable and were in 1933 filmed with Charles Laughton and Bela Lugosi. This story was set firmly in the present, but Wells showed that we might expect to find the "mad scientist" at work far into the future: "When The Sleeper Wakes" describes a world completely mechanised and full of robot men. As in so much of his work he was pointing the way for later writers. He excelled, too, in the art of short story writing, and "The Stolen Body" leads into the realms of thought transference and, even more astonishing, body transference. Perhaps there are the merest traces here of that other great horror classic of body change, "Dr. Jekyll and Mr. Hyde"—but apart from that it is pure Wells.

MR. BESSEL was the senior partner in the firm of Bessel, Hart, and Brown, of St. Paul's Churchyard, and for many years he was well known among those interested in psychical research as a liberal-minded and conscientious investigator. He was an unmarried man, and instead of living in the suburbs, after the fashion of his class, he occupied rooms in the Albany, near Piccadilly. He was particularly interested in the questions of thought transference and of apparitions of the living, and in November, 1896, he commenced a series of experiments in conjunction with Mr. Vincey, of Staple Inn, in order to test the alleged possibility of projecting an apparition of oneself by force of will through space.

Their experiments were conducted in the following manner: At a pre-arranged hour Mr. Bessel shut himself in one of his rooms in the Albany and Mr. Vincey in his sitting-room in Staple Inn, and each then fixed his mind as resolutely as possible on the other. Mr. Bessel had acquired the art of self-hypnotism, and, so far as he could, he attempted first to hypnotise himself and then to project himself as a 'phantom of the living' across the intervening space of nearly two miles into Mr. Vincey's apartment. On several evenings this was tried without any satisfactory result, but on the fifth or sixth occasion Mr. Vincey did actually see or imagine he saw an apparition of Mr. Bessel standing in his room. He states that the appearance, although brief, was very vivid and real. He noticed that Mr. Bessel's face was white and his expression anxious, and, moreover, that his hair was disordered. For a moment Mr. Vincey, in spite of his state of expectation, was too surprised to speak or move, and in that moment it seemed to him as though the figure glanced over its shoulder and incontinently vanished.

It had been arranged that an attempt should be made to photograph any phantasm seen, but Mr. Vincey had not the instant presence of mind to snap the camera that lay ready on the table beside him, and when he did so he was too late. Greatly elated, however, even by this partial success, he made a note of the exact time, and at once took a cab to the Albany to inform Mr. Bessel of this result.

He was surprised to find Mr. Bessel's outer door standing open to the night, and the inner apartments lit and in an extraordinary disorder. An empty champagne magnum lay smashed upon the floor; its neck had been broken off against the inkpot on the bureau and lay beside it. An octagonal occasional table, which carried a bronze statuette and a number of choice books, had been rudely overturned, and down the primrose paper of the wall inky fingers had been drawn, as it seemed for the mere pleasure of defilement. One of the delicate chintz curtains had been violently torn from its rings and thrust upon the fire, so that the smell of its smouldering filled the room. Indeed the whole place was disarranged in the strangest fashion. For a few minutes Mr. Vincey, who had entered sure of finding Mr. Bessel in his easy chair awaiting him, could scarcely believe his eyes, and stood staring helplessly at these unanticipated things.

Then, full of a vague sense of calamity, he sought the porter at the entrance lodge. 'Where is Mr. Bessel?' he asked. 'Do you know that all the furniture is broken in Mr. Bessel's room?' The porter said nothing, but, obeying his gestures, came at once to Mr. Bessel's apartment to see the state of affairs. 'This settles it,' he said, surveying the lunatic confusion. 'I didn't know of this. Mr. Bessel's gone off. He's mad!'

He then proceeded to tell Mr. Vincey that about half an hour previously, that is to say, at about the time of Mr. Bessel's apparition in Mr. Vincey's rooms, the missing gentleman had rushed out of the gates of the Albany into Vigo Street, hatless and with disordered hair, and had vanished into the direction of Bond Street. 'And as he went past me,' said the porter, 'he laughed—a sort of gasping laugh, with his mouth open and his eyes glaring—I tell you, sir, he fair scared me!—like this.'

According to his imitation it was anything but a pleasant laugh. 'He waved his hand, with all his fingers crooked and clawing—like that. And he said, in a sort of fierce whisper, "*Life*." Just that one word, "*Life*!" '

'Dear me,' said Mr. Vincey. 'Tut, tut,' and 'Dear me!' He could think of nothing else to say. He was naturally very much surprised. He turned from the room to the porter and from the porter to the room in the gravest perplexity. Beyond his suggestion that probably Mr. Bessel would come back presently and explain what had happened, their conversation was unable to proceed. 'It might be a sudden tooth-ache,' said the porter, 'a very sudden and violent tooth-ache, jumping on him suddenly-like and driving him wild. I've broken things myself before now in such a case . . .' He thought. 'If it was, why should he say "*life*" to me as he went past?'

Mr. Vincey did not know. Mr. Bessel did not return, and at last Mr. Vincey, having done some more helpless staring, and having addressed a note of brief inquiry and left it in a conspicuous position on the bureau, returned in a very perplexed frame of mind to his own premises in Staple Inn. This affair had given him a shock. He was at a loss to account for Mr. Bessel's conduct on any sane hypothesis. He tried to read, but he could not do so; he went for a short walk, and was so preoccupied that he narrowly escaped a cab at the top of Chancery Lane; and at last—a full hour before his usual time—he went to bed. For a considerable time he could not sleep because of his memory of the silent confusion of Mr. Bessel's apartment, and when at length he did attain an uneasy slumber it was at once disturbed by a very vivid and distressing dream of Mr. Bessel.

He saw Mr. Bessel gesticulating wildly, and with his face white and contorted. And, inexplicably mingled with his appearance, suggested perhaps by his gestures, was an intense fear, an urgency to act. He even believed that he heard the voice of his fellow experimenter calling distressfully to him, though at the time he considered this to be an illusion. The vivid impression remained though Mr. Vincey awoke. For a space he lay awake and trembling in the darkness, possessed with that vague, unaccountable terror of unknown possibilities that comes out of dreams upon even the bravest men. But at last he roused himself, and turned over and went to sleep again, only for the dream to return with enhanced vividness.

He awoke with such a strong conviction that Mr. Bessel was in overwhelming distress and need of help that sleep was no longer possible. He was persuaded that his friend had rushed out to some dire calamity. For a time he lay reasoning vainly against this belief, but at last he gave way to it. He arose, against all reason, lit his gas and dressed, and set out through the deserted streets—deserted, save for a noiseless policeman or so and the early news carts—towards Vigo Street to inquire if Mr. Bessel had returned.

But he never got there. As he was going down Long Acre some unaccountable impulse turned him aside out of that street towards Covent Garden, which was just waking to its nocturnal activities. He saw the market in front of him—a queer effect of glowing yellow lights and busy black figures. He became aware of a shouting, and perceived a figure turn the corner by the hotel and run swiftly towards him. He knew at once that it was Mr. Bessel. But it was Mr. Bessel transfigured. He was hatless and dishevelled, his collar was torn open, he grasped a bone-handled walking-cane near the ferrule end, and his mouth was pulled awry. And he ran, with agile strides, very rapidly. Their encounter was the affair of an instant. 'Bessel!' cried Vincey.

The running man gave no sign of recognition either of Mr. Vincey or of his own name. Instead, he cut at his friend savagely with the stick, hitting him in the face within an inch of the eye. Mr. Vincey, stunned and astonished, staggered back, lost his footing, and fell heavily on the pavement. It seemed to him that Mr. Bessel leapt over him as he fell. When he looked again Mr. Bessel had vanished, and a policeman and a number of garden porters and salesmen were rushing past towards Long Acre in hot pursuit.

With the assistance of several passers-by—for the whole street was speedily alive with running people—Mr. Vincey struggled to his feet. He at once became the centre of a crowd greedy to see his injury. A multitude of voices competed to reassure him of his safety, and then to tell him of the behaviour of the madman, as they regarded Mr. Bessel. He had suddenly appeared in the middle of the market screaming '*Life! Life!*' striking left and right with a blood-stained walking-stick, and dancing and shouting with laughter at each successful blow. A lad and two women had broken heads, and he had smashed a man's wrist; a little child had been knocked insensible, and for a time he had driven everyone before him, so furious and resolute had his behaviour been. Then he made a raid upon a coffee stall, hurled its paraffin flare through the window of the post office, and fled laughing, after stunning the foremost of the two policemen who had the pluck to charge him.

Mr. Vincey's first impulse was naturally to join in the pursuit of his friend, in order if possible to save him from the violence of the indignant people. But his action was slow, the blow had half stunned him, and while this was still no more than a resolution came the news, shouted through the crowd, that Mr. Bessel had eluded his pursuers. At first Mr. Vincey could scarcely credit this, but the universality of the report, and presently the dignified return of two futile policemen, convinced him. After some aimless inquiries he returned towards Staple Inn, padding a handkerchief to a now very painful nose.

He was angry and astonished and perplexed. It appeared to him indisputable that Mr. Bessel must have gone violently mad in the midst of his experiment in thought transference, but why that should make him appear with a sad white face in Mr. Vincey's dreams seemed a problem beyond solution. He racked his brains in vain to explain this. It seemed to him at last that not simply Mr. Bessel, but the order of things must be insane. But he could think of nothing to do. He shut himself carefully into his room, lit his fire—it was a gas fire with asbestos bricks—and, fearing fresh dreams if he went to bed, remained bathing his injured face, or holding up books in a vain attempt to read, until dawn. Throughout that vigil he had a curious persuasion that Mr. Bessel was endeavouring to speak to him, but he would not let himself attend to any such belief.

About dawn, his physical fatigue asserted itself, and he went to bed and slept at last in spite of dreaming. He rose late, unrested and anxious and in considerable facial pain. The morning papers had no news of Mr. Bessel's aberration —it had come too late for them. Mr. Vincey's perplexities, to which the fever of his bruise added fresh irritation, became at last intolerable, and, after a fruitless visit to the Albany, he went down to St. Paul's Churchyard to Mr. Hart, Mr. Bessel's partner, and so far as Mr. Vincey knew, his nearest friend.

He was surprised to learn that Mr. Hart, although he knew nothing of the outbreak, had also been disturbed by a vision, the very vision that Mr. Vincey had seen—Mr. Bessel, white and dishevelled, pleading earnestly by his gestures for help. That was his impression of the import of his signs. 'I was just going to look him up in the Albany when you arrived,' said Mr. Hart. 'I was so sure of something being wrong with him.'

As the outcome of their consultation the two gentlemen decided to inquire at Scotland Yard for news of their missing friend. 'He is bound to be laid by the heels,' said Mr. Hart. 'He can't go on at that pace for long.' But the police authorities had not laid Mr. Bessel by the heels. They confirmed Mr. Vincey's overnight experiences and added fresh circumstances, some of an even graver character than those he knew—a list of smashed glass along the upper half of Tottenham Court Road, an attack upon a policeman in Hampstead Road, and an atrocious assault upon a woman. All these outrages were committed between half-past twelve and a quarter to two in the morning, and between those hours—and, indeed, from the very moment of Mr. Bessel's first rush from his rooms at half-past nine in the evening —they could trace the deepening violence of his fantastic career. For the last hour, at least from before one, that is, until a quarter to two, he had run amuck through London, eluding with amazing agility every effort to stop or capture him.

But after a quarter to two he had vanished. Up to that hour witnesses were multitudinous. Dozens of people had seen him, fled from him or pursued him, and then things suddenly came to an end. At a quarter to two he had been seen running down the Euston Road towards Baker Street, flourishing a can of burning colza oil and jerking splashes of flame therefrom at the windows of the houses he passed. But none of the policemen on Euston Road beyond the Waxwork Exhibition, nor any of those in the side streets down which he must have passed had he left the Euston Road, had seen anything of him. Abruptly he disappeared. Nothing of his subsequent doings came to light in spite of the keenest inquiry.

Here was a fresh astonishment for Mr. Vincey. He had found considerable comfort in Mr. Hart's conviction: 'He is bound to be laid by the heels before long,' and in that assurance he had been able to suspend his mental perplexities.

But any fresh development seemed destined to add new impossibilities to a pile already heaped beyond the powers of his acceptance. He found himself doubting whether his memory might not have played him some grotesque trick, debating whether any of these things could possibly have happened; and in the afternoon he hunted up Mr. Hart again to share the intolerable weight on his mind. He found Mr. Hart engaged with a well-known private detective, but as that gentleman accomplished nothing in this case, we need not enlarge upon his proceedings.

All that day Mr. Bessel's whereabouts eluded an unceasingly active inquiry, and all that night. And all that day there was a persuasion in the back of Mr. Vincey's mind that Mr. Bessel sought his attention, and all through the night Mr. Bessel with a tear-stained face of anguish pursued him through his dreams. And whenever he saw Mr. Bessel in his dreams he also saw a number of other faces, vague but malignant, that seemed to be pursuing Mr. Bessel.

It was on the following day, Sunday, that Mr. Vincey recalled certain remarkable stories of Mrs. Bullock, the medium, who was then attracting attention for the first time in London. He determined to consult her. She was staying at the house of that well-known inquirer, Dr. Wilson Paget, and Mr. Vincey, although he had never met that gentleman before, repaired to him forthwith with the intention of invoking her help. But scarcely had he mentioned the name of Bessel when Doctor Paget interrupted him. 'Last night—just at the end,' he said, 'we had a communication.'

He left the room, and returned with a slate on which were certain words written in a handwriting, shaky indeed, but indisputably the handwriting of Mr. Bessel!

'How did you get this?' said Mr. Vincey. 'Do you mean——?'

'We got it last night,' said Doctor Paget. With numerous interruptions from Mr. Vincey, he proceeded to explain how the writing had been obtained. It appears that in her *séances*, Mrs. Bullock passes into a condition of trance, her eyes rolling up in a strange way under her eyelids, and her body becoming rigid. She then begins to talk very rapidly, usually in voices other than her own. At the same time one or both of her hands may become active, and if slates and pencils are provided they will then write messages simultaneously with and quite independently of the flow of words from her mouth. By many she is considered an even more remarkable medium than the celebrated Mrs. Piper. It was one of these messages, the one written by her left hand, that Mr. Vincey now had before him. It consisted of eight words written disconnectedly 'George Bessel . . . trial excav^n . . . Baker Street . . . help . . . starvation'. Curiously enough, neither Doctor Paget nor the two other inquirers who were present had heard of the disappearance of Mr. Bessel—the news of it appeared only in the evening papers of Saturday—and they had put the message aside with many others of a vague and enigmatical sort that Mrs. Bullock has from time to time delivered.

When Doctor Paget heard Mr. Vincey's story, he gave himself at once with great energy to the pursuit of this clue to the discovery of Mr. Bessel. It would serve no useful purpose here to describe the inquiries of Mr. Vincey and himself; suffice it that the clue was a genuine one, and that Mr. Bessel was actually discovered by its aid.

He was found at the bottom of a detached shaft which had been sunk and abandoned at the commencement of the work for the new electric railway near Baker Street Station. His arm and leg and two ribs were broken. The shaft is protected by a hoarding nearly 20 feet high, and over this, incredible as it seems, Mr. Bessel, a stout, middle-aged gentleman, must have scrambled in order to fall down the shaft. He was saturated in colza oil, and the smashed tin lay beside him, but luckily the flame had been extinguished by his fall. And his madness had passed from him altogether. But he was, of course, terribly enfeebled, and at the sight of his rescuers he gave way to hysterical weeping.

In view of the deplorable state of his flat, he was taken to the house of Dr. Hatton in Upper Baker Street. Here he was subjected to a sedative treatment, and anything that might recall the violent crisis through which he had passed was carefully avoided. But on the second day he volunteered a statement.

Since that occasion Mr. Bessel has several times repeated this statement—to myself among other people—varying the details as the narrator of real experiences always does, but never by any chance contradicting himself in any particular. And the statement he makes is in substance as follows.

In order to understand it clearly it is necessary to go back to his experiments with Mr. Vincey before his remarkable attack. Mr. Bessel's first attempts at self-projection, in his experiments with Mr. Vincey, were, as the reader will remember, unsuccessful. But through all of them he was concentrating all his power and will upon getting out of the body—'willing it with all my might,' he says. At last, almost against expectation, came success. And Mr. Bessel asserts that he, being alive, did actually, by an effort of will, leave his body and pass into some place or state outside this world.

The release was, he asserts, instantaneous. 'At one moment I was seated in my chair, with my eyes tightly shut, my hands gripping the arms of the chair, doing all I could to concentrate my mind on Vincey, and then I perceived myself outside my body—saw my body near me, but certainly not containing me, with the hands relaxing and the head drooping forward on the breast.'

Nothing shakes him in his assurance of that release. He describes in a quiet, matter-of-fact way the new sensation he experienced. He felt he had become impalpable—so much he had expected, but he had not expected to find himself enormously large. So, however, it would seem he became. 'I was a great cloud—if I may express it that way —anchored to my body. It appeared to me, at first, as if I had discovered a greater self of which the conscious being in my brain was only a little part. I saw the Albany and Piccadilly and Regent Street and all the rooms and places in the houses, very minute and very bright and distinct, spread out below me like a little city seen from a balloon. Every now and then vague shapes like drifting wreaths of smoke made the vision a little indistinct, but at first I paid little heed to them. The thing that astonished me most, and which astonishes me still, is that I saw quite distinctly the insides of the houses as well as the streets, saw little people dining and talking in the private houses, men and women dining, playing billiards, and drinking in restaurants and hotels, and several places of entertainment crammed with people. It was like watching the affairs of a glass hive.'

Such were Mr. Bessel's exact words as I took them down when he told me the story. Quite forgetful of Mr. Vincey, he remained for a space observing these things. Impelled by curiosity, he says, he stooped down, and with the shadowy arm he found himself possessed of attempted to touch a man walking along Vigo Street. But he could not do so, though his finger seemed to pass through the man. Something prevented his doing this, but what it was he finds it hard to describe. He compares the obstacle to a sheet of glass.

'I felt as a kitten may feel,' he said, 'when it goes for the first time to pat its reflection in a mirror.' Again and again, on the occasion when I heard him tell this story, Mr. Bessel returned to that comparison of the sheet of glass. Yet it was not altogether a precise comparison, because, as the reader will speedily see, there were interruptions of this generally impermeable resistance, means of getting through the barrier to the material world again. But, naturally, there is a very great difficulty in expressing these unprecedented impressions in the language of everyday experience.

A thing that impressed him instantly, and which weighed upon him throughout all this experience, was the stillness of this place—he was in a world without sound.

At first Mr. Bessel's mental state was an unemotional wonder. His thought chiefly concerned itself with where he might be. He was out of the body—out of his material body, at any rate—but that was not all. He believes, and I for one believe also, that he was somewhere out of space, as we understand it, altogether. By a strenuous effort of will he had passed out of his body into a world beyond this world, a world undreamt of, yet lying so close to it and so strangely situated with regard to it that all things on this earth are clearly visible both from without and from within in this other world about us. For a long time, as it seemed to him, this realisation occupied his mind to the exclusion of all other matters, and then he recalled the engagement with Mr. Vincey, to which this astonishing experience was, after all, but a prelude.

He turned his mind to locomotion in this new body in which he found himself. For a time he was unable to shift himself from his attachment to his earthly carcass. For a time this new strange cloud body of his simply swayed, contracted, expanded, coiled, and writhed with his efforts to free himself, and then quite suddenly the link that bound him snapped. For a moment everything was hidden by what appeared to be whirling spheres of dark vapour, and then through a momentary gap he saw his drooping body collapse limply, saw his lifeless head drop sideways, and found he was driving along like a huge cloud in a strange place of shadowy clouds that had the luminous intricacy of London spread like a model below.

But now he was aware that the fluctuating vapour about him was something more than vapour, and the temerarious excitement of his first essay was shot with fear. For he perceived, at first indistinctly, and then suddenly very clearly, that he was surrounded by *faces!* that each roll and coil of the seeming cloud-stuff was a face. And such faces! Faces of thin shadow, faces of gaseous tenuity. Faces like those faces that glare with intolerable strangeness upon the sleeper in the evil hours of his dreams. Evil, greedy eyes that were full of a covetous curiosity, faces with knit brows and snarling, smiling lips; their vague hands clutched at Mr. Bessel as he passed, and the rest of their bodies was but an elusive streak of trailing darkness. Never a word they said, never a sound from the mouths that seemed to gibber. All about him they pressed in that dreamy silence, passing freely through the dim mistiness that was his body, gathering ever more numerously about him. And the shadowy Mr. Bessel, now suddenly fear-stricken, drove through the silent, active multitude of eyes and clutching hands.

So inhuman were these faces, so malignant their staring eyes, and shadowy, clawing gestures, that it did not occur to Mr. Bessel to attempt intercourse with these drifting creatures. Idiot phantoms, they seemed, children of vain desire, beings unborn and forbidden the boon of being, whose only expressions and gestures told of the envy and craving for life that was their one link with existence.

It says much for his resolution that, amidst the swarming cloud of these noiseless spirits of evil, he could still think of Mr. Vincey. He made a violent effort of will and found himself, he knew not how, stooping towards Staple Inn, saw Vincey sitting attentive and alert in his armchair by the fire.

And clustering also about him, as they clustered ever about all that lives and breathes, was another multitude of these vain voiceless shadows, longing, desiring, seeking some loophole into life.

For a space Mr. Bessel sought ineffectually to attract his friend's attention. He tried to get in front of his eyes, to move the objects in his room, to touch him. But Mr. Vincey remained unaffected, ignorant of the being that was so close to his own. The strange something that Mr. Bessel has compared to a sheet of glass separated them impermeably.

And at last Mr. Bessel did a desperate thing. I have told how that in some strange way he could see not only the outside of a man as we see him, but within. He extended his shadowy hand and thrust his vague black fingers, as it seemed, through the heedless brain.

Then, suddenly, Mr. Vincey started like a man who recalls his attention from wandering thoughts, and it seemed to Mr. Bessel that a little dark-red body situated in the middle of Mr. Vincey's brain swelled and glowed as he did so. Since that experience he has been shown anatomical figures of the brain, and he knows now that this is that useless structure, as doctors call it, the pineal eye. For, strange as it will seem to many, we have, deep in our brains—where it cannot possibly see any earthly light—an eye! At the time this, with the rest of the internal anatomy of the brain, was quite new to him. At the sight of its changed appearance, however, he thrust forth his finger, and, rather fearful still of the consequences, touched this little spot. And instantly Mr. Vincey started, and Mr. Bessel knew that he was seen.

And at that instant it came to Mr. Bessel that evil had happened to his body, and behold! a great wind blew through all that world of shadows and tore him away. So strong was this persuasion that he thought no more of Mr. Vincey, but turned about forthwith, and all the countless faces drove back with him like leaves before a gale. But he returned too late. In an instant he saw the body that he had left inert and collapsed—lying, indeed, like the body of a man just dead—had arisen, had arisen by virtue of some strength and will beyond his own. It stood with staring eyes, stretching its limbs in dubious fashion.

For a moment he watched it in wild dismay, and then he stooped towards it. But the pane of glass had closed against him again, and he was foiled. He beat himself passionately against this, and all about him the spirits of evil grinned and pointed and mocked. He gave way to furious anger. He compares himself to a bird that has fluttered heedlessly into a room and is beating at the window-pane that holds it back from freedom.

And behold! the little body that had once been his was now dancing with delight. He saw it shouting, though he could not hear its shouts; he saw the violence of its movements grow. He watched it fling his cherished furniture about in the mad delight of existence, rend his books apart, smash bottles, drink heedlessly from the jagged fragments, leap and smite in a passionate acceptance of living. He watched these actions in paralysed astonishment. Then once more he hurled himself against the impassable barrier, and then, with all that crew of mocking ghosts about him, hurried back in dire confusion to Vincey to tell him of the outrage that had come upon him.

But the brain of Vincey was now closed against apparitions, and the disembodied Mr. Bessel pursued him in vain as he hurried out into Holborn to call a cab. Foiled and terror-stricken, Mr. Bessel swept back again, to find his desecrated body whooping in a glorious frenzy down the Burlington Arcade. . . .

And now the attentive reader begins to understand Mr. Bessel's interpretation of the first part of this strange story. The being whose frantic rush through London had inflicted so much injury and disaster had indeed Mr. Bessel's body, but it was not Mr. Bessel. It was an evil spirit out of that strange world beyond existence, into which Mr. Bessel had so rashly ventured. For twenty hours it held possession of him, and for all those twenty hours the dispossessed spirit-body of Mr. Bessel was going to and fro in that unheard-of middle world of shadows seeking help in vain.

He spent many hours beating at the minds of Mr. Vincey and of his friend Mr. Hart. Each, as we know, he roused by his efforts. But the language that might convey his situation to these helpers across the gulf he did not know; his feeble fingers groped vainly and powerlessly in their brains. Once, indeed, as we have already told, he was able to turn Mr. Vincey aside from his path so that he encountered the stolen body in its career, but he could not make him understand the thing that had happened: he was unable to draw any help from that encounter. . . .

All through those hours the persuasion was overwhelming in Mr. Bessel's mind that presently his body would be killed by its furious tenant, and he would have to remain in this shadow-land for evermore. So that those long hours were a growing agony of fear. And ever as he hurried to and fro in his ineffectual excitement innumerable spirits of that world about him mobbed him and confused his mind. And ever an envious applauding multitude poured after their successful fellow as he went upon his glorious career.

For that, it would seem, must be the life of these bodiless things of this world that is the shadow of our world. Ever they watch, coveting a way into a mortal body, in order that they may descend, as furies and frenzies, as violent lusts and mad, strange impulses, rejoicing in the body they have won. For Mr. Bessel was not the only human soul in that place. Witness the fact that he met first one, and afterwards several shadows of men, men like himself, it seemed, who had lost their bodies even it may be as he had lost his, and wandered, despairingly, in that lost world that is neither life nor death. They could not speak because that world is silent, yet he knew them for men because of their dim human bodies, and because of the sadness of their faces.

But how they had come into that world he could not tell, nor where the bodies they had lost might be, whether they still raved about the earth, or whether they were closed for ever in death against return. That they were the spirits of the dead neither he nor I believe. But Doctor Wilson Paget thinks they are the rational souls of men who are lost in madness on the earth.

At last Mr. Bessel chanced upon a place where a little

crowd of such disembodied silent creatures was gathered, and thrusting through them he saw below a brightly-lit room, and four or five quiet gentlemen and a woman, a stoutish woman dressed in black bombazine and sitting awkwardly in a chair with her head thrown back. He knew her from her portraits to be Mrs. Bullock, the medium. And he perceived that tracts and structures in her brain glowed and stirred as he had seen the pineal eye in the brain of Mr. Vincey glow. The light was very fitful; sometimes it was a broad illumination, and sometimes merely a faint twilight spot, and it shifted slowly about her brain. She kept on talking and writing with one hand. And Mr. Bessel saw that the crowding shadows of men about him, and a great multitude of the shadow spirits of that shadow land, were all striving and thrusting to touch the lighted regions of her brain. As one gained her brain or another was thrust away, her voice and the writing of her hand changed. So that what she said was disorderly and confused for the most part; now a fragment of one soul's message, and now a fragment of another's, and now she babbled the insane fancies of the spirits of vain desire. Then Mr. Bessel understood that she spoke for the spirit that had touch of her, and he began to struggle very furiously towards her. But he was on the outside of the crowd and at that time he could not reach her, and at last, growing anxious, he went away to find what had happened meanwhile to his body.

For a long time he went to and fro seeking it in vain and fearing that it must have been killed, and then he found it at the bottom of the shaft in Baker Street, writhing furiously and cursing with pain. Its leg and an arm and two ribs had been broken by its fall. Moreover, the evil spirit was angry because his time had been so short and because of the pain —making violent movements and casting his body about.

And at that Mr. Bessel returned with redoubled earnestness to the room where the *séance* was going on, and so soon as he had thrust himself within sight of the place he saw one of the men who stood about the medium looking at his watch as if he meant that the *séance* should presently end. At that a great number of the shadows who had been striving turned away with gestures of despair. But the thought that the *séance* was almost over only made Mr. Bessel the more earnest, and he struggled so stoutly with his will against the others that presently he gained the woman's brain. It chanced that just at that moment it glowed very brightly, and in that instant she wrote the message that Doctor Wilson Paget preserved. And then the other shadows and the cloud of evil spirits about him had thrust Mr. Bessel away from her, and for all the rest of the *séance* he could regain her no more.

So he went back and watched through the long hours at the bottom of the shaft where the evil spirit lay in the stolen body it had maimed, writhing and cursing, and weeping and groaning, and learning the lesson of pain. And towards dawn the thing he had waited for happened, the brain glowed brightly and the evil spirit came out, and Mr. Bessel entered the body he had feared he should never enter again. As he did so, the silence—the brooding silence—ended; he heard the tumult of traffic and the voices of people overhead, and that strange world that is the shadow of our world—the dark and silent shadows of ineffectual desire and the shadows of lost men—vanished clean away.

He lay there for the space of about three hours before he was found. And in spite of the pain and suffering of his wounds, and of the dim damp place in which he lay; in spite of the tears—wrung from him by his physical distress —his heart was full of gladness to know that he was nevertheless back once more in the kindly world of men.

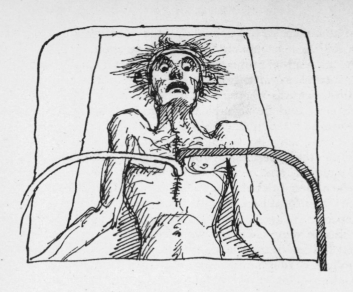

THE VIVISECTOR VIVISECTED

Sir Ronald Ross

(1857–1932)

*This story is certainly the most unique in the collection, for while all
the others are by professional writers about those who search for the
secrets of creation, Sir Ronald Ross was himself a scientific researcher
who made some remarkable discoveries. Though by no stretch of the
imagination could he be called a "mad scientist" or even a "monster
maker", some of his work earned him both scepticism and ridicule
from society. He was born in India and after studying medicine in
England returned to his native land where he served in the Indian
Medical Service and began research into tropical diseases. His
inquiries led him to discover the malaria parasite and in 1902 he
was awarded the Nobel prize for medicine. Much of his early writing*

was done in scientific papers and journals, but when he returned to be Professor of Tropical Medicine at Liverpool, he branched out into the fields of poetry and general fiction. His pronouncements on the scientific possibilities for the prolonging of life made him a celebrated figure (see the next story, "The Incubator Man") and caused him to write the following short story, published just before his death in 1932.

IN the year 1860, I, having completed my medical studies in London, and being a man of some small independence, determined upon visiting the various universities and scientific societies of the world. I travelled through Germany, France, Spain, Italy, Russia, Persia, Turkey, India and China. Having seen much physic poured down many throats, and having listened to the opposing views of five thousand professors, I became in the end assured that for most diseases the best medicine is water, taken internally. I was also convinced of the necessity for a better knowledge of physiology; for unless we know the working of a watch or machine, how can we hope to mend it? Truly hot oil poured in *may* do good; but it can also possibly clog the wheels. Hygiene is the better part of medicine; physiology, the best part of both: for without it we put on spectacles in the dark. Those great mysteries of Life and Death, birth, maintenance, action and thought were to me Mexicos, their solution El Dorados. Accordingly I set foot in America, the land of experiment, with enthusiasm. I passed eastward, calling on persons long known to me through their works; but I was not satisfied.

At the large city of Snogginsville I met the well-known Dr. Silcutt, famous for his excellent work on the encephalon of politicians. He was as ardent a physiologist as myself; and was at the time much excited by his recent excellent discovery that gold produces effects different from those of copper when approached to the different nerves of those engaged in public services. Titillation of the palm with the former metal produces contraction of the flexors, with the latter, contraction of the extensors. He was personally tall, sombre, and not of a humorous disposition. He lived in his private chambers at the Infirmary where I stayed with him so long that we became friends. With him there resided an old gentleman, suffering from dementia, whom at first I took to be his father.

The day before the one on which I intended leaving Snogginsville, Silcutt exhibited to me his private museum of medical curiosities. I remember that when we entered the room, he, being interested in argument, left the door ajar. Passing from specimen to specimen we at last arrived before a most curious contrivance. Roughly described, one would have considered it a double kind of pump with four tubes (two tubes from each pump) leading to a central mechanism. Each pump was a heavy square mass meant to be placed on the ground, with a piston action; the piston being so disposed as to require pushing down and pulling up without a lever. Silcutt seemed inclined to pass it, but I inquired its use; no sooner, however, were the words out of my mouth, than I heard a kind of scream behind me, muffled in laughter. The above-mentioned old gentleman was standing looking at the construction which had interested me. A quick frown passed over Silcutt's face, and he clutched the other by the arm. The old man lifted his right foot and placed it on a low bench close by. His face became tumid with blood until his white hair, eye-brows and scanty whiskers started out, as it were, in contrast. The veins of his neck swelled, and perspiration broke out on his forehead. His teeth were clenched and his eyes bloodshot; and though all this transformation occurred in a few seconds, yet he had every appearance of a man who had undergone severe bodily exercise. He stooped down as if to lift a heavy weight with both hands, and began to pull up and push down with his arms, as if, as I thought, he was working one of the pumps described above. He laughed and screamed alternately; until, after a few seconds more, a foam gathered on his lips, he shrieked, and fell down in an epileptic seizure.

Silcutt said, 'He is not my father. He is accustomed to these fits. He has been located with me for twenty years. Tonight, I will give you a manuscript, fully describing this occurrence and that machine; upon the condition that you do not divulge its contents until the death of both of us.'

Upon retiring to rest, I found on my bedroom table a manuscript signed 'William Silcutt, U.Sc.Phil.' Opening it, I read:—

'I attended Snogginsville Infirmary as a medical student from 1838 to 1840. Patrick Maculligan, a man of about forty years of age, was resident medical officer. He was at the time deeply engaged in experimental research on both physiology and therapeutics; and needing an assistant, he fixed on me. I was intensely fond of both these subjects; and we were often engaged together in the laboratory for the whole day. The Infirmary is situated on a hill, and is a long building, turreted at either end. At the time I speak of only one half of the structure was occupied by patients. At the top of the turret belonging to the empty wing, our laboratory was situated. Here we worked, ate, and often slept without seeing anyone but ourselves for twenty-four hours at a stretch. The laboratory consisted of five rooms; an animals' room for keeping live-stock; a chemical room; a micro-scopical room; a workshop for making implements; and the operation room. This last chamber was the top central one of the turret and had a window facing westward. It was painted black so as not to show the blood that was often spurted upon its walls. In a corner were a basin and ewer. Tables with various knives, tweezers, forceps, saws, etc., stood round. At a yard from one wall there was the usual stove with a pipe leading through the roof. In the middle stood the operating-table, which we called the altar of science. It was a complicated contrivance, padded and covered with leather, with a waterproof over all. It could be so drawn out, or pushed in, as to afford room for holding either a donkey or a guinea-pig at will. Numbers of fastening straps were attached. The door and window were padded to prevent the egress of any sound which might disturb the patients below.

'Maculligan was an Irish immigrant. He was of middle stature, pale of complexion, with light sandy hair. He was very grave and had large white front teeth. His hands were long and hairy; and owing to his studies, he was slightly bowed and weakly. A long scar cut from his left eye to the mouth, and the deformity made him the more shy. He was a Protestant, and when not engaged in vivisection, it was his great delight to read over a book of hymns, which he often hummed to himself. He told me that he was the son of an Irish physician and had left home owing to family quarrels, when a lad of seventeen.

'We had often discussed the awful problem of death. Could it be prevented? May not science hope to find its antidote? He said: "Seeing that most tissues are repairable, like bone, re-formable, or like skin to be mended by another structure, I believe that death does not originate in these parts which may be called rather the appurtenances of life than life itself. The older the man, the less able is he to obtain healing of wounds. Why? Because the healing power is older and less vigorous. What is the healing power? Where is it? Either in the nervous system or in the blood, I should say. A man dies, not because his muscles and organs decay; but because either the mechanism of his brain, cord, or ganglia is so attrite, and worn out, or his blood is so changed by continual use, as to be of no further service to the body. We cannot give an animal a new brain; but we can provide him with fresh blood. Let us try then whether the blood be not the seat of life. The plan we will adopt is this: I have constructed an artificial heart which may be filled with the fresh blood of an animal recently killed. Now we must obtain a corpse which has died of loss of blood alone: we must quickly after death cut down to his heart, and apply the apparatus to his blood-vessels, pour in a fresh circulation. By this means," he ended, rubbing his hands, "I hope to bring the dead to life." '

To understand the rest of Dr. Silcutt's narrative, the reader should know the course of the circulation. This is very simple. The heart is divided into two partitions, a right and a left one. The blood enters the right partition, whence it is squirted into the lungs; from the lungs it returns to the left partition, whence it is squirted all over the body; and from the body it finally returns back to the right partition, and so on *ad infinitum*. The apparatus now shown to Silcutt, described without the use of anatomical words, was an artificial heart, only the two partitions were quite separate, and to be worked by different pressure. The chest was opened and into the large blood-vessels, which convey the blood to and from the heart, long india-rubber tubes were inserted: so that the blood from the body was carried to the right artificial heart or pump, and thence squirted back to the lungs; from the lungs it passed to the left artificial heart or pump, and thence to the body, and so on. These artificial hearts were mere ordinary double-action pumps, with valves, which sucked in the fluid from one direction and expelled it in another; but having to be completely air-tight they were heavily constructed and the pistons were worked only with considerable difficulty. Each pump was placed in a hot-water bath to maintain the blood at the temperature of 100°; and one was to be put on either side of the dead body. To resume the manuscript:—

'It was some time before a fit subject was brought into the hospital. What was required was a person who had simply bled to death without much serious injury except the wound of the blood-vessels. A donkey was kept in readiness to supply the required fluid. We often practised the insertion of the india-rubber tubes into the blood-vessel on dead patients; and had become so skilful as to be able to finish the operation in five minutes.

'At last, on the morning of 5th October 1840, a patient was brought into the Infirmary with a cut wound on the head from which he had bled profusely. He had been cut with a knife in a street row. He was a tall, vigorous man, with an immense amount of red hair and beard and with a vicious leering kind of expression. When I saw him he was fast sinking; for the evident drunken habits of the patient did not predispose him to recovery. I only saw him and attended him (except the nurses); and had him removed to a private ward when he died at 2 p.m. Having previously acquainted Maculligan of the case, I waited below while that gentleman was preparing the apparatus. I sent the nurses out of the ward after the patient's death. I wrapt him in a blanket and drawing his hands over my shoulders carried him out. A violent storm, which had just broken, gave me greater security. I locked the door of the private ward and struggled as I best could with my burden up the narrow stairs of the turret. When I arrived in the laboratory, the apparatus was ready, and the pumps were standing in their baths of hot water (which was procured from the stove boiler). The donkey had been killed, and his fresh blood was in the cavities of our machine.

'Maculligan was flushed with excitement: "Now," he exclaimed, "we shall get at least some knowledge; either a useful negative result, or a world-reforming fact."

'I placed the body on the bed: on his left side was the pump which I was to work and which sent the blood all over his body; on his right side Maculligan supplied his lungs. In a minute I had fastened the limbs, and made bare the chest of the man. Maculligan seized the knife, and at one swoop cut down to the heart. I held apart the several parts. Almost immediately it seemed he had inserted the tubes into the arteries and veins, and a few seconds sufficed to sew up the chest again, joining the cartilages as well as the skin, and covering all the incision with a quickly congealing gum to exclude the air, and permit breathing. The whole was done by ten minutes after death. The corpse was pale, slightly cold, the eyelids half-open, and the eyes turned upwards beneath them. Blankets were thrown upon it to retain the heat. The storm outside had increased in fury; the rain drenched the window-panes, and the violence of the wind was such that the whole tower seemed to rock. Most unearthly noises, too, were caused by it; and the darkness was so great that we could barely see to do our experiment. I could observe Maculligan trembling with excitement. I myself, though generally stolid, was much moved.

' "Are you ready," said he, taking hold of his pump and speaking hoarsely. "Then away," and down went the pistons simultaneously.

'We told twelve strokes—no blood had oozed from the cut in the chest—all was satisfactory. Another twelve—a slight flushing the cheeks. Maculligan stopped, and we both took off our coats, the wind howling with tenfold fury. We resumed—suddenly the eyes closed. We went on for fully quarter of an hour.

' "He is breathing," cried my companion.

'Most certainly there was some slight action of the diaphragm. Maculligan suddenly motioned me to stop, and going up to the patient listened to hear the breathing. While he looked into the man's face the eyes suddenly opened, following my friend, who sprang back to his pump, trembling violently. We went on silently; the man, all the while, watching Maculligan whose hair seemed stiff, and whose face was so changed that I should hardly have known him. I myself was so astounded that I could not conceive the occurrence as real. We had never expected that there would be any recovery beyond a comatose condition.

'Suddenly the man, who appeared as if recovering from chloroform, said aloud, "Lave it, will you."

' "Lave what?" asked Maculligan, hoarsely.

' "Lave pulling that out of the ground, for sure it goes bang through the wurrld, and is clamped on the other side. It's o' no use."

' "Bedad," he continued, "but ye're the rummiest egg-flip iver I came across."

' "Egg-flip! Eh, boy?" cried Maculligan, laughing excitedly; "You're another."

' "What!" said the man, smiling with one side of his mouth, "you air a wag, you air—a kind o' wag as tells loodicrus tales to tay-totallers at taymatins, you air."

' "No, I ain't now," exclaimed my friend, lifting his chin, and winking in an excited, ready-boy kind of manner.

' "Wal, friend," continued the patient, "kep your 'air on, an' nobody 'ud tell you warn't a Quaker. But you're too quaky for your occupation—I tak it you're a water-works man, with that 'ere pump, eh, friend?" He then spat into the air.

' "What makes you think that, boy," answered my companion, putting his tongue in his cheek, and pumping vigorously.

' "Wal," returned the other, laughing roughly, "I guessed you war by your complexion. I say," he continued, winking, "you don't often git your pipes bunged in these parts by vivisections does yer—no vivisected babbies, now—eh?"

' "Not I, lad, not I," laughed Maculligan boisterously.

' "That's odd now! och! man, sure, an wasn't I a vivisector in ould Ireland, an a phesycian."

' "I hope you got many of 'em," laughed the other.

' "Many o' wot?"

' "Fees—you said you were a feesycian."

' "Wal," laughed the man, winking, "just you write that 'ere goak in yer diary and have a dinner on the annivassery of it, ivery year. Yes, sir, I was a physician, and, sure, an eminent one and got me thousand a year, and lived in Merion Square, bedad. But I went in for physiology—I went in for physiology, and so got ruined. I say! won't the devil give me hot for my vivisecting—for the cutting—eh? For the fastening up—eh? 'You should have taken the trouble to give chloroform,' he'll say. But I don't care a doight for the devil—eh?—till I am dead—eh? snifflewink?"

' "But what if you are," cried Maculligan, loudly. "Eh, boy, what if you are?"

' "Hey? Wal, stranger, I guess you air goin' it with that 'ere pump. I say," he called out suddenly, "stop it, will you! Every push sends a throb in me chist, you skippin' spalpeen."

'The patient seemed to become alarmed. He had kept his eyes fixed on my associate; he now turned them upon me, and I saw that he recognized me.

'He began to pull at his wrists and ankles, when Maculligan, not knowing what he was saying, kept on repeating, "But, what if you *are* dead?"

'All this while we were both pumping without intermission.

' "Aha!" hissed the man, his face wearing a horrible expression, "what is this? What is this? I am dead! Begorra, I died just now—I died of a cut on the head, and drank a bottle o' whiskey upon it to die drunk! Oh, Lord! I see it—ochone! I am in hell, and I am drunk still!" He wrenched again at his wrists, screaming.

' "So you are, Pat," cried my friend. "So you are."

' "Ah! Lord! What 'ull they say if I come up to court drunk! Maybe I have been in court already, but was so inebriate I did not know it, and have got damned out o' hand, with never a bit of a voice in the matter."

' "So you have, Pat, so you have. You were dead drunk in the dock, you were."

' "Ah! krimy," groaned the man, his eye wandering down to the instrument stuck in his chest, the stitches in his skin and the tubes leading to the pumps. "Och! St. Pathrick, I see it! And my punishment is, to be done to as I have been done by. And you are a couple of devils, and I a vivisection; and I shall be vivisected for iver and iver, wurrld without end—Oh! Lord—damn—damn—damn——"

'Here Maculligan inadvertently missed a stroke which caused the patient to gasp violently.

' "Now, don't do it again, honey," he continued. "I'll swear no more, purty deevil that ye are, I did not mane to chaffer ye just now—but ye're the wittiest devil, truly speaking, that I iver saw on earth, or in h—— or anywhere. You'll not be studyin' much on me now, will yer, dear?"

' "We shall not do more than tie up your bile duct and establish a fistula in your side today, friend," said Maculligan, winking at me.

' "And will you do that? Oh! crikey?"

' "To-morrow we are going to lay out a piece of your mesentery under the microscope to see the blood circulate."

' "Oh, sammy! And what 'ull yer do the day arter?"

' "See how much of your brains we can slice off without stopping your thinking."

' "Why, yer don't imagine I think with the pit of my stomich, do yer? One blessing yer'll have to lave it soon, for there 'ull never be a pickin' place left on me carcase."

' "Not a bit of it, my dear sir," roared Maculligan, who seemed mad from excitement. "You heal up in one place as soon as we go on to another."

' "Well, that knocks all hope out of me. But what are ye doin' now?"

' "Injecting you with donkey's blood to see if you will bray."

' "I'll not do that, anyway, but I tell you what, I feel uncommon sharp and witty like. I 'ud advise you to try a little of the same mixture. Yer not agoin' to have any alcoholic experiments on me, friend, air ye?"

' "No—why?"

' "Wal, yer might find out how much whuskey it 'ull take

to make me drunk, anyhow, honey. O Lord!" he ejaculated, looking round, "how well I know them scalpels, directors, retractors, bone-forceps, aneurism needles and the like, and I have often done all the experiments you have mentioned."

'At times the man dropped the coarser Irish brogue, and at other times used a Californian slang.

' "You see," he continued, "I was a man of some eminence in the medical profession."

' "And how did you lose that eminence?"

' "One day I was up to the ears in thought about me theory of diabetes, when a poodle happening to bark about me heels, instead of kicking it away, sure enough I put it in me pocket, thoughtlessly."

' "Well?"

' "Well, that poodle belonged to the vice-queen, or the vice-royess, who offered a hundred pound for it. Now a rapscallion saw me pockit the poodle, tould a policeman, who followed me as I went home one day, entered me house, got up to the laboratory and found the identical poodle with a pay in its fourth ventricle, and a pin in its curvickle ganglion. They had me up for dog-stealing, jist as I had complated me work on the subject in hand, and instid of putting me in the Royal Society, put me in a common prison. When I got out I took to drinking and went to America and the dogs; and I've got there now, begorra!—Yer will not give me chloroform, thin, honey; or a gin-cocktail now? Be Jesus, how the devils are howlin' round about!"

'During this extraordinary conversation the wind had risen still more, and the turret was plainly felt to rock to and fro. The evening, too, began to hasten in, aided by the black, scurrying rack that obscured the sky. We had been toiling for more than an hour, having to keep time like rowers. My arms were getting tired, and I was profusely perspiring. Maculligan was shouting and laughing like a maniac or drunkard, his face bloated with exertion and his long light hair hanging over his eyes. Suddenly I cast my eyes on the thermometer in the bath which maintained the heat of the blood at the necessary 100°. It stood at 97·4°. The fire in the stove was getting low.

'I said: "The fire is getting low; it must be replenished."

' "You pile it up then," said Maculligan; "we must both leave off together."

'At a signal from him we both ceased pumping and I, who was nearest, rushed to the stove, knocked the lid off and poured in, in my haste, the whole scuttle full of coals. When I returned the patient had fainted: we immediately resumed.

'I said: "He was nearly out then, Maculligan."

' "Wot's that?" muttered the patient, coming round. "Tarnation take you deevils, how did you gumption that my name was Maculligan?"

' "Is that so?" inquired Maculligan.

' "Is that so! I guess it is—Josephus Maculligan av Maculligan Castle, County Lietrim, son av old Maculligan av the same, and be damned to yer!"

'No sooner were these words uttered than my companion uttered the most horrible yell I ever heard.

' "You are my brother," he shrieked; "Ha! ha! look at this!" showing the long scar on his face. The patient's jaw dropped, and he struggled violently; but when my friend relaxed the speed of pumping he fell back, and began to groan.

' "Oh! oh! Is it me brother they have put to plague me, me twin brother, who I knocked about and gashed down the cheek because he was after bein' five munutes older than myself and had got all the proparty? Ye are not dead, Pathrick dear? Ye are no ghost, avic? Ye will not tormint me though your father and me druv you to Ameriky?"

' "No, no," shouted Maculligan. "I am alive! You are alive! We are all alive! I am surgeon of the Snogginsville Infirmary. I have made an invention for reviving the dead by means of injecting hot, fresh blood into his veins. I required a case for experiment, which had merely bled to death.

You were the first that presented. If we leave off pumping for five minutes, or the stove goes out, letting the hot water cool, the blood will clot in the machine and you will die immediately."

'I cannot describe the face of Josephus Maculligan during this recital. He burst forth into oaths, upbraiding his brother for attempting such an experiment, and shrieking for help. But the wind out-shrieked him. He prayed and cried alternately. My arms were getting intensely tired, and my back was aching, owing to the necessary stoop of the body. Suddenly the setting sun, which was almost touching the horizon, gleamed out from the clouds, and poured a red glow on Patrick Maculligan's face. I shall never forget its expression: he seemed to have become more like an ape than a man. His face was turbid and red; his mouth drawn back at the corners, showing all his teeth and the very gums. His tongue hung out, the large veins of the throat and forehead stood prominent, the long scar on the cheek glistened white, and seemed to have contracted in length, drawing up the upper lip, and showing the canine tooth of that side. His necktie and collar had burst open, and he panted quickly like a dog; while his eyes, round and lidless, glared on his brother, not with anger or fear, but without any expression at all. The one beam of blood-red light, streaming in from the window seemed to rest upon him on purpose, and, as it were, moved and twined amongst his hair. He alone was visible: all the rest of the room was dark; for the ray, after touching him passed into the workshop beyond. I could see that his hands which were working the pump were swollen and veined.

'He said: "You have wronged me. We are twin brothers, and I being the weaker should have been protected by you, rather than bullied. We both loved Lucy Hagan; but she preferred me. One day I said: 'I have brains; I don't want the property; I will ask Lucy to marry me, and we will go to America!' I went to ask her passing through a wood. You were there felling trees. You threw the hatchet at me, saying: 'I'll knock the Polly Beloy dear out of you!' The steel cut my cheek. A week afterwards I presented myself to Lucy. She said she would think about it, and in the evening sent me a refusal written in French and a hymn-book with her favourite hymns marked. She informed me that she was going to marry you. I called upon her to thank her for the hymn-book, and murdered her on the spot. I then proceeded to America when I heard that my father was found dead in bed. I said: 'My brother Joseph has murdered him.' Both of us being murderers, it was natural enough that we should go a step further and become vivisectors, and this is our punishment."

' "Wal," returned the other, spitting into the ray of light, "I guess I'd rayther be you than me in this here investigation of nature. You are payin' interest and principal together of that 'ere loan across the cheek I gave yer. If yer cannot kep up that elber-jiggerin work much longer, I will be much obleeged if you will ax someone to come up and relieve yer, and bring up a drop or two o' somethin' cooling, cas I am feeling tarnation warrum."

' "If either of us stop for two minutes you are dead, clear; and there are no more donkeys in the establishment," answered Patrick. "It won't do for only one to pump, because that will burst up your vessels. And it won't do to call, because no one will hear. It would take at least four minutes to get to the occupied wing of the building and back and by that time clots would be sure to form, any one of which getting in your brain would kill you slick."

' "Wal," asked Josephus, "and cud not both of you go and divide the distance atween yer? I am getting as hot as a tay-pot."

'Looking at the thermometer in the water-bath of my pump, I observed it stood at 102°. The fire in the stove, drawn by the violent wind, was beginning to roar through the heap of coals.

' "Turn on the cold water," said Patrick.

'It came from the tap with a gush, then stopped—*the water-pipe had been broken by the storm.* The thermometer was rising—if it passed 120° the blood would be heated to the same temperature, and would certainly become coagulated, or would coagulate the nervous matter of the patient. We left off, and I rushed to the stove—*the poker and shovel had both been sent to be mended.* The patient was gasping.

' "If you stop me circulation again, yer spalpeens, I'll skin yer," he said.

'We resumed. The light had left Patrick's face, but the stove glowed out in the darkness, and we heard the roaring of the flames. Patrick was staggering like a drunkard, and breathing stertorously. His tongue was hanging further out; the corners of his mouth were drawn more and more backwards; and at every stroke he pulled, his ears twitched. In my hands there was no feeling left, for as said before, the pumps were very stiff. I pushed and pulled mechanically; there was a dead pain at my heart; I could think of nothing, my eyes were glazed; all I saw was the thermometer slowly rising. Josephus was struggling and howling.

' "Arrah, now," he cried, "ye're running fire into me. Lave it will yer. I guess I'll get up and pummel yer both."

'We stopped for a second, when he yelled out, "Go on yer hell-sparks, or I'll report yer behaviour to the deevil. O Lord," he groaned, "here's faver and no ague."

'The thermometer had reached 106°.

' "Wal," continued Josephus, "this 'ull put me in the very best trainin' for hell cud be imagined. I shall ask for a place as head stoker after this, for I shan't flinch at no fire agin."

'Patrick tried to speak but could not. The flames in the stove shot up through the coaling-hole at top. The thermometer stood at 108°, a temperature seldom reached by the most violent fevers.

' "Josephus said, "I poisoned me father with opium and

drove me brother to murder his sweetheart, but they ought
to let me into heaven arter this, for it's punishment enough
sure. It's plaguey hard on a poor boy to make him die twice
—to make him pay over agin for his ticket to tarnation. Ah!
lads kep it up, lads. Though ye're a runnin' the red-hot blood
o' ten thousand jackasses biled in the boilers av the cintre
of the wurrld into me Ah-orta, kep it up! Though ye are a
sweatin' away yerselves, till there is nothin' left av yer but
yer skilitons, and a little ile in yer boots, yet kep it up, lads,
kep it up! Brayvo, brayvo! oh! but the warrmth—the
warrmth! I'll tak me whusky cold, I thank you. Ice! Thanks,
I wull jist tak a limp o' the same."

'He then ceased talking and struggled violently. The last
he said was, "Good-bye, Pathrick; I'll vivisect yer, t' other
side o' Jourdan!"

'The thermometer had reached 116·5°. The howling of
the wind was awful. Patrick was rolling from side to side.
The perspiration ran down over my eyes. I could not feel
my arms below the shoulders. Patrick suddenly drew in his
breath sharply, gave a yell, threw up his arms and fell on
his face. Josephus by a last effort wrenched his arms loose,
sat up, clutched at his throat and fell back. At the same
moment the storm blew in the window with a crash. In came
the tempest and rain, a spiral of flame shot up from the
stove, and I was hurled to the ground.

'It was morning when I woke. The stove was out and
Patrick sleeping soundly. I could not stand, nor move the
arms below the elbows. As best I could I crawled downstairs
for assistance.

'Josephus Maculligan was stone dead, and was soon
buried. Patrick lives, but he is demented and suffers from
attacks of epilepsy. I am myself quite well.

'(Signed) WILLIAM SILCUTT.'

Such was the remarkable manuscript I read, and I may
well be believed when I state that so great was the horror of

vivisection which I derived from the perusal of this account of the impaling and exhaustion to death of living beings, that I took to collecting butterflies in the summer, and hunting in the winter, neglecting the medical profession altogether. After the death of Silcutt and Maculligan, I related the story to the President of the Club for the Total Abolition of Vivisection. He asked me down to the country branch of that club, where I was to read the manuscript.

After our interesting pigeon battue, where more than two hundred birds were killed, we dined. I then read the work; which filled the members with such horror that they passed forty-five resolutions upon the spot, and finished the day with an oyster and white-bait supper. I am sure that the reader who believes this atrocious and fearful tale cannot become anything but a *Total Anti-vivisectionist.*

THE INCUBATOR MAN

Wallace West

(1907–   )

The stories which Sir Ronald Ross wrote during the closing years of his life were just as popular in America as in England, and Wallace West was not the only writer to have utilised some of his theories as a starting point for Fantasy Fiction. West came to prominence during the boom for S. F. magazines during and after the Second World War. Perhaps his most notable triumph was "Eddie for Short", written in 1953, in which the last woman left alive on earth—who is pregnant

—realises she must have a boy if the human race is to continue. He had written "The Incubator Man" many years earlier in 1928 when the statements by Sir Ronald and the interviews with him were head-line news—as the opening paragraphs of the story indicate. Even after all these years both the concept and the storytelling remain fresh and vivid—and not a little moving. This is the first story in the collection to be told by a "monster" from his own viewpoint, and the links with that great original, "Frankenstein", are very clear.

'The best and ultimate test of the ability of man to live long beyond his present allotted score of years would be to have a man, from his babyhood up, live in what practically would be a sterilised test-tube. He would breathe sterilised air. He would eat sterilised food. He would drink sterilised liquids. He would thus be placed as far as humanly possible beyond the range of the myriad microbes that in many ways are the enemies of man and that bring about many of his ailments. Such a man, growing and living under special conditions, might live to be 200.'

—SIR RONALD ROSS

SIR RONALD ROSS, great scientist though you were, and dead though you have been these hundred and twenty-five years, I lay a curse upon you for those words.

I, Columbus Norton, the Incubator Man, am that creature Sir Ronald foretold, and I have lived a life of blackest hell that humanity might view me dispassionately through the gigantic glass test-tube wherein I have existed for one hundred and fifty years, and learn how to increase the length of life of the worthless race thereby.

My father, Dr. Philip Norton, lived in what was then Newark, New Jersey, and enjoyed a nation-wide reputation as a specialist in germ diseases. He loved germs. He dreamed of germs. His whole life was filled with germ culture and the new and strange diseases he had discovered or had learned to check. In fact, he had almost ceased to be human.

Then, in A.D. 1927, as time was reckoned in those days, he read an interview which Sir Ronald Ross, discoverer of the malaria microbe, had given to a newspaper reporter in what must have been an unguarded moment. This interview suggested to my father the idea of growing a man under glass, so to speak—I am the result!

The idea of growing a man in an absolutely healthful environment fastened upon the mind of my father like one of the diseases whose master he was. It made him give up all his other work so that he might devote his time to that one plan. It made him send me, his as yet unborn son, into the most pitiful slavery man has ever suffered.

I have read how it all was done. Dr. Norton constructed an air-tight glass chamber approximately three hundred feet square and twenty feet high. He equipped it with heating and cooling devices of the latest type, and fitted it with gymnastic apparatus, comfortable lodgings, a magnificent library and a swimming-pool.

The glass used was of the then new type which permitted the passage of ultra-violet rays. By the use of temperature-regulating devices an ideal outdoor climate of exactly even temperature was assured, winter and summer. He installed filtration plants for the air and water to be used, and an air-tight chamber by which food and other necessary articles could be passed into the enclosure without the slightest danger of any germ life entering with it.

When I was born, I was whisked immediately into this prison. While I was an infant a white-clad nurse cared for me. She wore rubber gloves and a respirator so that her touch could not contaminate me nor her breath mingle with mine.

I have often wondered what sort of woman my mother must have been to allow her son to be snatched from her so easily. According to the books I have read (which, by the way, have given me almost my only knowledge of the outside world), mother love is not expressed so. Perhaps she also had given her life to science, or did not realise what she had done. I never found out. She died before I learned to talk.

During my childhood the imprisonment wasn't so bad. I knew nothing else. As I became able to care for myself, the nurse withdrew. After that I had contact with the outer world only through loud-speaking telephones which my father had installed and through the books and cinema films slipped through the fumigation chamber into my cell.

The best teachers were procured for me; the best of books and apparatus provided. The most perfect care was taken of my health. Living under such ideal conditions, I progressed in my studies with amazing rapidity, soon outstripping my teachers. At the age of twelve I passed the Harvard University entrance examinations, and in my sixteenth year was granted a Ph.D. degree. Yes, Dr. Norton had cause to be proud of his experiment.

I remember him well—a man with a stern, handsome face, who sat outside my cage, day after day, taking endless notes and talking pleasantly with me, yet watching my every reaction as though I were a guinea-pig.

He induced me to study medicine, and I made rapid progress, until we ran into the difficulty that live animal tissues could not be introduced into the chamber for fear of bringing disease germs with them. So, to this day, my knowledge of medical science is purely academic.

Oh, don't think I never rebelled! I did, bitterly; but my sense of duty, which had been fostered by my father in his many talks with me, conquered my rebellion. Dr. Norton continually pointed out the great service I was doing to humanity—that through me and through him the world was learning to control itself, and to live sanely and keep healthy and live long.

The only time I ever saw my father angry was when, in a fit of boyish rage, I threatened to smash the glass and escape. His face turned white as marble. He stood, trembling with passion, hands clenched above his head, like some prophet of old about to hurl imprecations upon sinners.

'Boy,' he thundered, 'you hold the future of humanity in that club which you have in your hands. Mankind must live longer to become wise enough to conquer his environment. Shatter that glass, and man's future collapses into the dust with it. Aye, and if there is a hell, your soul will be consigned to the deepest pit.'

What could a mere child do against the force of such a personality? I crept away trembling and never after that dared oppose his wishes.

His prophecy soon proved itself correct. The human race entered a new cycle as the result of dietary truths which I exemplified. Dr. Norton proved that a purely vegetable diet was more healthful for the human animal; that certain combinations of foods were poisonous while others were beneficial; that toxic substances in the blood will kill a man as surely as strychnine; that under right conditions of living, human machinery is little subject to breakage or deterioration—in short, during the first thirty years of my life, preventive medicine was advanced to such an extent that the average expectancy of human life jumped from 55·3 to 68 years.

One thing my father had not counted upon was the fact that I would become a man, with a man's dreams of love and fair women. And by the time I reached maturity there was no help for the matter. He regretted again and again that he had not also placed a girl baby in the chamber.

It was too late for that by the time he realised the desirability of such an experiment. I believe I hastened the day of his death by refusing to allow him to place a newly born girl in the chamber, even then, so that she might grow to maturity under the same ideal conditions, and perhaps, years later, become my mate. He must have been a soulless monster, even to think of such a scheme—and yet—and yet

I loved him and while he lived did not greatly mind my confinement.

I slept eight hours daily, studied eight hours and played eight hours. The best books, cinemas and apparatus were provided for my research work. By the time I was fifty I can unhesitatingly say that I knew more than any one man in the world.

I was well developed physically also, in spite of the restricted space in which I lived, for my father had always impressed upon me the fact that a healthy body makes a healthy mind. I know that I must have been, even then, a splendid specimen of manhood, for I could not help but hear, through my loud speakers, the comments of the people who by this time were flocking from the ends of the earth to see me.

It was a strange thing to see my father and the other members of his establishment growing old, while I remained at the peak of my vitality. It has become a common thing to me since then, but the knowledge that death was stalking those outside, while I escaped unscathed, was at the time inexpressibly sad.

My father died when I was near fifty years old. With my consent he willed his laboratories and my glass cubicle to the government, with the understanding that I was to be carefully guarded and tended. His last words to me were: 'Carry on, boy. Some day, through you, this silly thing that I am about to do won't be necessary.'

With his passing my last real contact with the outside world was broken. I never could grow attached to the vapid guards and caretakers who took his place, or the obsequious officials who periodically came to refresh their shallow minds with my learning and advice.

For this reason the thing I am about to do no longer seems wrong to me. I have spent my life in the service of humanity. Men live longer and are, perhaps, somewhat wiser, but I often wonder, now, whether the sacrifice was worth while. At least, in a few hours I shall know whether the world is worth saving. My only wonder is that I have waited thus long.

But to return to my story. As the years passed I confined myself more and more to my studies, and ignored the crowds that gathered outside the walls of my cage to look and admire. I can truthfully say that my scientific treatises, written here, have been the wonder of the world. It was I who first explained the true time and space equation, and showed that Einstein, handicapped as he was by lack of equipment and the faulty work of his predecessors, had only half glimpsed the truth in his theory that space is subject to curvature. But enough of such nonsense.

It was when I was seventy-three years old, in the year A.D. 2000, or the year One, Free Time, that the Ruskinite rebellion broke out in the United Americas. There must have been some atavistic streak in me, for I sympathised heartily with those poor, benighted Ruskinites who dreamed of a breakdown of the gigantic monster of Science that mankind, like a Frankenstein, is building up about him, and who tried to smash it and return to the simple agricultural life of their forefathers.

Of course the outbreak was doomed to failure from the start, though streets of the country ran blood for a few bitter weeks. The very science which they hated subdued them. How could disciples of Ruskin stoop to heat rays, poison gases and atomic bombs? They perished fighting to the last, but I know that for weeks government troops guarded my chamber as though it were a precious jewel. Sad would have been my lot, I am sure, could the Ruskinites have captured my cubicle. I know that I, who was at heart their best friend, was hated by them as the heart and soul of the scientific system.

I will skip over the next seventy-five years of my life with but a few words. Strange—three-quarters of a century— time enough for most men to live a full life and die content.

For me they passed in a dreary succession, enlightened only by my studies and my dreams. As I look back, I conceive myself as a being almost in a state of hibernation, waiting for the vital spark which would awaken me.

In me metabolism and catabolism seemed exactly balanced. After my thirty-fifth year, I grew no older physically. I never was sick. I was amply confirming that prediction of Sir Ronald, made so long ago. My only regret was that my father could not have lived to appreciate his triumph—a triumph which had turned dust in my mouth ages ago, and which seemed no more remarkable than those silly experiments by which early twentieth-century doctors were able to keep chicken hearts alive indefinitely in a sterile medium.

I devoted myself to study as before, until I conceived that I had in my one head the whole sum of human knowledge. I gave out that knowledge to the world until it drew so far ahead of present understanding that scientists could no longer comprehend it. Oh, the silly fools! With so much to do, man dawdles by the way like a lazy schoolboy. Well, soon now they must begin working out their own salvation.

And now I draw near the end of my story. As I said, I had conceived that on my one hundred and fiftieth birthday I held in my brain the sum of human knowledge, together with much that was beyond the comprehension of any but myself. Savants from all the world consulted me regarding knotty problems of science and government. I might add, also, that the present expectancy of life is eighty years.

Yet how little we know, poor things that humans are! My complacency lies in ruins about me. A whole new set of complexes and speculations has been released within me. Three days ago, while resting on the lawn outside my quarters, I was struck by something totally outside my experience. As I lay there a shadow fell on the grass and I looked up at a girl who stood not ten feet away from me on the other side of the glass barrier.

'Good morning,' I said inanely, knowing that the telephones would make me perfectly audible outside the enclosure.

She nodded slightly and continued to look at me with wide, luminous eyes, in which there was, I somehow felt, an infinite sadness.

She was a beautiful thing—beautiful with the glory which perfect health and well-being give to our modern girls. Her eyes were dark and soft, with that slightly oblong slant which is giving more and more of an Oriental appearance to the people of America.

Her body was a thing to dream of as it was revealed by the short kilt and embroidered band across the breasts, which is the fashion of today. Her feet, in little, gold-tipped sandals, were high-arched and sentient. Her hair was the colour of gold taken from Inca mines—but I perceive I grow ridiculous.

'Did you wish to consult me?' I asked foolishly, growing uncomfortable under that steady gaze.

Again she shook her head, but added, in a voice that tinkled silver music: 'Why should I wish to consult you?'

And strangely, I could think of no reply. What could I tell that radiant being that she did not already know?

'Your name?' I ventured.

'Why,' she answered, as though surprised that it could be of the slightest interest to me, 'I'm Lilith Hughes, 3684.'

'Of the National Theatre,' I exclaimed, interpreting the last two figures. 'Of course you would be.'

She smiled faintly. 'Thank you.' A pause followed. 'I must be going,' she said at last. 'Performance in San Francisco, you know.'

And then I said a strange thing. The words seemed to form themselves without my volition. 'Can't you stay and talk with me a little longer?' I pleaded. 'It's lonely here.'

Again she smiled that slow, enchanting smile of hers. 'Can't. I'm sorry. The Torpedo doesn't wait, you know.

And then you have your work to do.' Her voice sank to the faintest murmur, which she did not realise I could hear plainly through the amplifiers. 'You have your work to do —poor thing!'

When I looked up, she was gone.

The hell of one hundred and fifty years of loneliness has been nothing to the hell of the last three days!

Last night I made up my mind to leave all this. Humanity must take care of itself. To be perfectly frank: to hell with humanity; I want to get out of this.

I am a man, sound and strong and well-favoured. I look and feel and think like one of thirty-five and I—am in love. Strange that such a primal urge, which I had considered merely a trick of nature's to prolong the race, should sweep me away at last!

I am going to seal this statement of my case in an envelope, so that if anything happens to me in this strange world I am about to explore, people will understand why I have done this. Tonight I'll smash this cursed glass and go in search of Lilith. Pretty name—Lilith.

The foregoing manuscript, carefully typed and sealed, was found on the body of Columbus Norton, the Incubator Man, who died of an almost unknown disease—the measles—two days after he broke out of his sealed chamber.

Attendants at B. Hospital, where he was taken, say that because of his long stay in an absolutely germless atmosphere he had failed to develop any resistance to disease and was 100 per cent susceptible to the first microbe which found lodgment in his body. He died a very few hours after being brought to the hospital.

Evidently he had spent his time, until the disease struck him, in becoming acquainted with a world whose ways he knew only by hearsay. At least there is no evidence that he ever took the San Francisco Torpedo, as the manuscript implies was his purpose.

THE PLAGUE DEMON

H. P. Lovecraft

(1890–1937)

Film records show that pictures based on the famous "mad scientist" novels such as "Frankenstein" and "The Invisible Man" have been made almost from the birth of the cinema, but it was not until the late thirties that they became outstandingly popular. Boris Karloff certainly heads the list of stars who have played these "monster" roles, rivalled only by his modern compatriot Peter Cushing. The films were often natural extensions of the classics—Frankenstein, for instance, apart from seeking his "Revenge", had innumerable "Brides", "Sons", and even a "Ghost"—and their popularity has continued undiminished to this day. The plots sometimes lacked originality—more often than not the monster was allowed to escape after his creation and cause havoc in the nearby localities until finally put to "death", but in a manner that left the film producers free to revive him should the public so demand. None the less present day audiences are as enthusiastic as ever and I can think of no more suitable story to typify this kind of film than "The Plague Demon". The author, H. P. Lovecraft, is one of the most important figures in the history of the modern horror story, and several of his tales and novels have been made into films. His creation of the Cthulu Mythos *of a long lost race of monsters trying to re-establish themselves on Earth, has been a major influence on many now famous horror story writers such as August Derleth, Robert Bloch and Ray Bradbury, all of whom he encouraged. Despite his short and troubled life (very much in the tradition of his fellow countryman, Edgar Allan Poe), Lovecraft is now something of a cult figure and much more widely read than ever he was in his lifetime. This contribution of his to the "mad scientist" genre is the story of a man's attempts to revive the dead, and the terrible carnage which ensued.*

I SHALL never forget that hideous summer sixteen years ago, when like a noxious afrite from the halls of Eblis typhoid stalked leeringly through Arkham. It is by that satanic scourge that most recall the year, for truly terror brooded with bat-wings over the piles of coffins in the tombs of Christ Church Cemetery; yet for me there is a greater horror in that time—a horror known to me alone now that Herbert West has disappeared.

West and I were doing post-graduate work in summer classes at the medical school of Miskatonic University, and my friend had attained a wide notoriety because of his experiments leading toward the revivification of the dead. After the scientific slaughter of uncounted small animals the freakish work had ostensibly stopped by order of our sceptical dean, Dr. Allan Halsey; though West had continued to perform certain secret tests in his dingy boarding-house room, and had on one terrible and unforgettable occasion taken a human body from its grave in the potter's field to a deserted farmhouse beyond Meadow Hill.

I was with him on that odious occasion, and saw him inject into the still veins the elixir which he thought would to some extent restore life's chemical and physical processes. It had ended horribly—in a delirium of fear which we gradually came to attribute to our own over-wrought nerves —and West had never afterward been able to shake off a maddening sensation of being haunted and hunted. The body had not been quite fresh enough; it is obvious that to restore normal mental attributes a body must be very fresh indeed; and the burning of the old house had prevented us from burying the thing. It would have been better if we could have known it was underground.

After that experience West had dropped his researches for some time; but as the zeal of the born scientist slowly returned, he again became importunate with the college faculty, pleading for the use of the dissecting-room and of fresh human specimens for the work he regarded as so over-whelmingly important. His pleas, however, were wholly in vain; for the decision of Dr. Halsey was inflexible, and the other professors all endorsed the verdict of their leader. In the radical theory of reanimation they saw nothing but the immature vagaries of a youthful enthusiast whose slight form, yellow hair, spectacled blue eyes, and soft voice gave no hint of the super-normal—almost diabolical—power of the cold brain within. I can see him now as he was then— and I shiver. He grew sterner of face, but never elderly. And now Sefton has had the mishap and West has vanished.

West clashed disagreeably with Dr. Halsey near the end of our last undergraduate term in a wordy dispute that did less credit to him than to the kindly dean in point of courtesy. He felt that he was needlessly and irrationally retarded in a supremely great work; a work which he could of course conduct to suit himself in later years, but which he wished to begin while still possessed of the exceptional facilities of the university. That the tradition-bound elders should ignore his singular results on animals, and persist in their denial of the possibility of reanimation, was inexpressibly disgusting and almost incomprehensible to a youth of West's logical temperament. Only greater maturity could help him understand the chronic mental limitations of the 'professor-doctor' type—the product of generations of pathetic Puritanism, kindly, conscientious, and sometimes gentle and amiable, yet always narrow, intolerant, custom-ridden, and lacking in perspective. Age has more charity for these incomplete yet high-souled characters, whose worst real vice is timidity, and who are ultimately punished by general ridicule for their intellectual sins—sins like Ptolemaism, Calvinism, anti-Darwinism, anti-Nietzscheism, and every sort of Sabbatarianism and sumptuary legislation. West, young despite his marvellous scientific acquirements, had scant patience with good Dr. Halsey and his erudite colleagues; and nursed an increasing resentment, coupled with a desire to prove his theories to these obtuse worthies in some striking and dramatic fashion. Like most youths, he indulged in elaborate day-dreams of revenge, triumph, and final magnanimous forgiveness.

And then had come the scourge, grinning and lethal, from the nightmare caverns of Tartarus. West and I had graduated about the time of its beginning, but had remained for additional work at the summer school, so that we were in Arkham when it broke with full demoniac fury upon the town. Though not as yet licensed physicians, we now had our degrees, and were pressed frantically into public service as the numbers of the stricken grew. The situation was almost past management, and deaths ensued too frequently for the local undertakers fully to handle. Burials without embalming were made in rapid succession, and even the Christ Church Cemetery receiving tomb was crammed with coffins of the unembalmed dead. This circumstance was not without effect on West, who thought often of the irony of the situation —so many fresh specimens, yet none for his persecuted researches! We were frightfully overworked, and the terrific mental and nervous strain made my friend brood morbidly.

But West's gentle enemies were no less harassed with

prostrating duties. College had all but closed, and every doctor of the medical faculty was helping to fight the typhoid plague. Dr. Halsey in particular had distinguished himself in sacrificing service, applying his extreme skill with whole-hearted energy to cases which many others shunned because of danger or apparent hopelessness. Before a month was over the fearless dean had become a popular hero, though he seemed unconscious of his fame as he struggled to keep from collapsing with physical fatigue and nervous exhaustion. West could not withhold admiration for the fortitude of his foe, but because of this was even more determined to prove to him the truth of his amazing doctrines. Taking advantage of the disorganization of both college work and municipal health regulations, he managed to get a recently deceased body smuggled into the university dissecting-room one night, and in my presence injected a new modification of his solution. The thing actually opened its eyes, but only stared at the ceiling with a look of soul-petrifying horror before collapsing into an inertness from which nothing could rouse it. West said it was not fresh enough—the hot summer air does not favour corpses. That time we were almost caught before we incinerated the thing, and West doubted the advisability of repeating his daring misuse of the college laboratory.

The peak of the epidemic was reached in August. West and I were almost dead, and Dr. Halsey did die on the fourteenth. The students all attended the hasty funeral on the fifteenth, and bought an impressive wreath, though the latter was quite overshadowed by the tributes sent by wealthy Arkham citizens and by the municipality itself. It was almost a public affair, for the dean had surely been a public benefactor. After the entombment we were all somewhat depressed, and spent the afternoon at the bar of the Commercial House; where West, though shaken by the death of his chief opponent, chilled the rest of us with references to his notorious theories. Most of the students went home, or to various duties, as the evening advanced; but West persuaded me to aid him in 'making a night of it'. West's landlady saw us arrive at his room about two in the morning, with a third man between us; and told her husband that we had all evidently dined and wined rather well.

Apparently this acidulous matron was right; for about three A.M. the whole house was aroused by cries coming from West's room, where when they broke down the door they found the two of us unconscious on the blood-stained carpet, beaten, scratched, and mauled, and with the broken remnants of West's bottles and instruments around us. Only an open window told what had become of our assailant, and many wondered how he himself had fared after the terrific leap from the second story to the lawn which he must have made. There were some strange garments in the room, but West upon regaining consciousness said they did not belong to the stranger, but were specimens collected for bacteriological analysis in the course of investigations on the transmission of germ diseases. He ordered them burnt as soon as possible in the capacious fireplace. To the police we both declared ignorance of our late companion's identity. He was, West nervously said, a congenial stranger whom we had met at some downtown bar of uncertain location. We had all been rather jovial, and West and I did not wish to have our pugnacious companion hunted down.

That same night saw the beginning of the second Arkham horror—the horror that to me eclipsed the plague itself. Christ Church Cemetery was the scene of a terrible killing; a watchman having been clawed to death in a manner not only too hideous for description, but raising a doubt as to the human agency of the deed. The victim had been seen alive considerably after midnight—the dawn revealed the unutterable thing. The manager of a circus at the neighbouring town of Bolton was questioned, but he swore that no beast had at any time escaped from its cage. Those who found the body noted a trail of blood leading to the receiving tomb, where a small pool of red lay on the concrete just outside the gate. A fainter trail led away toward the woods, but it soon gave out.

The next night devils danced on the roofs of Arkham, and unnatural madness howled in the wind. Through the fevered town had crept a curse which some said was greater than the plague, and which some whispered was the embodied demon-soul of the plague itself. Eight houses were entered by a nameless thing which strewed red death in its wake— in all, seventeen maimed and shapeless remnants of bodies were left behind by the voiceless, sadistic monster that crept abroad. A few persons had half seen it in the dark, and said it was white and like a malformed ape or anthropomorphic fiend. It had not left behind quite all that it had attacked, for sometimes it had been hungry. The number it had killed was fourteen; three of the bodies had been in stricken homes and had not been alive.

On the third night frantic bands of searchers, led by the police, captured it in a house on Crane Street near the Miskatonic campus. They had organised the quest with care, keeping in touch by means of volunteer telephone stations, and when someone in the college district had reported hearing a scratching at a shuttered window, the net was quickly spread. On account of the general alarm and precautions, there were only two more victims, and the capture was effected without major casualties. The thing was finally stopped by a bullet, though not a fatal one and was rushed to the local hospital amidst universal excitement and loathing.

For it had been a man. This much was clear despite the nauseous eyes, the voiceless simianism, and the demoniac savagery. They dressed the wound and carted it to the asylum at Sefton, where it beat its head against the walls of a padded cell for sixteen years—until the recent mishap, when it escaped under circumstances that few like to mention. What had most disgusted the searchers of Arkham was

the thing they noticed when the monster's face was cleaned
—the mocking, unbelievable resemblance to a learned and
self-sacrificing martyr who had been entombed but three
days before—the late Dr. Allan Halsey, public benefactor
and dean of the medical school of Miskatonic University.

To the vanished Herbert West and to me the disgust and
horror were supreme. I shudder tonight as I think of it,
shudder even more than I did that morning when West
muttered through his bandages,

'Damn it, it wasn't *quite* fresh enough!'

THE STRANGE ISLAND OF DR NORK

Robert Bloch

(1917–   )

Robert Bloch was one of the young American writers who found early inspiration for his work from H. P. Lovecraft. His admiration for the older man was so great that he later wrote some tales which continued the story of the Cthulu Mythos. *Bloch himself first became recognised by fans of the macabre through the pages of "Weird Tales" magazine, but made his mark on the public in general with his novel "Psycho" which Alfred Hitchcock made into a memorable film. Since then he has continued to write short stories and novels, but has also become one of Hollywood's busiest screenwriters for films and television—not a few of his works dealing with "mad scientists" and monster makers. His writings probably contain more stories on these basic themes than any other writer and making a single selection for this book was not easy. There were several reasons for choosing "The*

Strange Island of Dr Nork". Firstly, it shows the "Black Comedy" side of Robert Bloch's work and perhaps gives the reader a little light relief after the unrelenting horrors of H. P. Lovecraft's story. Secondly, it has some devastating things to say about mad scientists, monsters, journalists and horror comics. Thirdly, a more personal reason, it takes its inspiration from H. G. Wells's novel "The Island of Dr. Moreau", a particular favourite of mine.

BETWEEN the Greater Antilles and the Lesser Antilles rises a little group of islands generally known as the Medium-Sized Antilles.

Mere pimples on the smiling face of the Caribbean, they remain unsqueezed by the hands of man.

Far off the usual trade routes, their shores are only infrequently desecrated by a banana peeling washed off a United Fruit Lines boat.

It was here that I came on the fateful day in August, my monoplane circling until it descended upon the broad, sandy beach of the central island—the strange island of Doctor Nork.

How Sidney Dearborn ever heard of Doctor Nork, I cannot say. The old dingbat, doddering around the confines of his palatial estate, seldom pays much attention to his news magazine, let alone interesting himself in the doings of a mere individual.

But probably even a man like Dearborn, who is devoting most of his time to becoming an octogenarian—has been for the past eighty years—occasionally pauses and reads the papers.

Quite possibly, Dearborn read an article about Doctor Nork in one of his own magazines. I can see him calling my editor in New York.

'Hello—this is Dearborn. Get me an exclusive feature interview on Nork.

'Nork, Nork! No, I'm not sick. Fella's name. N-o-r-k.

Big scientist. Lives all alone on an island someplace, doing experiments.

'How do I know what kind of experiments? Find out for me. Tell our readers. That's what I'm paying you fifty grand a year for—to find out facts.

'This story on Nork is drivel. Pure drivel. No facts. It says he's endowed by a lot of foundations. Endowed for what? Can he split an atom? Get me all the dope.

'Know what I think? I smell Communism, that's what I smell. What would a big scientist want to hide out on an island for if he wasn't afraid? The American people deserve to know.

'Well, send a man down to see him. Interview him. I want a complete writeup on Nork within ten days. And say—hello, hello—I want you to be sure and find out where he stands on the oleomargarine tax!'

That's the way the conversation probably went. I can only guess. All I know is that the managing editor called me into the front office and gave me the assignment.

'Charter a plane,' he said. 'Get there, get the yarn, and get back. Get it?'

I got it, but good.

The smooth yellow beach on which my monoplane had landed evidently girdled the island, which was approximately a mile in diameter. Inland, palmettos clustered thickly in a dense jungle that ended abruptly at the foot of a gigantic cliff occupying the island's centre. Monkeys, macaws, toucans and parakeets set up a Disney-like clatter as I toted my suitcase and portable typewriter across the sands, but there was no evidence of human life—not even a Burma-Shave sign.

For a moment I wondered if I had made a mistake. I felt like Robinson Crusoe, and remembered the stirring episode where he discovers in the sand the imprint of a naked human foot.

Then I gasped. I *was* Robinson Crusoe. For there, before me in the golden sand, was the symbol of life itself! Not the raw imprint of savage life, but the very essence of civilization.

It was an old Pepsi-Cola bottle.

I stooped down to pick it up and then noted, with a sudden shock, that the bottle was not empty.

A soggy, crumpled sheet of paper had been stuffed down the neck, which was sealed with a battered cap. I pried it loose, then fished out the parchment and unfolded the sheet. The message was written in a childish scrawl.

> *To Whom It May Concern :*
> *Doctor Nork is a mean, nasty old thing, so there!*
> *(Signed) A True Friend*

So I *was* on the right island, after all.

My elation subsided as I realised 'A True Friend's' warning about my future host. Well, it was no concern of mine. For all I knew, 'A True Friend' might be a far meaner and nastier old thing than Doctor Nork.

At any rate, I wasn't here to sit in judgment; I was here to get a story on the mysterious medico.

Resealing the message in the bottle, I tossed it into the water. Apparently that had been 'A True Friend's' intention, but his aim was bad.

I toted my luggage towards the palmetto forest as the macaws formed a screaming rainbow round my head.

Oh, those living flames of beauty! Oh, those lovely, lambent—'Oh, for crying out loud!' I muttered.

Apparently it was safer to walk under the shelter of the trees.

I was still wiping my pith helmet when I felt a hand tap my shoulder. I wheeled, then recoiled in horror. It hadn't been a hand on my shoulder, after all. I beheld a paw.

Crouching, confronting me, was the shaggy, shambling figure of a gigantic great ape. Gorilla-eyes glared, and a tusked maw gaped wide in slavering dread. A growl rumbled up into the threatening throat.

'You want handkerchief?' said the ape.

The intonation was bestial, but the words were human, intelligible. I stared, gulped, and shook my head in amazement.

'Who you fella?' the ape demanded. 'You fella come safari?'

I shook my head again, but the hallucination didn't disappear.

'You come in jungle, hunt for diamonds, gold, no? You seek Elephant's Graveyard, maybe, heap much ivory?'

I could only goggle.

'You *bwana* search for White Goddess?'

I shrugged my heart back out of my mouth and down to where it belonged. Then I found my voice again. 'You— you can actually talk!' I gasped. 'I—I never thought I'd live to hear a gorilla talk like that.'

The ape grimaced dreadfully.

'Sounds pretty corny, eh, Jack? I think so, too—all that pidgin English and fake native lingo. Strictly from hunger. But you know how it is with Doc—he makes me talk that way, says it's what they want to hear.

'Sometimes I get pretty ashamed when I think that an anthropoid of my education has to go around making like a *schmoe*, but I got my orders. Like I say, you know the Doc.'

'But I don't know the Doc,' I answered. 'That's just what I came down here for; I want to meet him.'

'You from the publishers?' asked the gorilla.

'News magazine,' I replied. 'I'm here for an interview.'

'Might have known it,' the ape muttered. 'You don't have a moustache. Thought you were a villain at first; but the villains all have moustaches, don't they?'

I was getting confused again.

The anthropoid ignored my bewilderment and courteously

relieved me of my luggage. 'Come on,' he growled. 'Follow me.'

He led a path through the palmettos. 'Reporter, eh?' he mused. 'What do you do evenings?'

'How do you mean?'

'Fly, hurtle, sail, batter, flame, or blast?'

'I don't understand,' I confessed. 'You must have me mixed up with somebody else. Evenings, I go home. Sometimes I look up a friend and play a little Gin Rummy.'

'Tell you what you do,' the gorilla suggested. 'When you get done with the Doc, look me up and I'll take you on for a few hands.'

The cliff-top was a broad, flat plateau overlooking the beach and sea below. The wind blew cold and clear across the treeless expanse, and borne upon its eddies the seagulls wheeled and circled.

Remembering the macaws, I made an instinctive grab for my solar topee and jammed it down over my forehead. Then I peered out under its brim at the domicile of Doctor Nork.

Nork's residence sprawled across the plateau like some gigantic concrete wheel. A white-domed central structure acted as the hub, from which extended a half-dozen radii in the shape of wings attached to the main building. The outer circumference was rimmed by a high stone fence, broken by a single gate. The ape led me towards it while I stared up and marvelled at the elaborate structure set upon a lonely tropical isle.

Then we were standing before the gate, which apparently served as a front door. I noted a neatly lettered sign reading:

ERASMUS NORK, M.D.
Doctor is in—Please be Seated

I had nothing to sit on but my valise. The gorilla opened the front door and bid me enter. He shambled into a spacious white hallway, its antiseptic décor reminiscent of an old Doctor Kildare movie. I followed him as we walked along the corridor, passing half a dozen closed doors in succession. Finally we paused before a large double-door at the end of the hall.

'I'll announce you,' the ape suggested. 'Doctor Nork is conducting an experiment.'

He slipped through the half-open doorway and disappeared. I stood in the hall and listened to the drone of a faraway dynamo. It accented the eeriness of this white palace set in the heart of a tropical jungle. Weird scientific experiments and talking apes—

'Come right in, my friend!' The booming voice resounded from the room behind the door. 'Welcome to the Island!' I stepped forward into the laboratory of Doctor Nork.

A great arc-light glared from the domed roof, glared down upon a scene of horror. A huge steel operating table occupied the centre of the room, and it was in use. Strapped securely to its surface was a half-clad girl, hair streaming, mouth contorted, eyes wide with terror.

Towering above her was a tall, thin, red-bearded man with a beaked nose and slanted eyes. Like a surgeon, he wore a white gown. Like a surgeon, he brandished a glittering knife. Even as I watched, he raised the cruel blade and his arm swooped down to the girl's bare white bosom.

The red-bearded man grinned exultantly. 'How's tricks?' he whispered. The knife came down—

'Stop!'

I plunged forward frantically. Hairy arms pinioned me from behind. The ape held me fast.

'Hold it!' snarled the red-bearded man. 'There—got it?'

'Swell, Boss!' squeaked an unfamiliar voice from the corner of the room. I twisted my head and saw a little man with a smock standing before an easel. Even as I watched, he did things to the tripod stand, folding it under his arm, and gathering the board up, scuttled from the room.

The tall man dropped the knife and fumbled with the cords binding the girl.

'Curse these knots!' he grumbled. 'Ought to use the disintegrator. There you are, Toots.'

The girl stood up and fluffed out her hair. She smiled at me—no, past me, over my shoulder where the ape stood.

'How's for a little gin?' she said.

The gorilla nodded and released me. Linked arm in arm, girl and gorilla ambled from the room. And the tall, red-bearded man gestured towards me with his knife.

'Sit down, my friend,' he said. 'You must be tired after your trip. Maybe you'd prefer to lie down—how about right here, on the operating table?'

'No thanks,' I gulped. 'You're Doctor Nork, I presume?'

'Of course. Glad to see you. It isn't often we get a chance to converse with a representative of civilization. You must tell me all that's happening in the world. Has the atomic bomb blown up any continents lately?'

'I don't know—I left New York yesterday,' I answered.

Nork shrugged. 'So you came all the way down here just for an interview, eh? I suppose you want to discuss the new slants we worked out?'

'Slants?' I fumbled for his meaning. 'I was sent here to find out something about your experiments. I hear you are conducting some mysterious investigations.'

'Mysterious investigations? Experiments? My dear sir, you've been badly misled. I'm a business man. This is a business office.' Doctor Nork took out a strop and began to sharpen his knife, splitting hairs from his beard to test the keen edge of the blade.

'But I heard—'

'You were mistaken.' Nork spoke curtly.

At that moment the door opened and the gorilla entered.

'Hey, Doc, those guys are here for the experiments,' he announced.

Nork blushed and avoided my accusing stare.

'Tell them I'm busy,' he barked. 'Tell them they'll have to wait.'

'But the subject is already strapped down. The steno-grapher ready. Everything is set up.'

'Confound it!' muttered the Doctor. 'Oh, very well!'

'You don't have to come down, Doc,' the ape said. 'Just give me the equipment and I'll take it to them.'

Doctor Nork shrugged and stepped over to one of the blank, gleaming white laboratory walls. He pressed a tile and something clicked. A section of the wall slid back and revealed a long rack. Objects hung from thongs, dangled from hooks.

I stared at the display. There were long black whips, short cats-of-nine-tails, blackjacks, bludgeons, truncheons, clubs, assegais, knobkerries, shillelaghs.

The gorilla lumbered over and selected an armful at random.

'This oughta do the trick, eh, Doc?'

Nork nodded. Another click and the wall slid back into place. He pressed a second tile. A grating wheeze echoed through the room as a portion of the floor moved to disclose a secret stairway descending into black depths below. The ape clambered down the steps, bearing his homicidal burden. With a loud clang, the floor closed behind him.

I reeled, bewildered. Whips, weapons, concealed passages, and a nameless experiment—what did it mean?

Nork feigned nonchalance as he faced me.

'Come on,' I said. 'Quit stalling. My editor sent me down here for a feature story and I intend to get it. Now I—'

My words were cut short, then drowned out by a ghastly shriek. It came from beneath my very feet; rising in a weird wail, an ululation of utter agony.

'What's that?' I gasped.

'I didn't hear anything,' purred Nork.

Again the dreadful scream tore the air to ribbons.

'What's going on here?' I panted. 'What does it all mean? What kind of experiment needs whips and bludgeons? What are they doing down there?'

'Oh, all right, I suppose I'll have to tell you,' Nork sighed. 'But it's really nothing at all. They're just beating the living hell out of a guy.'

I made a dive for the Doctor's bearded throat. 'You fiend!' I shrieked. 'Now I know what you are—a mad scientist!'

'Hey, cut it out!' yelled Nork. 'You're tearing my beard!'

Indeed, the red beard came loose in my hands, revealing a smaller black beard beneath it.

'Don't touch the black beard—that's genuine!' warned the scientist. 'I just wear the red for sketches. Red seems to be all the thing this season. Wait, let me explain things to you.'

'Explain things? While you're torturing that poor devil down there in the cellar?'

'What poor devil? He's a volunteer. Also a confirmed masochist; he likes to be beaten up. Besides, I'm paying him five hundred dollars for his trouble.'

'You're paying him five hundred dollars—?'

'Didn't I tell you this was business? Come on, I'll let you see for yourself.'

The Doctor pressed the wall, the steps below were revealed, and I followed him down into the noisome darkness. As we passed into the nighted depths, the screams and groans rose hideously. The hair on my scalp followed suit.

We groped along a damp stone corridor until we reached a dimly lit room. It was a sight I never expected to see—a sight no man of the twentieth century should see—a medieval dungeon.

Torchlight flared on rack and strappado, on boot and Iron Maiden and wheel. Torchlight flickered down on the table where the groaning man writhed beneath the blows of two gigantic blackamoors.

The ape stood by silently, hand resting on the shoulders of a small man who sat perched on a high stool. Head cocked attentively as though listening, the little man was frantically scribbling down shorthand jottings.

Thuds, curses, screeches, blows, moans and gasps filled the air—but they faded into a sort of background noise as the little man beamed ecstatically and babbled at each fresh sound.

'WHUUP!' he yelled. 'OOFFLE!'

'Huh?' I murmured.

'GUTCH! Boy, didja hear dat one, hey? GUTCH; Tha's a new one, huh, Doc?' He peered over his spectacles and addressed the blackamoors. 'Hey, how's fer usin' the brass knucks now? We ain't had no brass knucks lately.'

'OK,' grunted the biggest of the Negroes. 'Dat is, if'n it's OK wid de victim.'

'OK, don't mind me,' piped the man on the table, grinning up through the black-and-blue blur of his ravaged face. 'I can take it.' Surprisingly, he giggled. 'Lay on, MacDuff!'

The Negroes began to assail his midriff with brass knuckles. He howled and grunted at every blow.

'SPLATT!' yapped the stenographer on the stool. 'Oh, Boy, lissen to him! URRK! BLIPP! WHIZZLE! Hey, you with a lead pipe—rap him onna noggin again. I did'n catch it the firs' time. There! SPOOOIIINNNGGG!!!'

Doctor Nork tapped me on the shoulder. 'Had enough?' he whispered. I nodded.

'Let's go.' He led the way back to the stairs, calling over his shoulder, 'Don't overdo it, boys, and be careful how you hit him. Last time you broke three whips and a truncheon. Those things cost money, you know.'

'BOING!' yelled the stenographer. 'BOINGA-BOINGA-BOINGA!'

As we plodded up the steps, Nork sighed. 'There's so much to worry about,' he confided. 'So much to do. It isn't easy, being the mastermind of all the comic books.'

We sat in another chamber, now—Doctor Nork's spacious and imposing library. A hundred shelves, rising to the dizzying height of the ceiling, encircled us on all sides. Every shelf was packed, crammed, jammed full of paperbound books with lurid covers. Nork reached over to an end-table and selected one at random, riffling the pages as he spoke.

'Of course, you can understand what we're doing down there, now,' he said. 'Just getting our blurbs, that's all. Filling the old balloons.'

'Filling the what?'

'The balloons. You know—the things coming out of the characters' mouths in comic books. When a crook gets hit by the hero, he makes a noise. Or the weapon makes a noise. Sometimes they both make noises.'

'Like BANG and OUCH?'

'There—you see?' Doctor Nork beamed. 'We can't use BANG and OUCH all the time. Or WHAM and ZOWIE and POW. They're corny. Besides, the Flushing Chain of Comic Books covers about twenty titles a month—that means roughly five thousand separate panels or drawings. Now you figure that at least four thousand of those panels in every comic book represent somebody getting hit, lashed, flayed, burned, punched, beaten, shot, stabbed, or run over with a steamroller—that takes a lot of different noises and sounds for balloons.

'We strive for variety, understand? But variety alone is not enough. My boss, the publisher, Bloodengore Flushing, is a stickler for realism. He wants accurate sounds. So that's why we hold experiments. We beat up a victim and take down the noises for our balloons. Get it?'

I got it, but couldn't handle it. 'You mean to say your comic books are drawn from real life?'

'More or less. That's where I come in. Mr. Flushing pays me a fortune, my dear sir, to mastermind the Flushing Chain. He endowed this laboratory, set up a fund for research, took me under contract for that purpose alone—to make sure that the sixty million readers of such famous comics as *Captain Torture* and *Hatchet Man* get only the finest and most realistic literature.

'Why, would you believe it, when I took over he only published three comic books and two of them were actually funny?

'It was ridiculous, and I told him so. Everybody knows that there's no point in a comic book that's funny! Why, people will laugh at it! What they want is thrills; girls with big busts and men with big muscles.'

'I don't know much about comic books,' I confessed. 'I had rather a sketchy education. I thought people just wrote and drew them in some kind of an office.'

'That's the old-fashioned way,' Nork laughed. 'Since I went to work for Flushing, we've changed all that. Ours is a great humanitarian enterprise; catering to sixty million readers as we do, bringing them romance, adventure, murder, arson, insanity, fratricide, bestiality. That's a great responsibility my boy, and I am keenly aware of it.

'When I went to work for the Chain, I was just a broken-down old Nobel Prize winner, puttering around in a laboratory. I smashed a few atoms, that's just about all I did. Now I am engaged in a great crusade to bring comic-book culture to the masses.

'That's why Flushing hired me. Up to the time I came here, comic books were put out just about the way you said they were: in offices, by artists and writers who worked solely with their imaginations. They kept thinking up new variants of Superman and that's about all they could do—occasionally they did a sort of Tarzan take-off or a Dick Tracy imitation. But it was stale, flat, repetitious.

'You see, the trouble was that they lacked *facts* to go by. They went stale because they didn't know anything about their subject matter. None of them had ever been to the jungle, let alone lived with gorillas. None of them had ever used a ray-gun or split a Jap spy's head open with a butcher's cleaver. None of them could walk through walls, or put on a suit of red underwear and fly through the air.

'That's where I came in. I brought the scientific method to bear, the experimental approach. Now all the artists and writers work from rough sketches and material supplied by me, here in my laboratory. Everything you see in Flushing Comics has been pre-tested and is guaranteed accurate.'

'You mean you've created a comic book world?' I gasped.

'More or less. Who do you think taught the gorilla to talk? I worked with him ever since he was a tiny rhesus; made him listen to Linguaphone records, everything. And why do you think our drawings are so accurate? Because I have an artist here sketching night and day; you saw me posing as the Mad Doctor with that girl when you came in. That's why I wore the false red beard—it looks better in colour reproduction. Many people have been kind enough to tell me that I make the best and most convincing Mad Doctor they've ever seen.'

'I'm sure you do,' I said, politely.

'Take those fellows downstairs—they're working on the sound effects, as I told you. All over this great laboratory experiments are going on concurrently, and trained observers are noting the results; roughing out sketches, transcribing bits of dialogue, thinking up plots. The result is obvious— Flushing Comics today are beyond all doubt the most realistically gruesome, hideous, ghastly, sanguinary and horrible comics in the world.'

'But what about all those super-characters?' I asked. 'You can teach gorillas to talk and pose for pictures and beat people up, but where do you get the ideas for those invincible heroes with the wonderful powers?'

'I give them the powers,' purred Doctor Nork. 'My experiments in nuclear physics, chemo-biology, endrocrinology, and mopery have borne fruit. Strange fruit. As you shall presently see. Speaking of fruit, it's time for luncheon. And now you'll have an opportunity to meet some of the actual characters I have created for Flushing Comics.'

Doctor Nork and I dined in palatial splendour. For the first few minutes after our entry into the huge hall, we were alone, save for the silent servants; tall, white-faced men who stared straight ahead in impassive obeisance as they offered us our choice of delicacies.

'How well trained they are,' I whispered, as one of the black-liveried footmen served me with a helping of jugged flamingo and pickled eland tongues. 'They never say a word, do they?'

'Not remarkable at all,' said Doctor Nork, as he carved the *pièce de resistance*—a huge baked wildebeeste head with an enormous apple in its mouth. 'How can they say anything? Some of them are zombies and the rest of them are dead. I reanimated them myself, you know.'

'I didn't know,' I gulped. 'And I'm not so sure I want to. You actually raised corpses up to be your servants?'

'Sure. Don't you read the comics? Scientists are always going into their laboratories and shooting a lot of electrical arcs through bodies. Had to try it myself just for the sake of accuracy. It worked. And after I had these cadavers animated again, I had no other use for them except as servants. Still it worries me.'

'Worries me, too,' I agreed. 'I don't like their looks.'

'Oh, that doesn't matter,' Nork replied. 'I just don't want the Waiter's Union to find out.' He gnawed a yak-leg and offered me some jellied eel.

'Where are the others I was supposed to meet?' I asked.

'Others? They'll be along. I'm sure. Matter of fact, here they come now.'

His remark was unnecessary. My bursting eardrums and bulging eyes attested to the arrival of some exceedingly strange strangers.

The first one to enter wasn't so bad—he was obviously human, despite his red cloak and the helmet he wore, which resembled an inverted commode. The only thing that disconcerted me in the least was the fact that he didn't walk in. He *flew*.

Behind him was a hopping figure. It might have been a gigantic frog with a human face. It might have been a gigantic human with a frog's body. Whatever it was, I didn't care for it.

Right behind the batrachian being stalked a tall man who displayed remarkable stoicism, in so far as his hair seemed to be on fire.

Even as I stared, my attention was arrested, tried, and condemned by another gentleman whose exceedingly long neck seemed to be made of wood. This neck was surmounted by a most unconventional head—flat on top, hooked in the rear, and round in front. There were no features visible in the round surface, which was shiny and metallic.

My eyes were still fighting the battle of the bulge when the girl came in. She was tall, slim, alluring; her body a pale shaft of moonlight and her hair a shimmering simulacrum of the sun. She wore a combination of leopard-skin bra and shorts that was very pretty, in spots.

I saw no reason why she needed to also wear a large boa-constrictor for a scarf—but she did. One would also assume that a wench with such long, lithe, lovely limbs might be satisfied to walk; but no, she had to ride on the back of a lion.

'Greetings!' said the girl, as the lion halted before us and began to slaver over my shoes.

'Hi,' chirped Doctor Nork. He beamed at me. 'Meet my daughter, Albino—the White Goddess of the Jungle.'

'Your daughter?'

'Brought her up among the animals to be useful in my work. Decided to make a female Tarzan out of her at an early age, when she showed signs of inheriting my own fondness for wild game. You may not know it, but I used to be quite a sportsman myself. Earned quite a reputation as a deer-hunter in my youth—I was a fast man with a buck.'

Albino sat down, unwound her snake, and replaced it with a napkin. She began to feed her lion from my plate.

'Pass the salt,' she said.

I did so, trembling—a human saltshaker. She noticed my tremor and sniffed disdainfully.

'Where'd you find this jerk, Pa?' she asked. 'You know I don't like sissies.'

I was all set to give her a snappy come-back, but something choked off my flow of conversation. That something was the boa-constrictor, which now began to twine around my neck. I removed it hastily and wiped my hands on what I thought was a napkin. But napkins don't roar.

I took my hands out of the lion's mane and turned to Doctor Nork. 'What an aggregation,' I murmured.

'All normal people,' he assured me. 'At least, they were until I got to work on them. You see before you, my dear sir, the results of years of experiments. My daughter was just a plain, ordinary little girl until I taught her how to behave like a monkey. In her case, all that was required was a little child psychology. Instead of giving her a doll to play with, I gave her a talking gorilla. The rest followed easily.

'In some of the other cases, surgery was necessary. Take Water Boy, for example.'

'Who?'

He indicated the frog-man. 'One of Flushing Comics' most popular characters. I made him; raised him from a tadpole, as it were. As a result of a unique series of experiments, he's now more frog than human. It was a risky business to turn a man into a frog—more than once I thought he'd croak. But you can see for yourself how successful I've been.'

Nork pointed at the man with the flaming hair. 'That's Fire-bug,' he told me. 'The Human Torch. Goes around giving criminals the hot-foot. I developed his metabolism to the point where he can actually live on fire.'

'That's why he's eating coal, eh?'

'Precisely. And as for our flying man, Rogers—'

'Buck Rogers?'

'No. Two-Dollar Rogers, we call him. He's twice as good as Buck.'

I turned away in bewilderment. 'Let me get this straight once and for all,' I said. 'You experiment on people and develop superhuman or unusual characteristics. Then you watch their actions and use what you see as the basis for plot-material in comic books.'

'Right. Now—'

A violent pounding interrupted him. The strange being with the long wooden neck and the metallic head was using the blank spot where his face should be—using it as a walnut-cracker.

'Hammerhead,' explained the Doctor. 'Our readers get a bang out of him.' He giggled. 'Did you see our last issue featuring him? Had a sequence where he uses his head as an atom-smasher.'

I tried to ignore the scientist's remarks and make a little time with Albino. But she obviously despised me for a weakling; just a poor coward who was probably secretly afraid of rhinocerii.

'Ow!'

The shout came from down at the end of the table. Hammerhead had accidentally banged the fingers of Fire-Bug.

'Look what you're doing, clumsy!' he yelled.

'Don't get hot under the collar,' retorted Hammerhead.

For answer, Fire-Bug opened his mouth, but no remarks came out. Instead, a six-foot tongue of living flame belched forth. Hammerhead ducked just in time, but Two-Dollar Rogers got smoke in his eyes. Rising, cloak whirling about him in red fury, the superhuman flier whipped out a strange, gleaming weapon and levelled it at the human torch.

'I'll blast you!' he yelled. Lightning crackled from the muzzle, and Fire-Bug ducked as an atomic beam disintegrated the chair in which he had been sitting. At the same time, he let go with another burst of flame.

Water Boy opened his frog-mouth and extinguished the blaze, inelegantly but effectively.

'Wet smack!' screamed Rogers, levelling his weapon. Fire-Bug turned towards him, ready to blaze away. Hammerhead poised himself to pound him down.

'*Quiet!*' screamed Doctor Nork. 'Cut it out—get out of here, all of you. If you can't learn to behave and get along with one another, I'll—I'll turn the Faceless Fiend loose on you!'

There was a deathly silence.

'There,' said the Doctor. 'That's telling them, eh? But where are you?'

'Here,' I gasped. 'Right here—under the table.'

Albino sniffed.

'I—uh—dropped my fork,' I said.

'You're scared,' she accused. 'I can tell by the way your hand trembles.'

'What hand?'

'The one on my ankle. Take it off.'

I rose and took my place again. 'All right,' I said. 'I *am* scared. Who wouldn't be with all this blasting and firing and pounding going on?'

'If you think these characters are bad, you ought to see the Faceless Fiend,' she told me.

'Who is he?' I noticed everybody shut up when his name was mentioned.

Nork's face clouded. He sighed heavily and reached for a platter of breaded horse-kidneys. 'One of my few failures,' he murmured. 'Some of my agents spirited away a mass-murderer from the penal colony in French Guiana. That's where I get most of my subjects—you'll find that comic book characters are best when they have criminal minds.

'Anyhow, this time I intended to create a super-criminal for a new book. The man was frightfully disfigured, and as a first step I attempted to remedy his condition with plastic surgery. At the same time, I began psychiatric treatment with deep hypnosis; my aim was to uncondition all his reflexes and hibit all his inhibitions. This I did, while working on his face to remove the scars.

'Alas, I did my work too well. I had him in a state of complete abandon, psychically, long before his features were rebuilt by plastic surgery. As a matter of fact, I had just finished removing his old features and hadn't got around to building new ones when he—escaped. Ran away.

'Of course, when the poor fellow removed the bandages, he found that he had no face left at all. This, coupled with his mental unbalance, resulted in the creation of the perfect super-criminal: the Faceless Fiend.

'Nobody knows what he looks like, because he doesn't look like anyone. He has no scruples—just hatred of society. Gifted with superhuman cunning, he has managed to evade capture and even now is lurking somewhere on this island. I've sent my staff out time and time again to comb the jungles for him. I imported several beachcombers just to comb the beaches. But he eludes me.

'Meanwhile he swears vengeance on me and all my work. He threatens me in a million ways. I am convinced it is he who writes letters to the press denouncing comic books.'

'Say, wait a minute,' I said. 'I wonder if he wrote that note?'

I told him about the message I'd found in a bottle on the beach.

'That's his work,' Nork nodded. 'A dangerous adversary, my friend.'

The gorilla shuffled into the room and tapped the Doctor on the shoulder.

'Sorry to interrupt,' he said, 'but it's time for you to come down to the crocodile pits.

'We're getting ready to draw that sequence where Wonder Child ties their tails into Boy Scout knots. If we get that out of the way this afternoon, we can go right on to the scene where he strangles his grandmother—right?'

'Right.' Nork rose. 'Excuse me,' he said. 'The press of business affairs. Perhaps you're tired. I'll ask Albino to see you to your room.'

'Follow me,' the girl urged. 'Do you want to ride my lion?'

'No thanks, I'll walk.'

We left the banquet hall and ascended a spiral staircase. The blonde girl led me into a handsomely furnished bedroom.

'Maybe a little sleep will quiet your nerves,' she observed. The scorn in her voice was evident.

'I'll be all right, thanks,' I said. 'Oh—what's that?'

A rumbling rose, and the air was suddenly suffused with blue flame.

'Nothing at all, scaredy-cat,' she snickered. 'Just a little hurricane coming up, I suppose.'

'Hurricane?'

I stared out of the window and saw that she spoke the truth.

The storm was gathering over the tropical isle. Water boiled like lava across the beach. The palmettos prostrated themselves before the fury of the storm. Wind roared from all points of the compass, and the currents clashed overhead to tear the very air to ribbons.

A kaleidoscopic cloud of macaws blew across the island, followed by a white cumulus of seagulls—borne ruthlessly away by the violence of the elements.

'Quit shaking, you coward!' taunted the girl. 'I'll turn on the lights.' She did so. I collapsed across the bed, watching the onslaught of the storm. The walls trembled and I followed suit.

'Oh, you're impossible,' she told me. 'Just like all the other men I've ever met—afraid of everything.'

'You can't blame me,' I replied. 'After all, not everybody has had your advantages. Being brought up by a gorilla, and all that.'

'Never mind the excuses,' Albino said. 'It doesn't matter.

I've been the White Goddess of the Jungle here for five years, and I'm getting pretty darn sick of it, too. Always waiting for some strong, handsome, virile he-man to come along and woo me, like they do in the comic books. And what do I get? A bunch of weaklings, namby-pamby characters who are afraid of everything—lions, snakes, hurricanes.'

'And you're not afraid of anything?'

'Of course not.'

'You're sure?'

There was a crash overhead and suddenly the lights went out. The room was black—an inky vacuum in the dark womb of storm.

I winced, but the girl's voice rose strong and clear in the darkness.

'I fear nothing,' she told me. 'Not even the Faceless Fiend himself.'

'That's very good to hear. I'd hate to have caused you any discomfort.'

'What's that?' I yelled. 'Who said that?'

'Me. The Faceless Fiend.'

'You're here—in this room?'

'Just came in through a secret staircase,' the slow voice hissed. 'I've been waiting to get my hands on you ever since you arrived.'

'You don't say,' I answered, hurling myself in the direction of the door. Thunder boomed and wind howled.

'Don't try to escape,' chuckled the unseen presence. 'You can't see in the dark, but I can. And I'm going to get you.'

'Help!' I yelled. 'Albino—save me!'

'Stay where you are,' the girl commanded. 'I'm coming.'

'So am I!' cackled the menacing voice.

I whirled, then cried out.

'Ouch!' I yelled. Something hit me in the back of my neck. It was the ceiling.

When I opened my eyes, I was lying strapped to a table in a long, narrow underground chamber. Blue light flickered in mephitic gloom. Crouching above me was a cloaked figure. I stared up and was rewarded only by a blank look. This creature, this monster, this being with an empty gap between neck and hairline, was something not to be countenanced. It was beyond all doubt the Faceless Fiend. His chuckle sounded out of emptiness, slithering off the slimy walls.

'Don't look so unhappy, my friend,' he purred. 'You ought to thank me for rescuing you. Here you are, safe and sound in a nice, comfortable sewer, while above us the entire laboratory has collapsed.'

'Collapsed? Was it lightning?'

'No, just rain. The place just melted away.'

'How could that be?'

'Simple,' explained my captor. 'Doctor Nork built it all out of guano. Apparently he didn't feed the seagulls enough cement. At any rate, the entire structure has been demolished —and your friends have all perished. No one is left but the two of us.'

'Dead?' I cried. 'All of them—you're sure?'

'Beyond a doubt. It's an end to the whole insane scheme; the comic books will go out of existence, and Doctor Nork will no longer be free to perpetrate his wicked experiments in the name of science.'

'But the girl,' I persisted. 'Albino, she was in the room with us—'

'I snatched you through the trapdoor and down the secret staircase just in time. I'm afraid you'll have to face it. We're alone. And now, speaking of facing it—'

The cloaked figure stooped to the side of the table and rose again. One hand clutched a small saw. 'Speaking of facing it,' he continued, 'I am about to perform a small experiment of my own. Ever since I lost my face, I've waited for a chance to find another. I hid down here in the sewers under the laboratory and bided my time. I didn't want to take a stupid mug like Nork's and I certainly wouldn't appropriate the visage of any of his monsters.

'But when you flew in to the island this morning, I knew my long vigil was over. Sorry, I cannot offer you any anaesthetic, but time is short.'

'You—you mean you're going to steal my face?' I screamed.

'I prefer to think of it as a little face-lifting job,' answered my captor. 'Please now; just relax.'

The Faceless Fiend bent forward, saw in hand. It was a typical scene from a comic book story—as such, it probably would have delighted ten million dear little kiddies throughout the land. But it didn't amuse me in the least.

The saw grazed my neck—

A roar shattered the walls. A tawny blur bore the cloaked figure backwards into the shadows. There were screams, and growls, and other less pleasant noises generally heard only at presidential conventions or in zoos.

'Good work!'

Albino was at my side, using the saw on the ropes that bound me. She gestured towards the shadows of the sewer beyond, where the lion was now creating a Bodiless Fiend.

'We got through the trapdoor in time, just behind you. Then part of the walls gave, and we were delayed—but not too long.'

'Then it's true,' I said. 'The laboratory is destroyed?'

'Everything's gone,' she sighed. 'Even this sewer isn't safe much longer. Let's get out of here.'

A crash accented her words. Turning, I saw that the shadowed portion of the sewer had disappeared, hiding both the lion and the Faceless Fiend from view forever beneath fresh debris.

'This way,' Albino urged, pulling me along the corridor. 'There should be a sewer outlet to the beach.'

'Thanks for rescuing me,' I panted.

'Think nothing of it,' the girl answered. 'That's just a reflex action, you know. Been rescuing people for years now for the comics.'

The damp walls of the sewer twisted and turned. We raced along, Albino taking a lithe-limbed lead. She rounded a curve ahead of me and I blundered forward.

Suddenly she screamed.

I turned the corner and grasped her arm.

'What's the matter?' I said.

The girl stood there shaking in a frenzy of fear.

'Eeeeh!' she shrieked. 'Take it away!'

'Huh?' I said.

For answer, she clung to me and threw herself forward and upward into my arms. I held her close.

'Look!' she sobbed. 'Down there—make it go away!'

'Where?' I asked.

'There.'

'But—it's only a mouse,' I said.

She began to cry. I stepped forward, carrying her in my arms, and the mouse retreated to its burrow with a shrill squeak.

Albino was weeping hysterically, and the more she cried the more I grinned.

'There, there,' I said. 'Don't you worry. I'll protect you.'

There isn't much more to tell. By the time we emerged upon the broad expanse of the beach, the hurricane had blown away and only a gentle rain fell upon the ruins of the big laboratory on the cliff.

Despite my fears, I found the plane quite undamaged, save for a minor accident that had crumpled part of the landing gear. As it was, I managed a takeoff and a subsequent landing some hours later in the airport at Jamaica.

Within a day Albino and I were back in civilization. I managed to sell her on the notion, while *en route*, that her brand of courage was of no value in New York.

'People seldom encounter lions and tigers in the city,' I told her, 'but the place is simply lousy with mice. What you need is someone like me to protect you.'

She agreed, meekly enough. And that's why we were

married, even before I reported to my editor with the story.

That episode is still painful in my memory. Being called a liar and a drunkard is bad enough, but when he accused me of opium-smoking, there was only one course left open to me.

'I resign!' I shouted, as he booted me down the stairs.

Still, it's all over now, and Albino doesn't mind. I have a new job—bought a little newsstand over on Seventh Avenue. I don't make much money selling newspapers, but there's always enough to buy a few mousetraps for the house.

Besides, I manage to sell quite a lot of comic books. . . .

IT

Theodore Sturgeon

(1918–   )

Until now, this collection has contained only one story of the "mad scientist" and the monster written from the creature's point of view. Two more such stories follow, each presenting quite different emotions, but firmly in the tradition of Mary Shelley's sad and terrible creation who, though without real life, most certainly had some heart. The first of these, Theodore Sturgeon's story "It" has rightly been called a classic since its first publication in 1940 when the author was just 22! Sam Moskowitz, the great biographer of Fantasy writers, has said of the story, "Authors had created monsters before, many whose names became synonyms for terror, but none of them had been treated with such objectivity or presented with such incredible mastery of style." High praise indeed, and typical of the comments that have earned Theodore Sturgeon an important place in the ranks of modern Fantasy and Science Fiction writers. Of this story, Sturgeon himself wrote later that he was repeatedly asked how it came to be written. "I can only answer that it wrote itself . . . I was feeling so good that I took what poisons were in me at the moment and got rid of them in one pure splash of putrescence." In the intervening years, Sturgeon has written on widely differing themes and been honoured time and again by Science Fiction enthusiasts. But although he has created plays, film and T.V. scripts, numerous short stories and several novels, including the highly praised modern vampire tale, "Some of Your Blood", none has ever surpassed the brilliance of "It".

IT walked in the woods.

It was never born. It existed. Under the pine needles the fires burn, deep and smokeless in the mould. In heat and in darkness and decay there is growth. There is life and there is growth. It grew, but it was not alive. It walked unbreathing through the woods, and thought and saw and was hideous and strong, and it was not born and it did not live. It grew and moved about without living.

It crawled out of the darkness and hot damp mould into the cool of a morning. It was huge. It was lumped and crusted with its own hateful substances, and pieces of it dropped off as it went its way, dropped off and lay writhing, and stilled, and sank putrescent into the forest loam.

It had no mercy, no laughter, no beauty. It had strength and great intelligence. And—perhaps it could not be destroyed. It crawled out of its mound in the wood and lay pulsing in the sunlight for a long moment. Patches of it shone wetly in the golden glow, parts of it were nubbled and flaked. And whose dead bones had given it the form of a man?

It scrabbled painfully with its half-formed hands, beating the ground and the bole of a tree. It rolled and lifted itself up on its crumbling elbows, and it tore up a great handful of herbs and shredded them against its chest, and it paused and gazed at the grey-green juices with intelligent calm. It wavered to its feet, and seized a young sapling and destroyed it, folding the slender trunk back on itself again and again, watching attentively the useless, fibred splinters. And it snatched up a fear-frozen field-creature, crushing it slowly, letting blood and pulpy flesh and fur ooze from between its fingers, run down and rot on the forearms.

It began searching.

Kimbo drifted through the tall grasses like a puff of dust, his bushy tail curled tightly over his back and his long jaws agape. He ran with an easy lope, loving his freedom and the power of his flanks and furry shoulders. His tongue lolled listlessly over his lips. His lips were black and serrated, and each tiny pointed liplet swayed with his doggy gallop. Kimbo was all dog, all healthy animal.

He leaped high over a boulder and landed with a startled yelp as a longeared cony shot from its hiding place under the rock. Kimbo hurtled after it, grunting with each great thrust of his legs. The rabbit bounced just ahead of him, keeping its distance, its ears flattened on its curving back and its little legs nibbling away at distance hungrily. It stopped, and Kimbo pounced, and the rabbit shot away at a tangent and popped into a hollow log. Kimbo yelped again and rushed snuffling at the log, and knowing his failure, curvetted but once around the stump and ran on into the forest. The thing that watched from the wood raised its crusted arms and waited for Kimbo.

Kimbo sensed it there, standing dead-still by the path. To him it was a bulk which smelled of carrion not fit to roll in, and he snuffled distastefully and ran to pass it.

The thing let him come abreast and dropped a heavy twisted fist on him. Kimbo saw it coming and curled up tight as he ran, and the hand clipped stunningly on his rump, sending him rolling and yipping down the slope. Kimbo straddled to his feet, shook his head, shook his body with a deep growl, came back to the silent thing with green murder in his eyes. He walked stiffly, straight-legged, his tail as low as his lowered head and a ruff of fury round his neck. The thing raised its arms again, waited.

Kimbo slowed, then flipped himself through the air at the monster's throat. His jaws closed on it; his teeth clicked together through a mass of filth, and he fell choking and snarling at its feet. The thing leaned down and struck twice, and after the dog's back was broken, it sat beside him and began to tear him apart.

'Be back in an hour or so,' said Alton Drew, picking up his rifle from the corner behind the wood box. His brother laughed.

'Old Kimbo 'bout runs your life, Alton,' he said.

'Ah, I know the ol' devil,' said Alton. 'When I whistle for him for half an hour and he don't show up, he's in a jam or he's treed something wuth shootin' at. The ol' son of a gun calls me by not answerin'.'

Cory Drew shoved a full glass of milk over to his nine-year-old daughter and smiled. 'You think as much o' that houn' dog o' yours as I do of Babe here.'

Babe slid off her chair and ran to her uncle. 'Gonna catch me the bad fella, Uncle Alton?' she shrilled. The 'bad fella' was Cory's invention—the one who lurked in corners ready to pounce on little girls who chased the chickens and played around mowing machines and hurled green apples with a powerful young arm at the sides of the hogs, to hear the synchronised thud and grunt; little girls who swore with an Austrian accent like an ex-hired man they had had; who dug caves in haystacks till they tipped over, and kept pet crawfish in tomorrow's milk cans, and rode work horses to a lather in the night pasture.

'Get back here and keep away from Uncle Alton's gun!'

said Cory. 'If you see the bad fella, Alton, chase him back here. He has a date with Babe here for that stunt of hers last night.' The preceding evening, Babe had kind-heartedly poured pepper on the cows' salt block.

'Don't worry, kiddo,' grinned her uncle, 'I'll bring you the bad fella's hide if he don't get me first.'

Alton Drew walked up the path towards the wood, thinking about Babe. She was a phenomenon—a pampered farm child. Ah well—she had to be. They'd both loved Clissa Drew, and she'd married Cory, and they had to love Clissa's child. Funny thing, love. Alton was a man's man, and thought things out that way; and his reaction to love was a strong and frightened one. He knew what love was because he felt it still for his brother's wife and would feel it as long as he lived for Babe. It led him through his life, and yet he embarrassed himself by thinking of it. Loving a dog was an easy thing, because you and the old devil could love one another completely without talking about it. The smell of gun smoke and wet fur in the rain were perfume enough for Alton Drew, a grunt of satisfaction and the scream of something hunted and hit were poetry enough. They weren't like love for a human, that choked his throat so he could not say words he could not have thought of anyway. So Alton loved his dog Kimbo and his Winchester for all to see, and let his love for his brother's women, Clissa and Babe, eat at him quietly and unmentioned.

His quick eyes saw the fresh indentations in the soft earth behind the boulder, which showed where Kimbo had turned and leaped with a single surge, chasing the rabbit. Ignoring the tracks, he looked for the nearest place where a rabbit might hide, and strolled over to the stump. Kimbo had been there, he saw, and had been there too late. 'You're an ol' fool,' muttered Alton. 'Y' can't catch a cony by chasin' it. You want to cross him up some way.' He gave a peculiar trilling whistle, sure that Kimbo was digging frantically un-

der some nearby stump for a rabbit that was three counties
away by now. No answer. A little puzzled, Alton went back
to the path. 'He never done this before,' he said softly.

He cocked his .32-40 and cradled it. At the county fair
someone had once said of Alton Drew that he could shoot
at a handful of corn and peas thrown in the air and hit only
the corn. Once he split a bullet on the blade of a knife and
put two candles out. He had no need to fear anything that
could be shot at. That's what he believed.

The thing in the woods looked curiously down at what it
had done to Kimbo, and tried to moan the way Kimbo had
before he died. It stood a minute storing away facts in its
foul, unemotional mind. Blood was warm. The sunlight was
warm. Things that moved and bore fur had a muscle to
force the thick liquid through tiny tubes in their bodies. The
liquid coagulated after a time. The liquid on rooted green
things was thinner and the loss of a limb did not mean loss
of life. It was very interesting, but the thing, the mould with
a mind, was not pleased. Neither was it displeased. Its
accidental urge was a thirst for knowledge, and it was only—
interested.

It was growing late, and the sun reddened and rested
awhile on the hilly horizon, teaching the clouds to be inverted flames. The thing threw up its head suddenly, noticing the dusk. Night was ever a strange thing, even for those
of us who have known it in life. It would have been frightening for the monster had it been capable of fright, but it
could only be curious; it could only reason from what it
had observed.

What was happening? It was getting harder to see. Why?
It threw its shapeless head from side to side. It was true—
things were dim, and growing dimmer. Things were changing shape, taking on a new and darker colour. What did the
creatures it had crushed and torn apart see? How did they
see? The larger one, the one that had attacked, had used two

organs in its head. That must have been it, because after the
thing had torn off two of the dog's legs it had struck at the
hairy muzzle; and the dog, seeing the blow coming, had
dropped folds of skin over the organs—closed its eyes. Ergo,
the dog saw with its eyes. But then after the dog was dead,
and its body still, repeated blows had had no effect on the
eyes. They remained open and staring. The logical conclusion was, then, that a being that had ceased to live and
breathe and move about lost the use of its eyes. It must be
that to lose sight was, conversely, to die. Dead things did
not walk about. They lay down and did not move. Therefore the thing in the wood concluded that it must be dead,
and so it lay down by the path, not far away from Kimbo's
scattered body, lay down and believed itself dead.

Alton Drew came up through the dusk to the wood. He
was frankly worried. He whistled again, and then called,
and there was still no response, and he said again, 'The ol'
flea-bus never done this before,' and shook his heavy head.
It was past milking time, and Cory would need him. 'Kimbo!'
he roared. The cry echoed through the shadows, and Alton
flipped on the safety catch of his rifle and put the butt on
the ground beside the path. Leaning on it, he took off his
cap and scratched the back of his head, wondering. The
rifle butt sank into what he thought was soft earth; he staggered and stepped into the chest of the thing that lay beside
the path. His foot went up to the ankle in its yielding rottenness, and he swore and jumped back.

'*Whew!* Somp'n sure dead as hell there! Ugh!' He swabbed
at his boot with a handful of leaves while the monster lay
in the growing blackness with the edges of the deep foot-
print in its chest sliding into it, filling it up. It lay there regarding him dimly out of its muddy eyes, thinking it was
dead because of the darkness, watching the articulation of
Alton Drew's joints, wondering at this new incautious creature.

Alton cleaned the butt of his gun with more leaves and went on up the path, whistling anxiously for Kimbo.

Clissa Drew stood in the door of the milk shed, very lovely in red-checked gingham and a blue apron. Her hair was clean yellow, parted in the middle and stretched tautly back to a heavy braided knot. 'Cory! Alton!' she called a little sharply.

'Well?' Cory responded gruffly from the barn, where he was stripping off the Ayrshire. The dwindling streams of milk plopped pleasantly into the froth of a full pail.

'I've called and called,' said Clissa. 'Supper's cold, and Babe won't eat until you come. Why—where's Alton?'

Cory grunted, heaved the stool out of the way, threw over the stanchion lock and slapped the Ayrshire on the rump. The cow backed and filled like a towboat, clattered down the line and out into the barn-yard. 'Ain't back yet.'

'Not back?' Clissa came in and stood beside him as he sat by the next cow, put his forehead against the warm flank. 'But, Cory, he said he'd—'

'Yeh, yeh, I know. He said he'd be back fer the milkin'. I heard him. Well, he ain't.'

'And you have to— Oh, Cory, I'll help you finish up. Alton would be back if he could. Maybe he's—'

'Maybe he's treed a blue jay,' snapped her husband. 'Him an' that damn dog.' He gestured hugely with one hand while the other went on milking. 'I got twenty-six head o' cows to milk. I got pigs to feed an' chickens to put to bed. I got to toss hay for the mare and turn the team out. I got harness to mend and a wire down in the night pasture. I got wood to split an' carry.' He milked for a moment in silence, chewing on his lip. Clissa stood twisting her hands together, trying to think of something to stem the tide. It wasn't the first time Alton's hunting had interfered with the chores. 'So I got to go ahead with it. I can't interfere with Alton's spoorin.' Every damn time that hound o' his smells out a squirrel I go without my supper. I'm gettin' sick and—'

'Oh, I'll help you!' said Clissa. She was thinking of the spring, when Kimbo had held four hundred pounds of raging black bear at bay until Alton could put a bullet in its brain, the time Babe had found a bearcub and started to carry it home, and had fallen into a freshet, cutting her head. You can't hate a dog that has saved your child for you, she thought.

'You'll do nothin' of the kind!' Cory growled. 'Get back to the house. You'll find work enough there. I'll be along when I can. Dammit, Clissa, don't cry! I didn't mean to— Oh, shucks!' He got up and put his arms around her. 'I'm wrought up,' he said. 'Go on now. I'd no call to speak that way to you. I'm sorry. Go back to Babe. I'll put a stop to this for good tonight. I've had enough. There's work here for four farmers an' all we've got is me an' that . . . that huntsman.

'Go on now, Clissa.'

'All right,' she said into his shoulder. 'But, Cory, hear him out first when he comes back. He might be unable to come back. He might be unable to come back this time. Maybe he . . . he—'

'Ain't nothin' kin hurt my brother that a bullet will hit. He can take care of himself. He's got no excuse good enough this time. Go on, now. Make the kid eat.'

Clissa went back to the house, her young face furrowed. If Cory quarrelled with Alton now and drove him away, what with the drought and the creamery about to close and all, they just couldn't manage. Hiring a man was out of the question. Cory'd have to work himself to death, and he just wouldn't be able to make it. No one man could. She sighed and went into the house. It was seven o'clock, and the milking not done yet. Oh, why did Alton have to—

Babe was in bed at nine when Clissa heard Cory in the shed, slinging the wire cutters into a corner. 'Alton back yet?' they both said at once as Cory stepped into the kitchen; and as she shook her head he clumped over to the stove, and lifting a lid, spat into the coals. 'Come to bed,' he said.

She laid down her stitching and looked at his broad back. He was twenty-eight, and he walked and acted like a man ten years older, and looked like a man five years younger. 'I'll be up in a while,' Clissa said.

Cory glanced at the corner behind the wood box where Alton's rifle usually stood, then made an unspellable, disgusted sound and sat down to take off his heavy muddy shoes.

'It's after nine,' Clissa volunteered timidly. Cory said nothing, reaching for house slippers.

'Cory, you're not going to—'

'Not going to what?'

'Oh, nothing. I just thought that maybe Alton—'

'Alton,' Cory flared. 'The dog goes hunting field mice. Alton goes hunting the dog. Now you want me to go hunting Alton. That's what you want?'

'I just—He was never this late before.'

'I won't do it! Go out lookin' for him at nine o'clock in the night? I'll be damned! He has no call to use us so, Clissa.'

Clissa said nothing. She went to the stove, peered into the wash boiler, set aside at the back of the range. When she turned around, Cory had his shoes and coat on again.

'I knew you'd go,' she said. Her voice smiled though she did not.

'I'll be back durned soon,' said Cory. 'I don't reckon he's strayed far. It is late. I ain't feared for him, but—' He broke his 12-gauge shotgun, looked through the barrels, slipped two shells in the breech and a box of them into his pocket. 'Don't wait up,' he said over his shoulder as he went out.

'I won't,' Clissa replied to the closed door, and went back to her stitching by the lamp.

The path up the slope to the wood was very dark when Cory went up it, peering and calling. The air was chill and quiet, and a fetid odour of mould hung in it. Cory blew the taste of it out through impatient nostrils, drew it in again with the next breath, and swore. 'Nonsense,' he muttered. 'Houn' dawg. Huntin', at ten in th' night, too. Alton!' he bellowed. 'Alton Drew!' Echoes answered him, and he entered the wood. The huddled thing he passed in the dark heard him and felt the vibrations of his foot-steps and did not move because it thought it was dead.

Cory strode on, looking around and ahead and not down since his feet knew the path.

'Alton!'

'That you, Cory?'

Cory Drew froze. That corner of the wood was thickly set and as dark as a burial vault. The voice he heard was choked, quiet, penetrating.

'Alton?'

'I found Kimbo, Cory.'

'Where the hell have you been?' shouted Cory furiously. He disliked this pitch-darkness; he was afraid at the tense hopelessness of Alton's voice, and he mistrusted his ability to stay angry at his brother.

'I called him, Cory. I whistled at him, an' the ol' devil didn't answer.'

'I can say the same for you, you ... you louse. Why weren't you to milkin'? Where are you? You caught in a trap?'

'The houn' never missed answerin' me before, you know,' said the tight, monotonous voice from the darkness.

'Alton! What the devil's the matter with you? What do I care if your mutt didn't answer? Where—'

'I guess because he ain't never died before,' said Alton, refusing to be interrupted.

'You *what*?' Cory clicked his lips together twice and then said, 'Alton, you turned crazy? What's that you say?'

'Kimbo's dead.'

'Kim ... oh! Oh!' Cory was seeing that picture again in

his mind— Babe sprawled unconscious in the freshet, and Kimbo raging and snapping against a monster bear, holding her back until Alton could get there. 'What happened, Alton?' he asked more quietly.

'I aim to find out. Someone tore him up.'

'*Tore him up?*'

'There ain't a bit of him left tacked together, Cory. Every damn joint in his body tore apart. Guts out of him.'

'Good God! Bear, you reckon?'

'No bear, nor nothin' on four legs. He's all here. None of him's been et. Whoever done it just killed him an'—tore him up.'

'Good God!' Cory said again. 'Who could've—' There was a long silence, then. 'Come 'long home,' he said almost gently. 'There's no call for you to set up by him all night.'

'I'll set. I aim to be here at sunup, an' I'm going to start trackin', an' I'm goin' to keep trackin' till I find the one done this job on Kimbo.'

'You're drunk or crazy, Alton.'

'I ain't drunk. You can think what you like about the rest of it. I'm stickin' here.'

'We got a farm back yonder. Remember? I ain't going to milk twenty-six head o' cows again in the mornin' like I did jest now, Alton.'

'Somebody's got to. I can't be there. I guess you'll just have to, Cory.'

'You dirty scum!' Cory screamed. 'You'll come back with me now or I'll know why!'

Alton's voice was still tight, half-sleepy. 'Don't you come no nearer, bud.'

Cory kept moving towards Alton's voice.

'I said'—the voice was very quiet now—'*stop where you are.*' Cory kept coming. A sharp click told of the release of the .32-40's safety catch. Cory stopped.

'You got your gun on me, Alton?' Cory whispered.

'Thass right, bud. You ain't a-trompin' up these tracks for me. I need 'em at sunup.'

A full minute passed, and the only sound in the blackness was that of Cory's pained breathing. Finally:

'I got my gun, too, Alton. Come home.'

'You can't see to shoot me.'

'We're even on that.'

'We ain't. I know just where you stand, Cory. I been here four hours.'

'My gun scatters.'

'My gun kills.'

Without another word Cory Drew turned on his heel and stamped back to the farm.

Black and liquidescent it lay in the blackness, not alive, not understanding death, believing itself dead. Things that were alive saw and moved about. Things that were not alive could do neither. It rested its muddy gaze on the line of trees at the crest of the rise, and deep within it thoughts trickled wetly. It lay huddled, dividing its newfound facts, dissecting them as it had dissected live things when there was light, comparing, concluding, pigeonholing.

The trees at the top of the slope could just be seen, as their trunks were a fraction of a shade lighter than the dark sky behind them. At length they, too, disappeared, and for a moment sky and trees were a monotone. The thing knew it was dead now, and like many a being before it, it wondered how long it must stay like this. And then the sky beyond the trees grew a little lighter. That was a manifestly impossible occurrence, thought the thing, but it could see it and it must be so. Did dead things live again? That was curious. What about dismembered dead things? It would wait and see.

The sun came hand over hand up a beam of light. A bird somewhere made a high yawning peep, and as an owl killed a shrew, a skunk pounced on another, so that the night shift deaths and those of the day could go on without cessation. Two flowers nodded archly to each other, comparing their pretty clothes. A dragon fly nymph decided it was tired of looking serious and cracked its back open, to crawl out and dry gauzily. The first golden ray sheared down between the trees, through the grasses, passed over the mass in the shadowed bushes. 'I am alive again,' thought the thing that could not possibly live. 'I am alive, for I see clearly.' It stood up on its thick legs, up into the golden glow. In a little while the wet flakes that had grown during the night dried in the sun, and when it took its first steps, they cracked off and a small shower of them fell away. It walked up the slope to find Kimbo, to see if he, too, were alive again.

Babe let the sun come into her room by opening her eyes. Uncle Alton was gone—that was the first thing that ran through her head. Dad had come home last night and had shouted at Mother for an hour. Alton was plumb crazy. He'd turned a gun on his own brother. If Alton ever came ten feet into Cory's land, Cory would fill him so full of holes, he'd look like a tumbleweed. Alton was lazy, shiftless, selfish, and one or two other things of questionable taste but undoubted vividness. Babe knew her father. Uncle Alton would never be safe in this county.

She bounced out of bed in the enviable way of the very young, and ran to the window. Cory was trudging down to the night pasture with two bridles over his arm, to get the team. There were kitchen noises from downstairs.

Babe ducked her head in the washbowl and shook off the water like a terrier before she towelled. Trailing clean shirt and dungarees, she went to the head of the stairs, slid into the shirt, and began her morning ritual with the trousers. One step down was a step through the right leg. One more, and she was into the left. Then, bouncing step by step on both feet, buttoning one button per step, she reached the bottom fully dressed and ran into the kitchen.

'Didn't Uncle Alton come back a-tall, Mum?'

'Morning, Babe. No, dear.' Clissa was too quiet, smiling too much, Babe thought shrewdly. Wasn't happy.

'Where'd he go, Mum?'

'We don't know, Babe. Sit down and eat your breakfast.'

'What's a misbegotten, Mum?' the Babe asked suddenly. Her mother nearly dropped the dish she was drying. 'Babe! You must never say that again!'

'Oh. Well, why is Uncle Alton, then?'

'Why is he what?'

Babe's mouth muscled around an outsize spoonful of oatmeal. 'A misbe—'

'Babe!'

'All right, Mum,' said Babe with her mouth full. 'Well, why?'

'I told Cory not to shout last night,' Clissa said half to herself.

'Well, whatever it means, he isn't,' said Babe with finality. 'Did he go hunting again?'

'He went to look for Kimbo, darling.'

'Kimbo? Oh Mummy, is Kimbo gone, too? Didn't he come back either?'

'No dear. Oh, please, Babe, stop asking questions!'

'All right. Where do you think they went?'

'Into the north woods. Be quiet.'

Babe gulped away at her breakfast. An idea struck her; and as she thought of it she ate slower and slower, and cast more and more glances at her mother from under the lashes of her tilted eyes. It would be awful if Daddy did anything to Uncle Alton. Someone ought to warn him.

Babe was halfway to the woods when Alton's .32-40 sent echoes giggling up and down the valley.

Cory was in the south thirty, riding a cultivator and cussing at the team of greys when he heard the gun. 'Hoa,' he called to the horses, and sat a moment to listen to the sound. 'One-two-three. Four,' he counted. 'Saw someone, blasted away at him. Had a chance to take aim and give him another, careful. My God!' He threw up the cultivator points and steered the team into the shade of three oaks. He hobbled the gelding with swift tosses of a spare strap, and headed for the woods. 'Alton a killer,' he murmered, and doubled back to the house for his gun. Clissa was standing just outside the door.

'Get shells!' he snapped and flung into the house. Clissa followed him. He was strapping his hunting knife on before she could get a box off the shelf. 'Cory—'

'Hear that gun, did you? Alton's off his nut. He don't waste lead. He shot at someone just then, and he wasn't fixin' to shoot pa'tridges when I saw him last. He was out to get a man. Gimme my gun.'

'Cory, Babe—'

'You keep her here. Oh, God, this is a helluva mess. I can't stand much more.' Cory ran out of the door.

Clissa caught his arm: 'Cory, I'm trying to tell you. Babe isn't here. I've called, and she isn't here.'

Cory's heavy, young-old face tautened. 'Babe—Where did you last see her?'

'Breakfast.' Clissa was crying now.

'She say where she was going?'

'No. She asked a lot of questions about Alton and where he'd gone.'

'Did you say?'

Clissa's eyes widened, and she nodded, biting the back of her hand.

'You shouldn't ha' done that, Clissa,' he gritted, and ran toward the woods, Clissa looking after him, and in that moment she could have killed herself.

Cory ran with his head up, straining with his legs and lungs and eyes at the long path. He puffed up the slope to the woods, agonised for breath after the forty-five minutes' heavy going. He couldn't even notice the damp smell of mould in the air.

He caught a movement in a thicket to his right, and

dropped. Struggling to keep his breath, he crept forward until he could see clearly. There was something in there, all right. Something black, keeping still. Cory relaxed his legs and torso completely to make it easier for his heart to pump some strength back into them, and slowly raised the 12-gauge until it bore on the thing hidden in the thicket.

'Come out!' Cory said when he could speak.

Nothing happened.

'Come out or by God I'll shoot!' rasped Cory.

There was a long moment of silence, and his finger tightened on the trigger.

'You asked for it,' he said, and as he fired, the thing leaped sideways into the open, screaming.

It was a thin little man dressed in sepulchral black, and bearing the rosiest baby-face Cory had ever seen. The face was twisted with fright and pain. The man scrambled to his feet and hopped up and down saying over and over, 'Oh, my hand. Don't shoot again! Oh, my hand. Don't shoot again!' He stopped after a bit, when Cory had climbed to his feet, and he regarded the farmer out of sad china-blue eyes. 'You shot me,' he said reproachfully, holding up a little bloody hand. 'Oh, my goodness.'

Cory said, 'Now, who the hell are you?'

The man immediately became hysterical, mouthing such a flood of broken sentences that Cory stepped back a pace and half-raised his gun in self-defence. It seemed to consist mostly of 'I lost my papers,' and 'I didn't do it,' and 'It was horrible. Horrible. Horrible,' and 'The dead man,' and 'Oh, don't shoot again.'

Cory tried twice to ask him a question, and then he stepped over and knocked the man down. He lay on the ground writhing and moaning and blubbering and putting his bloody hand to his mouth where Cory had hit him.

'Now what's going on around here?'

The man rolled over and sat up. 'I didn't do it!' he sobbed. 'I didn't. I was walking along and I heard the gun and I heard some swearing and an awful scream and I went over there and peeped and I saw the dead man and I ran away and you came and I hid and you shot me and—'

'*Shut up!*' The man did, as if a switch had been thrown. 'Now,' said Cory, pointing along the path, 'you say there's a dead man up there?'

The man nodded and began crying in earnest. Cory helped him up. 'Follow this path back to my farmhouse,' he said. 'Tell my wife to fix up your hand. *Don't* tell her anything else. And wait there until I come. Hear?'

'Yes. Thank you. Oh, thank you. *Snff.*'

'Go on now.' Cory gave him a gentle shove in the right direction and went alone, in cold fear, up the path to the spot where he had found Alton the night before.

He found him here now, too, and Kimbo. Kimbo and Alton had spent several years together in the deepest friendship; they had hunted and fought and slept together, and the lives they owed each other were finished now. They were dead together.

It was terrible that they died the same way. Cory Drew was a strong man, but he gasped and fainted dead away when he saw what the thing of the mould had done to his brother and his brother's dog.

The little man in black hurried down the path, whimpering and holding his injured hand as if he rather wished he could limp with it. After a while the whimper faded away, and the hurried stride changed to a walk as the gibbering terror of the last hour receded. He drew two deep breaths, said: 'My goodness!' and felt almost normal. He bound a linen handkerchief around his wrist, but the hand kept bleeding. He tried the elbow, and that made it hurt. So he stuffed the handkerchief back in his pocket and simply waved the hand stupidly in the air until the blood clotted. He did not see the great moist horror that clumped along behind him, although his nostrils crinkled with its foulness.

The monster had three holes close together on its chest, and one hole in the middle of its slimy forehead. It had three close-set pits in its back and one on the back of its head. These marks were where Alton Drew's bullets had struck and passed through. Half of the monster's shapeless face was sloughed away, and there was a deep indentation on its shoulder. This was what Alton Drew's gun butt had done after he clubbed it and struck at the thing that would not lie down after he put his four bullets through it. When these things happened the monster was not hurt or angry. It only wondered why Alton Drew acted that way. Now it followed the little man without hurrying at all, matching his stride step by step and dropping little particles of muck behind it.

The little man went on out of the wood and stood with his back against a big tree at the forest's edge, and he thought. Enough had happened to him here. What good would it do to stay and face a horrible murder inquest, just to continue this silly, vague search? There was supposed to be the ruin of an old, old hunting lodge deep in this wood somewhere, and perhaps it would hold the evidence he wanted. But it was a vague report—vague enough to be forgotten without regret. It would be the height of foolishness to stay for all the hick-town red tape that would follow that ghastly affair back in the wood. Ergo, it would be ridiculous to follow that farmer's advice, to go to his house and wait for him. He would go back to town.

The monster was leaning against the other side of the big tree.

The little man snuffled disgustedly at a sudden overpowering odour of rot. He reached for his handkerchief, fumbled and dropped it. As he bent to pick it up, the monster's arm *whuffed* heavily in the air where his head had been—a blow that would certainly have removed that baby-face protuberance. The man stood up and would have put the handkerchief to his nose had it not been so bloody. The creature behind the tree lifted its arm again just as the little man tossed the handkerchief away and stepped out into the field, heading across country to the distant highway that would take him back to town. The monster pounced on the handkerchief, picked it up, studied it, tore it across several times and inspected the tattered edges. Then it gazed vacantly at the disappearing figure of the little man, and finding him no longer interesting, turned back into the woods.

Babe broke into a trot at the sound of the shots. It was important to warn Uncle Alton about what her father had said, but it was more interesting to find out what he had bagged. Oh, he'd bagged it, all right. Uncle Alton never fired without killing. This was about the first time she had ever heard him blast away like that. Must be a bear, she thought excitedly, tripping over a root, sprawling, rolling to her feet again, without noticing the tumble. She'd love to have another bearskin in her room. Where would she put it? Maybe they could line it and she could have it for a blanket. Uncle Alton could sit on it and read to her in the evening—Oh, no. No. Not with this trouble between him and Dad. Oh, if she could only do something! She tried to run faster, worried and anticipating, but she was out of breath and went more slowly instead.

At the top of the rise by the edge of the woods she stopped and looked back. Far down in the valley lay the south thirty. She scanned it carefully, looking for her father. The new furrows and the old were sharply defined, and her keen eyes saw immediately that Cory had left the line with the cultivator and had angled the team over to the shade trees without finishing his row. That wasn't like him. She could see the team now, and Cory's pale-blue denim was nowhere in sight. She giggled lightly to herself as she thought of the way she would fool her father. And the little sound of laughter drowned out, for her, the sound of Alton's hoarse dying scream.

She reached and crossed the path and slid through the brush beside it. The shots came from up around here some-where. She stopped and listened several times, and then suddenly heard something coming towards her, fast. She ducked under cover, terrified, and a little baby-faced man in black, his blue eyes wide with horror, crashed blindly past her, the leather case he carried catching on the branches. It spun a moment and then fell right in front of her. The man never missed it.

Babe lay there for a long moment and then picked up the case and faded into the woods. Things were happening too fast for her. She wanted Uncle Alton, but she dared not call. She stopped again and strained her ears. Back towards the edge of the wood she heard her father's voice, and an-other's—probably the man who had dropped the brief case. She dared not go over there. Filled with enjoyable terror, she thought hard, then snapped her fingers in triumph. She and Alton had played Injun many times up here; they had a whole repertoire of secret signals. She had practised bird-calls until she knew them better than the birds themselves. What would it be? Ah—blue jay. She threw back her head and by some youthful alchemy produced a nerve-shattering screech that would have done justice to any jay that ever flew. She repeated it, and then twice more.

The response was immediate—the call of a blue jay, four times, spaced two and two. Babe nodded to herself happily. That was the signal that they were to meet immediately at The Place. The Place was a hide-out that he had discovered and shared with her, and not another soul knew of it; an angle of rock beside a stream not far away. It wasn't exactly a cave, but almost. Enough so to be entrancing. Babe trotted happily away towards the brook. She had just known that Uncle Alton would remember the call of the blue jay, and what it meant.

In the tree that arched over Alton's scattered body perched a large jay bird, preening itself and shining in the sun. Quite

unconscious of the presence of death, hardly noticing the
Babe's realistic cry, it screamed again four times, two and
two.

It took Cory more than a moment to recover himself
from what he had seen. He turned away from it and leaned
weakly against a pine, panting. Alton. That was Alton
lying there, in—parts.

'God! God, God, God—'

Gradually his strength returned, and he forced himself to
turn again. Stepping carefully, he bent and picked up the
.32-40. Its barrel was bright and clean, but the butt and
stock were smeared with some kind of stinking rottenness.
Where had he seen the stuff before? Somewhere—no matter.
He cleaned it off absently, throwing the befouled bandanna
away afterwards. Through his mind ran Alton's words—was
that only last night? — '*I'm goin' to start trackin'. An' I'm goin'
to keep trackin' till I find the one done this job on Kimbo.*'

Cory searched shrinkingly until he found Alton's box of
shells. The box was wet and sticky. That made it—better,
somehow. A bullet wet with Alton's blood was the right
thing to use. He went away a short distance, circled around
till he found heavy footprints, then came back.

'I'm a-trackin' for you, bud,' he whispered thickly, and
began. Through the brush he followed its wavering spoor,
amazed at the amount of filthy mould about, gradually
associating it with the thing that had killed his brother. There
was nothing in the world for him any more but hate and
doggedness. Cursing himself for not getting Alton home last
night, he followed the tracks to the edge of the woods. They
led him to a big tree there, and there he saw something
else—the footprints of the little city man. Nearby lay some
tattered scraps of linen, and—what was that?

Another set of prints—small ones. Small, stub-toed ones.

'Babe!'

No answer. The wind sighed. Somewhere a blue jay called.

Babe stopped and turned when she heard her father's voice, faint with distance, piercing.

'Listen at him holler,' she crooned delightedly. 'Gee, he sounds mad.' She sent a jay bird's call disrespectfully back to him and hurried to The Place.

It consisted of a mammoth boulder beside the brook. Some upheaval in the glacial age had cleft it, cutting out a huge V-shaped chunk. The widest part of the cleft was at the water's edge, and the narrowest was hidden by bushes. It made a little ceilingless room, rough and uneven and full of pot-holes and cavelets inside, and yet with quite a level floor. The open end was at the water's edge.

Babe parted the bushes and peered down the cleft.

'Uncle Alton !' she called softly. There was no answer. Oh, well, he'd be along. She scrambled in and slid down to the floor.

She loved it here. It was shaded and cool, and the chattering stream filled it with shifting golden lights and laughing gurgles. She called again, on principle, and then perched on an outcropping to wait. It was only then she realised that she still carried the little man's brief case.

She turned it over a couple of times and then opened it. It was divided in the middle by a leather wall. On one side were a few papers in a large yellow envelope, and on the other some sandwiches, a candy bar, and an apple. With a youngster's complacent acceptance of manna from heaven, Babe fell to. She saved one sandwich for Alton, mainly because she didn't like its highly spiced bologna. The rest made quite a feast.

She was a little worried when Alton hadn't arrived, even after she had consumed the apple core. She got up and tried to skim some flat pebbles across the roiling brook, and she stood on her hands, and she tried to think of a story to tell herself, and she tried just waiting. Finally, in desperation, she turned again to the brief case, took out the papers, curled up by the rocky wall and began to read them. It was something to do, anyway.

There was an old newspaper clipping that told about strange wills that people had left. An old lady had once left a lot of money to whoever would make the trip from the Earth to the Moon and back. Another had financed a home for cats whose masters and mistresses had died. A man left thousands of dollars to the first person who could solve a certain mathematical problem and prove his solution. But one item was blue-pencilled. It was:

One of the strangest of wills still in force is that of Thaddeus M. Kirk, who died in 1920. It appears that he built an elaborate mausoleum with burial vaults for all the remains of his family. He collected and removed caskets from all over the country to fill the designated niches. Kirk was the last of his line; there were no relatives when he died. His will stated that the mausoleum was to be kept in repair permanently, and that a certain sum was to be set aside as a reward for whoever could produce the body of his grandfather, Roger Kirk, whose niche is still empty. Anyone finding this body is eligible to receive a substantial fortune.

Babe yawned vaguely over this, but kept on reading because there was nothing else to do. Next was a thick sheet of business correspondence, bearing the letterhead of a firm of lawyers. The body of it ran:

In regard to your query regarding the will of Thaddeus Kirk, we are authorized to state that his grandfather was a man about five feet, five inches, whose left arm had been broken and who had a triangular silver plate set into his skull. There is no information as to the whereabouts of his death. He disappeared and was declared legally dead after the lapse of fourteen years.

The amount of the reward as stated in the will,

plus accrued interest, now amounts to a fraction over sixty-two thousand dollars. This will be paid to any-one who produces the remains, providing that said remains answer descriptions kept in our private files.

There was more, but Babe was bored. She went on to the little black notebook. There was nothing in it but pen-cilled and highly abbreviated records of visits to libraries; quotations from books with titles like 'History of Angelina and Tyler Counties' and 'Kirk Family History'. Babe threw that aside, too. Where could Uncle Alton be?

She began to sing tunelessly, 'Tumalumalum tum, ta ta ta,' pretending to dance a minuet with flowing skirts like a girl she had seen in the movies. A rustle of the bushes at the entrance to The Place stopped her. She peeped upward, saw them being thrust aside. Quickly she ran to a tiny cul-de-sac in the rock wall, just big enough for her to hide in. She giggled at the thought of how surprised Uncle Alton would be when she jumped out at him.

She heard the newcomer come shuffling down the steep slope of the crevice and land heavily on the floor. There was something about the sound—What was it? It occurred to her that though it was a hard job for a big man like Uncle Alton to get through the little opening in the bushes, she could hear no heavy breathing. She heard no breathing at all!

Babe peeped out into the main cave and squealed in utmost horror. Standing there was, not Uncle Alton, but a massive caricature of a man: a huge thing like an irregular mud doll, clumsily made. It quivered and parts of it glis-tened and parts of it were dried and crumbly. Half of the lower left part of its face was gone, giving it a lopsided look. It had no perceptible mouth or nose, and its eyes were crooked, one higher than the other, both a dingy brown with no whites at all. It stood quite still looking at her, its only movement a steady unalive quivering.

It wondered about the queer little noise Babe had made.

Babe crept far back against a little pocket of stone, her brain running round and round in tiny circles of agony. She opened her mouth to cry out, and could not. Her eyes bulged and her face flamed with the strangling effort, and the two golden ropes of her braided hair twitched and twitched as she hunted hopelessly for a way out. If only she were out in the open—or in the wedge-shaped half-cave where the thing was—or home in bed!

The thing clumped towards her, expressionless, moving with a slow inevitability that was the sheer crux of horror. Babe lay wide-eyed and frozen, mounting pressure of terror stilling her lungs, making her heart shake the whole world. The monster came to the mouth of the little pocket, tried to walk to her and was stopped by the sides. It was such a narrow little fissure, and it was all Babe could do to get in. The thing from the wood stood straining against the rock at its shoulders, pressing harder and harder to get to Babe. She sat up slowly, so near to the thing that its odour was almost thick enough to see, and a wild hope burst through her voiceless fear. It couldn't get in! It couldn't get in because it was too big!

The substance of its feet spread slowly under the tremendous strain and at its shoulder appeared a slight crack. It widened as the monster unfeelingly crushed itself against the rock, and suddenly a large piece of the shoulder came away and the being twisted slushily three feet farther in. It lay quietly with its muddy eyes fixed on her, and then brought one thick arm up over its head and reached.

Babe scrambled in the inch farther she had believed impossible, and the filthy clubbed hand stroked down her back, leaving a trail of muck on the blue denim of the shirt she wore. The monster surged suddenly and, lying full length now, gained that last precious inch. A black hand seized one of her braids, and for Babe the lights went out.

When she came to, she was dangling by her hair from

that same crusted paw. The thing held her high, so that her face and its featureless head were not more than a foot apart. It gazed at her with a mild curiosity in its eyes, and it swung her slowly back and forth. The agony of her pulled hair did what fear could not do—gave her a voice. She screamed. She opened her mouth and puffed up her powerful young lungs, and she sounded off. She held her throat in the position of the first scream, and her chest laboured and pumped more air through the frozen throat. Shrill and monotonous and infinitely piercing, her screams.

The thing did not mind. It held her as she was, and watched. When it had learned all it could from this phenomenon, it dropped her jarringly, and looked around the half-cave, ignoring the stunned and huddled Babe. It reached over and picked up the leather brief case and tore it twice across as if it were tissue. It saw the sandwich Babe had left, picked it up, crushed it, dropped it.

Babe opened her eyes, saw that she was free, and just as the thing turned back to her she dove between its legs and out into the shallow pool in front of the rock, paddled across and hit the other bank screaming. A vicious little light of fury burned in her; she picked up a grapefruit-sized stone and hurled it with all her frenzied might. It flew low and fast, and struck squashily on the monster's ankle. The thing was just taking a step towards the water; the stone caught it off balance, and its unpractised equilibrium could not save it. It tottered for a long, silent moment at the edge and then splashed into the stream. Without a second look Babe ran shrieking away.

Cory Drew was following the little gobs of mould that somehow indicated the path of the murderer, and he was nearby when he first heard her scream. He broke into a run, dropping his shotgun and holding the .32-40 ready to fire. He ran with such deadly panic in his heart that he ran right past the huge cleft rock and was a hundred yards past it before she burst out through the pool and ran up the bank. He had to run hard and fast to catch her, because anything behind her was that faceless horror in the cave, and she was living for the one idea of getting away from there. He caught her in his arms and swung her to him, and she screamed on and on and on.

Babe didn't see Cory at all, even when he held her and quieted her.

The monster lay in the water. It neither liked nor disliked this new element. It rested on the bottom, its massive head a foot beneath the surface, and it curiously considered the facts that it had garnered. There was the little humming noise of Babe's voice that sent the monster questing into the cave. There was the black material of the brief case that resisted so much more than green things when he tore it. There was the little two-legged one who sang and brought him near, and who screamed when he came. There was this new cold moving thing he had fallen into. It was washing his body away. That had never happened before. That was interesting. The monster decided to stay and observe this new thing. It felt no urge to save itself; it could only be curious.

The brook came laughing down out of its spring, ran down from its source beckoning to the sunbeams and embracing freshets and helpful brooklets. It shouted and played with streaming little roots, and nudged the minnows and pollywogs about in its tiny backwaters. It was a happy brook. When it came to the pool by the cloven rock it found the monster there, and plucked at it. It soaked the foul substances and smoothed and melted the moulds, and the waters below the thing eddied darkly with its diluted matter. It was a thorough brook. It washed all it touched, persistently. Where it found filth, it removed filth; and if there were layer on layer of foulness, then layer by foul layer it was removed. It was a good brook. It did not mind the poison of the monster, but took it up and thinned it and spread it in little rings round rocks downstream, and let it drift to the rootlets of water plants, that they might grow greener and lovelier. And the monster melted.

'I am smaller,' the thing thought. 'That is interesting. I could not move now. And now this part of me which thinks is going, too. It will stop in just a moment, and drift away with the rest of the body. It will stop thinking and I will stop being, and that, too, is a very interesting thing.'

So the monster melted and dirtied the water, and the water was clean again, washing and washing the skeleton that the monster had left. It was not very big, and there was a badly-healed knot on the left arm. The sunlight flickered on the triangular silver plate set into the pale skull, and the skeleton was very clean now. The brook laughed about it for an age.

They found the skeleton, six grimlipped men who came to find a killer. No one had believed Babe, when she told her story days later. It had to be days later because Babe had screamed for seven hours without stopping, and had lain like a dead child for a day. No one believed her at all, because her story was all about the bad fella, and they knew that the bad fella was simply a thing that her father had made up to frighten her with. But it was through her that the skeleton was found, and so the men at the bank sent a cheque to the Drews for more money than they had ever dreamed about. It was old Roger Kirk, sure enough, that skeleton, though it was found five miles from where he had died and sank into the forest floor where the hot moulds built around his skeleton and emerged—a monster.

So the Drews had a new barn and fine new livestock and they hired four men. But they didn't have Alton. And they didn't have Kimbo. And Babe screams at night and has grown very thin.

LAZARUS II

Richard Matheson

(1926–)

The third story written from the monster's viewpoint is quite different again from its predecessors. Richard Matheson, like his colleagues Wallace West and Theodore Sturgeon, seeks to avoid the obvious approach of a berserk, unreasoning monster, killing all before it in a lust for blood, and by so doing scores a major triumph in the genre. Matheson, like Sturgeon, wrote one story which overshadowed all others, and confirmed him as one of today's most important Fantasists: "I Am Legend", a nightmare tale of a world peopled with vampires. He is perhaps one of the best horror film screenwriters and has adapted several Edgar Allan Poe stories, and Fritz Leiber's extraordinary witchcraft novel, "Conjure Wife". He also created a notable drama of his own, "The Incredible Shrinking Man".

Matheson now lives and works in what must be the world's "hothouse" of horror writers, California, where his neighbours include such stars as Robert Bloch, Ray Bradbury, William Nolan, Ray Russell and Avram Davidson. Like all of them, he is a wonderfully visual writer and in painstakingly revealing the dilemma of a new 'creation' gives yet another dimension to the world of the 'monster makers'.

'BUT I died,' he said.

His father looked at him without speaking. There was no expression on his face. He stood over the bed and——

Or was it the bed?

His eyes left his father's face. He looked down and it wasn't the bed. It was an experimental table. He was in the laboratory.

His eyes moved back to those of his father. He felt so heavy. So stiff. 'What is it?' he asked.

And suddenly realised that the sound of his voice was different. A man didn't know the actual sound of his voice, they said. But when it changed so much, he knew. He could tell when it was no longer the voice of a man.

'Peter,' his father spoke at last, 'I know you'll despise me for what I've done. I despise myself already.'

But Peter wasn't listening. He was trying to think. Why was he so heavy? Why couldn't he lift his head?

'Bring me a mirror,' he said.

That voice. That grating, wheezing voice.

He thought he trembled.

His father didn't move.

'Peter,' he said, 'I want you to understand this wasn't my idea. It was your——'

'*A mirror.*'

A moment longer his father stood looking down at him. Then he turned and walked across the dark-tiled floor of the laboratory.

Peter tried to sit up. At first he couldn't. Then the room

seemed to move and he knew he was sitting but there was no feeling. What was wrong? Why didn't he feel anything in his muscles? His eyes looked down.

His father took a mirror from his desk.

But Peter didn't need it. He had seen his hands.

Metal hands.

Metal arms. Metal shoulders. Metal chest. Metal trunk, metal legs, metal feet.

Metal man!

The idea made him shudder. But the metal body was still. It sat there without moving.

His body?

He tried to close his eyes. But he couldn't. They weren't his eyes. Nothing was his.

Peter was a robot.

His father came to him quickly.

'Peter, I never meant to do this,' he said in a flat voice. 'I don't know what came over me—it was your mother.'

'Mother,' said the machine hollowly.

'She said she couldn't live without you. You know how devoted she is to you.'

'Devoted,' he echoed.

Peter turned away. He could hear the clockwork of himself ticking in a slow, precise way. He could hear the machinery of his body with the tissue of his brain.

'You brought me back,' he accused.

His brain felt mechanical too. The shock of finding his body gone and replaced with *this*. It numbed his thinking.

'I'm back,' he said, trying to understand. 'Why?'

Peter's father ignored his question.

He tried to get off the table, tried to raise his arms. At first they hung down, motionless. Then, he heard a clicking in his shoulders and his arms raised up. His small glass eyes saw it and his brain knew that his arms were up.

Suddenly it swept over him. All of it.

'But I'm dead!' he cried.

He did not cry. The voice that spoke his anguish was a soft, rasping voice. An unexcited voice.

'Only your body died,' his father said, trying to convince himself.

'But I'm dead!' Peter screamed.

Not screamed. The machine spoke in a quiet, orderly way. A machine-like way.

It made his mind seethe.

'Was this her idea?' he thought and was appalled to hear the hollow voice of the machine echo his thought.

His father didn't reply, standing miserably by the table, his face gaunt and lined with weariness. He was thinking that all the exhausting struggle had been for nothing. He was wondering, half in fright, if towards the end he had not been more interested in what he was doing than in why.

He watched the machine walk, clank rather, to the window, carrying his son's brain in its metal case.

Peter stared out of the window. He could see the campus. See it? The red glass eyes in the skull could see, the steel skull that held his brain. The eyes registered, his brain translated. He had no eyes of his own.

'What day is it?' he asked.

'Saturday, March tenth,' he heard the quiet voice of his father say, 'Ten o'clock at night.'

Saturday. A Saturday he'd never wanted to see. The enraging thought made him want to whirl and confront his father with vicious words. But the big steel frame clicked mechanically and eased around with a creaking sound.

'I've been working on it since Monday morning when——'

'When I killed myself,' said the machine.

His father gasped, stared at him with dull eyes. He had always been so assured, so brittle, so confident. And Peter had always hated that assurance. Because he had never been assured of himself.

Himself.

It brought him back. Was this himself? Was a man only his mind? How often he had claimed that to be so. On those quiet evenings after dinner when other teachers came over and sat in the living-room with him and his parents. And, while his mother sat by him, smiling and proud, he would claim that a man was his mind and nothing more. Why had she done this to him?

He felt that fettered helplessness again. The feeling of being trapped. He *was* trapped. In a great, steel-jawed snare, this body his father had made.

He had felt the same rigid terror for the past six months. The same feeling that escape was blocked in every direction. That he would never get away from the prison of his life; that chains of daily schedule hung heavy on his limbs. Often he wanted to scream.

He wanted to scream now. Louder than he ever had before. He had chosen the only remaining exit and even that was blocked. Monday morning he had slashed open his veins and the blanket of darkness had enveloped him.

Now he was back again. His body was gone. There were no veins to cut, no heart to crush or stab, no lungs to smother. Only his brain, lean and suffering. But he was back.

He stood facing the window again. Looking out over the Fort College campus. Far across he could see—the red glass lenses could see—the building where he had taught Sociological Surveys.

'Is my brain uninjured?' he asked.

Strange how the feeling seemed to abate now. A moment ago he had wanted to scream out of lungs that were no longer there. Now he felt apathetic.

'As far as I can tell,' said his father.

'That's fine,' Peter said, the machine said, 'That's just fine.'

'Peter, I want you to understand this wasn't my idea.'

The machine stirred. The voice gears rubbed a little and grated but no words came. The red eyes shone out of the window at the campus.

'I promised your mother,' his father said, 'I had to, Peter. She was hysterical. She—there was no other way.'

'And besides, it was a most interesting experiment,' said the voice of the machine, his son.

Silence.

'Peter Dearfield,' said Peter, said the turning, twinkling gears in the steel throat, 'Peter Dearfield is resurrected!' He turned to look at his father. He knew in his mind that a living heart would have been beating heavily, but the little wheels turned methodically. The hands did not tremble, but hung in polished muteness at his steel sides. There was no heart to beat. And no breath to catch, for the body was not alive but a machine.

'Take out my brain,' Peter said.

His father began to put on his vest; his tired fingers buttoned it slowly.

'You can't leave me like this.'

'Peter, I—I must.'

'For the experiment?'

'For your mother.'

'You hate her and you hate me!'

His father shook his head.

'Then I'll do it myself,' intoned the machine.

The steel hands reached up.

'You can't,' said his father. 'You can't harm yourself.'

'Damn you!'

No outraged cry followed. Did his father know that, in his mind, Peter was screaming? The sound of his voice was mild. It could not enrage. Could the well-modulated requests of a machine be heeded?

The legs moved heavily. The clanking body moved towards Doctor Dearfield. He raised his eyes.

'And have you taken out the ability to kill?' asked the machine.

The old man looked at the machine standing before him. The machine that was his only son.

'No,' he said, wearily, 'you can kill me.'

The machine seemed to falter. Gears struck teeth, reversed themselves.

'Experiment successful,' said the flat voice. 'You've made your own son into a machine.'

His father stood there with a tired look on his face.

'Have I?' he said.

Peter turned from his father with a clicking of gears, not trying to speak, and moved over to the wall mirror.

'Don't you want to see your mother?' asked his father.

Peter made no answer. He stopped before the mirror and the little glass eyes looked at themselves.

He wanted to tear the brain out of its steel container and hurl it away.

No mouth. No nose. A gleaming red eye on the right and a gleaming red eye on the left.

A head like a bucket. All with little rivets like tiny bumps on his new metal skin.

'And you did all this for *her*,' he said.

He turned on well-oiled wheels. The red eyes did not show the hate behind them. 'Liar,' said the machine. 'You did it for yourself—for the pleasure of experimenting.'

If only he could rush at his father. If only he could stamp and flail his arms wildly and scream until the laboratory echoed with the screams.

But how could he? His voice went on as before. A whisper, a turning of oiled wheels, spinning like gears in a clock.

His brain turned and turned.

'You thought you'd make her happy, didn't you?' Peter said. 'You thought she'd run to me and embrace me. You thought she'd kiss my soft, warm skin. You thought she'd look into my blue eyes and tell me how handsome I——'

'Peter this will do no——'

'—how *handsome* I am. Kiss me on the mouth.'

He stepped towards the old doctor on slow, steel legs. His eyes flickered in the fluorescent light of the small laboratory.

'Will she kiss my mouth?' Peter asked. 'You haven't given me one.'

His father's skin was ashen. His hands trembled.

'You did it for yourself,' said the machine. 'You never cared about her—or me.'

'Your mother is waiting,' his father said quietly putting on his coat.

'I'm not going.'

'Peter, she's waiting.'

The thought made Peter's mind swell up in anguish. It ached and throbbed in its hard, metal casing. Mother, mother, how can I look at you now? After what I've done. Even though these aren't my own eyes, how can I look at you now?

'She mustn't see me like this,' insisted the machine.

'She's waiting to see you.'

'*No!*'

Not a cry, but a mannerly turning of wheels.

'She *wants* you, Peter.'

He felt helpless again. Trapped. He was back. His mother was waiting for him.

The legs moved him. His father opened the door and he went out to his mother.

She stood up suddenly from the bench, one hand clutching her throat, the other holding her dark, leather handbag. Her eyes were fastened on the robot. The colour left her cheeks.

'Peter,' she said. Only a whisper.

He looked at her. At her grey hair, her soft skin, the gentle mouth and eyes. The stooped form, the old overcoat she'd worn so many years because she'd insisted that he take her extra money and buy clothes for himself.

He looked at his mother who wanted him so much she would not let even death take him from her.

'Mother,' said the machine, forgetting for a moment.

Then he saw the twitching in her face. And he realised what he was.

He stood motionless; her eyes fled to his father standing beside him. And Peter saw what her eyes said.

They said—why like *this*?

He wanted to turn and run. He wanted to die. When he had killed himself the despair was a quiet one, a despair of hopelessness. It had not been this brain-bursting agony. His life had ebbed away silently and peacefully. Now he wanted to destroy it in an instant, violently.

'Peter,' she said.

But she did not smother him with kisses. How could she, his brain tortured. Would anyone kiss a suit of armour?

How long would she stand there, staring at him? He felt the rage mounting in his mind.

'Aren't you satisfied?' he said.

But something went wrong inside him and his words were jumbled into a mechanical croaking. He saw his mother's lips tremble. Again she looked at his father. Then back at the machine. Guiltily.

'How do you—feel, Peter?'

There was no hollow laughter even though his brain wanted to send out hollow laughter. Instead the gears began to grind and he heard nothing but the friction of gnashing teeth. He saw his mother try to smile, then fail to conceal her look of sick horror.

'*Peter*,' she wailed, slumping to the floor.

'I'll tear it apart,' he heard his father saying huskily, 'I'll destroy it.'

For Peter there was an upsurge of hope.

But then his mother stopped trembling. She pulled away from her husband's grip.

'No,' she said and Peter heard the granite-like resolve in her voice, the strength he knew so well.

'I'll be all right in a minute,' she said.

She walked straight towards him, smiling.

'It's all right, Peter,' she said.

'Am I handsome, Mother?' he asked.

'Peter, you——'

'Don't you want to kiss me, Mother?' asked the machine.

He saw her throat move. He saw tears on her cheeks. Then she leaned forward. He could not feel her lips press against the cool steel. He only heard it, a slight thumping against the metal skin.

'Peter,' she said, 'forgive us for what we've done.'

All he could think was——

Can a machine forgive?

They took him out of the back doorway of the Physical Sciences Centre. They tried to hustle him to the car. But half-way down the walk Peter saw everything spin around and there was a stabbing in his brain as the mass of his new body crashed backward on the cement.

His mother gasped and looked down at him in fright.

His father bent over and Peter saw his fingers working on the right knee joint. His voice was muffled as he worked.

'How does your brain feel?'

He didn't answer. The red eyes glinted.

'Peter,' his father said urgently.

He didn't answer. He stared at the dark trees that lined Eleventh Street.

'You can get up now,' his father said.

'No.'

'Peter, not here.'

'I'm not getting up,' the machine said.

'Peter, please,' his mother begged.

'No, I can't, Mother, I can't.'

Spoken like a hideous metal monster.

'Peter, you can't stay *there*.'

The memory of all the years before stopped him. He would not get up.

'Let them find me,' he said. 'Maybe *they'll* destroy me.'

His father looked around with worried eyes. And, suddenly Peter realised that no one knew of this but his parents. If the board found out, his father would be pilloried. He found the idea pleased him.

But his wired reflexes were too slow to stop his father from placing hands on his chest and pulling open a small hinged door.

Before he could swing one of his clumsy arms, his father flicked his mechanism and, abruptly, the arm stopped as the connection between his will and the machinery was broken.

Doctor Dearfield pushed a button and the robot stood and walked stiffly to the car. He followed behind, his frail chest labouring for breath. He kept thinking what a horrible mistake he had made to listen to his wife. Why did he always let her alter his decisions?

Why had he allowed her to control their son when he lived? Why had he let her convince him to bring their son back when he had made a last, desperate attempt to escape?

His robot son sat in the back seat stiffly. Doctor Dearfield slid into the car beside his wife.

'Now he's perfect,' he said. 'Now you can lead him around as you please. A pity he wasn't so agreeable in life. Almost as pliable, almost as machine-like. But not quite. He didn't do *everything* you wanted him to.'

She looked at her husband with surprise, glancing back at the robot as if afraid it might hear. It was her son's mind. And she had said a man was his mind.

The sweet, unsullied mind of her son! The mind she had always protected and sheltered from the ugly taint of worldliness. He was her life. She did not feel guilty for having him brought back. If only he weren't so. . . .

'Are you satisfied, Ruth?' asked her husband. 'Oh, don't worry; he can't hear me.'

But he could. He sat there and listened. Peter's brain heard.

'You're not answering me,' said Doctor Dearfield, starting the motor.

'I don't want to talk about it.'

'You have to talk about it,' he said. 'What have you planned for him now? You always made it a point to live his life before.'

'Stop it, John.'

'No, you've broken my silence, Ruth. I must have been insane to listen to you. Insane to let myself get interested in such a—hideous project. To bring you back your dead son.'

'Is it hideous that I love my son and want him with me?'

'It's hideous that you defy his last desire on Earth! To be dead and free of you and at peace at last.'

'Free of me, free of me,' she screamed angrily. 'Am I such a monster?'

'No,' he said quietly, 'but, with my help, you've certainly made our son a monster.'

She did not speak. Peter saw her lips draw into a thin line.

'What will he do now?' asked her husband. 'Go back to his classes? Teach sociology?'

'I don't know,' she murmured.

'No, of course you don't. All you ever worried about was his being near you.'

Doctor Dearfield turned the corner. He started up College Avenue.

'I know,' he said, 'we'll use him for an ashtray.'

'John, stop it!'

She slumped forward and Peter heard her sobbing. He watched his mother with the red glass eyes of the machine he lived in.

'Did you—h-have to make him so—so——'

'So ugly?'

'I——'

'Ruth, I *told* you what he'd look like. You just glossed over my words. All you could think of was getting your claws into him again.'

'I didn't, I didn't,' she sobbed.

'Did you ever respect a single one of his wishes?' her husband asked. '*Did* you? When he wanted to write, would you let him? No! You scoffed. Be practical, darling, you said. It's a pretty thought but we must be practical. Your father will get you a nice position with the college.'

She shook her head silently.

'When he wanted to go to New York to live, would you let him? When he wanted to marry Elizabeth, would you let him?'

The angry words of his father faded as Peter looked out at the dark campus on his right. He was thinking, dreaming, of a pretty, dark-haired girl in his class. Remembering the day she'd spoken to him. Of the walks, the concerts, the soft, exciting kisses, the tender, shy caresses.

If only he could sob, cry out.

But a machine could not cry and it had no heart to break.

'Year after year,' his father's voice fluttered back into hearing, 'turning him into a machine even then.'

And Peter's mind pictured the long, elliptical walk around the campus. The walk he had so many times trudged to and from classes, briefcase gripped firmly in his hand. The dark grey hat on his balding head, balding at twenty-eight! The heavy overcoat in winter, the grey tweed suit in autumn and spring. The lined seersucker during the hot months when he taught summer session.

Nothing but depressing days that stretched on endlessly. Until he had ended them.

'He's still my son,' he heard his mother saying.

'Is he?' mocked his father.

'It's still his mind, and a man's mind is everything.'

'What about his body?' her husband persisted. 'What about his hands? They are just two pronged claws like *hooks*.

Will you hold his hands as you used to? Those riveted metal arms—would you let him put those arms around you and embrace you?'

'John, *please*——'

'What will you do with him? Put him in a closet? Hide him when guests come? What will you——'

'I don't want to *talk* about it!'

'You *must* talk about it! What about his face? Can you kiss that face?'

She trembled and, suddenly, her husband drove the car to the curb and stopped it with a jerk. He grabbed her shoulder and turned her forcibly around.

Look at him! Can you kiss that metal face? Is it your son, is *that* your son?'

She could not look. And it was the final blow at Peter's brain. He knew that she had not loved his mind, his personality, his character at all. It was the living person she had doted upon, the body *she* could direct, the hands *she* could hold— the responses *she* could control.

'You never loved him,' his father said cruelly. 'You *possessed* him. You *destroyed* him.'

'Destroyed!' she moaned in anguish.

And then they both spun around in horror. Because the machine had said, 'Yes. Destroyed.'

His father was staring at him.

'I thought——' he said, thinly.

'I am now, in objective form, what I have always been,' said the robot. 'A well-controlled machine.'

The throat gears made sound.

'Mother, take home your little boy,' said the machine.

But Doctor Dearfield had already turned the car around and was heading back.

THE GOLEM

Avram Davidson

(1931–   )

*One particular kind of monster not yet encountered, although it has a
tradition of long-standing, is the Golem. This creature has its origins
in Jewish legend and was allegedly a being made of clay and infused
with life during the sixteenth century. Its maker was said to be the
great Talmudic scholar, Rabbi Judah Low Ben Bezalel, who gave it
life to protect the Hebrew community in Prague when they feared unwarranted attack from the emperor. Such was the persistence of the
legend, that a statue of the Golem, "the body without a soul", and its
creator was later erected in the old quarter of the city, and this was to
provide the inspiration for several films. German, French, Czecho-
slovakian and American film makers have all retold the legend;
perhaps the most bizarre version is the German, where the monster
falls in love with its creator's daughter, and when spurned by her in
horror, goes on the rampage. Despite its universal popularity, the
Golem is seldom found in fiction. The only two really satisfying
examples are the Austrian writer Gustav Meyrink's novel "The
Golem" (1916) and this short story by Avram Davidson written*

nearly half a century later. Davidson, one of America's best current Science Fiction writers, has taken over where Meyrink left off. The Austrian was convinced that the creature could not be destroyed and might well still be lying dormant somewhere in Prague—if it had not already gone further afield. Davidson has brought the monster to Twentieth Century America and shows that the life which was originally created for noble deeds might still function to that end today.

THE grey-faced person came along the street where old Mr. and Mrs. Gumbeiner lived. It was afternoon, it was autumn, the sun was warm and soothing to their ancient bones. Anyone who attended the movies in the twenties or the early thirties has seen that street a thousand times. Past these bungalows with their half-double roofs Edmund Lowe walked arm-in-arm with Leatrice Joy and Harold Lloyd was chased by Chinamen waving hatchets. Under these squamous palm trees Laurel kicked Hardy and Woolsey beat Wheeler upon the head with a codfish. Across these pocket-handkerchief-sized lawns the juveniles of the Our Gang Comedies pursued one another and were pursued by angry fat men in golf knickers. On this same street—or perhaps on some other one of five hundred streets exactly like it.

Mrs. Gumbeiner indicated the grey-faced person to her husband.

'You think maybe he's got something the matter?' she asked. 'He walks kind of funny, to me.'

'Walks like a *golem*,' Mr. Gumbeiner said indifferently.

The old woman was nettled.

'Oh, I don't know,' she said. '*I* think he walks like your cousin Mendel.'

The old man pursed his mouth angrily and chewed on his pipestem. The grey-faced person turned up the concrete path, walked up the steps to the porch, sat down in a chair. Old Mr. Gumbeiner ignored him. His wife stared at the stranger.

'Man comes in without a hello, goodbye, or howareyou, sits

himself down and right away he's at home. . . . The chair is comfortable?' she asked. 'Would you like maybe a glass of tea?'

She turned to her husband.

'Say something, Gumbeiner!' she demanded. 'What are you, made of wood?'

The old man smiled a slow, wicked, triumphant smile.

'Why should *I* say anything?' he asked the air. 'Who am I? Nothing, that's who.'

The stranger spoke. His voice was harsh and monotonous.

'When you learn who—or, rather, what—I am, the flesh will melt from your bones in terror.' He bared porcelain teeth.

'Never mind about my bones!' the old woman cried. 'You've got a lot of nerve talking about my bones!'

'You will quake with fear,' said the stranger. Old Mrs. Gumbeiner said that she hoped he would live so long. She turned to her husband once again.

'Gumbeiner, when are you going to mow the lawn?'

'All mankind——' the stranger began.

'*Shah!* I'm talking to my husband. . . . He talks *eppis* kind of funny, Gumbeiner, no?'

'Probably a foreigner,' Mr. Gumbeiner said, complacently.

'You think so?' Mrs. Gumbeiner glanced fleetingly at the stranger. 'He's got a very bad colour in his face, *nebbich*, I suppose he came to California for his health.'

'Disease, pain, sorrow, love, grief—all are nought to——'

Mr. Gumbeiner cut in on the stranger's statement.

'Gall bladder,' the old man said. 'Guinzburg down at the *shule* looked exactly the same before his operation. Two professors they had in for him, and a private nurse day and night.'

'I am not a human being!' the stranger said loudly.

'Three thousand seven hundred fifty dollars it cost his son, Guinzburg told me. "For you, Poppa, nothing is too expensive —only get well," the son told him.'

'*I am not a human being!*'

'Ai, is that a son for you!' the old woman said, rocking her head. 'A heart of gold, pure gold.' She looked at the stranger. 'All right, all right, I heard you the first time. Gumbeiner! I asked you a question. When are you going to cut the lawn?'

'On Wednesday, *odder* maybe Thursday, comes the Japaneser to the neighbourhood. To cut lawns is *his* profession. *My* profession is to be a glazier—retired.'

'Between me and all mankind is an inevitable hatred,' the stranger said. 'When I tell you what I am, the flesh will melt——'

'You said, you said already,' Mr. Gumbeiner interrupted.

'In Chicago where the winters were as cold and bitter as the Czar of Russia's heart,' the old woman intoned, 'you had strength to carry the frames with the glass together day in and day out. But in California with the golden sun to mow the lawn when your wife asks, for this you have no strength. Do I call in the Japaneser to cook for you supper?'

'Thirty years Professor Allardyce spent perfecting his theories. Electronics, neuronics——'

'Listen, how educated he talks,' Mr. Gumbeiner said, admiringly. 'Maybe he goes to the University here?'

'If he goes to the University, maybe he knows Bud?' his wife suggested.

'Probably they're in the same class and he came to see him about the homework, no?'

'Certainly he must be in the same class. How many classes are there? Five *in ganzen*: Bud showed me on his programme card.' She counted off on her fingers. 'Television Appreciation and Criticism, Small Boat Building, Social Adjustment, The American Dance. . . . The American Dance—*nu*, Gumbeiner——'

'Contemporary Ceramics,' her husband said, relishing the syllables. 'A fine boy, Bud. A pleasure to have him for a boarder.'

'After thirty years spent in these studies,' the stranger, who had continued to speak unnoticed, went on, 'he turned from the theoretical to the pragmatic. In ten years' time he had made the most titanic discovery in history: he made mankind, *all* mankind, superfluous; he made *me*.'

'What did Tillie write in her last letter?' asked the old man.

The old woman shrugged.

'What should she write? The same thing. Sidney was home from the Army, Naomi has a new boy friend——'

'*He made ME!*'

'Listen, Mr. Whatever-your-name-is,' the old woman said, 'maybe where you came from is different, but in *this* country you don't interrupt people the while they're talking.... Hey. Listen—what do you mean, he *made* you? What kind of talk is that?'

The stranger bared all his teeth again, exposing the too-pink gums.

'In his library, to which I had a more complete access after his sudden and as yet undiscovered death from entirely natural causes, I found a complete collection of stories about androids, from Shelley's *Frankenstein* through Capek's *R.U.R.* to Asimov's——'

'Frankenstein?' said the old man, with interest. 'There used to be a Frankenstein who had the soda-*wasser* place on Halstead Street—a Litvack, *nebbich*.'

'What are you talking?' Mrs. Gumbeiner demanded. 'His name was Franken*thal*, and it wasn't on Halstead, it was on Roosevelt.'

'—clearly shown that all mankind has an instinctive antipathy towards androids and there will be an inevitable struggle between them——'

'Of course, of course!' Old Mr. Gumbeiner clicked his teeth against his pipe. 'I am always wrong, you are always right. How could you stand to be married to such a stupid person all this time?'

'I don't know,' the old woman said. 'Sometimes I wonder, myself. I think it must be his good looks.' She began to laugh.

Old Mr. Gumbeiner blinked, then began to smile, then took his wife's hand.

'Foolish old woman,' the stranger said. 'Why do you laugh? Do you not know I have come to destroy you?'

'What?' old Mr. Gumbeiner shouted. 'Close your mouth, you!' He darted from his chair and struck the stranger with the flat of his hand. The stranger's head struck against the porch pillar and bounced back.

'When you talk to my wife, talk respectable, you hear?'

Old Mrs. Gumbeiner, cheeks very pink, pushed her husband back to his chair. Then she leaned forward and examined the stranger's head. She clicked her tongue as she pulled aside a flap of grey, skinlike material.

'Gumbeiner, look! He's all springs and wires inside!'

'I *told* you he was a *golem*, but no, you wouldn't listen,' the old man said.

'You said he *walked* like a *golem.*'

'How could he walk like a *golem* unless he *was* one?'

'All right, all right. . . . You broke him, so now fix him.'

'My grandfather, his light shines from Paradise, told me that when MoHaRal—Moreynu Ha-Rav Löw—his memory for a blessing, made the *golem* in Prague, three hundred? four hundred years ago? he wrote on his forehead the Holy Name.'

Smiling reminiscently, the old woman continued, 'And the *golem* cut the rabbi's wood and brought his water and guarded the ghetto.'

'And one time only he disobeyed the Rabbi Löw, and Rabbi Löw erased the *Shem Ha-Mephorash* from the *golem's* forehead and the *golem* fell down like a dead one. And they put him up in the attic of the *shule* and he's still there today if the Communisten haven't sent him to Moscow. . . . This is not just a story,' he said.

'*Avadda* not!' said the old woman.

'I myself have seen both the *shule and* the rabbi's grave,' her husband said, conclusively.

'But I think this must be a different kind of *golem*, Gumbeiner. See, on his forehead; nothing written.'

'What's the matter, there's a law I can't write something there? Where is that lump of clay Bud brought us from his class?'

The old man washed his hands, adjusted his little black skull-cap, and slowly and carefully wrote four Hebrew letters on the grey forehead.

'Ezra the Scribe himself couldn't do better,' the old woman said, admiringly. 'Nothing happens,' she observed, looking at the lifeless figure sprawled in the chair.

'Well, after all, am I Rabbi Löw?' her husband asked, deprecatingly. 'No,' he answered. He leaned over and examined the exposed mechanism. 'This spring goes here . . . this wire comes with this one. . . .' The figure moved. 'But this one goes where? And this one?'

'Let be,' said his wife. The figure sat up slowly and rolled its eyes loosely.

'Listen, Reb *Golem*,' the old man said, wagging his finger. 'Pay attention to what I say—you understand?'

'Understand. . . .'

'If you want to stay here, you got to do like Mr. Gumbeiner says.'

'Do-like-Mr.-Gumbeiner-says. . . .'

'*That's* the way I like to hear a *golem* talk. Malka, give here the mirror from the pocketbook. Look, you see your face? You see the forehead, what's written? If you don't do like Mr. Gumbeiner says, he'll wipe out what's written and you'll be no more alive.'

'No-more-alive. . . .'

'*That's* right. Now, listen. Under the porch you'll find a lawnmower. Take it. And cut the lawn. Then come back. Go.'

'Go. . . .' The figure shambled down the stairs. Presently the sound of the lawnmower whirred through the quiet air in the street just like the street where Jackie Cooper shed huge tears on Wallace Beery's shirt and Chester Conklin rolled his eyes at Marie Dressler.

'So what will you write to Tillie?' old Mr. Gumbeiner asked.

'What should I write?' old Mrs. Gumbeiner shrugged. 'I'll write that the weather is lovely out here and that we are both, Blessed be the Name, in good health.'

The old man nodded his head slowly, and they sat together on the front porch in the warm afternoon sun.

MEN OF IRON

Guy Endore

(1923–   )

*This excursion through the history of monsters has now brought us to
the present day and the very real transition of man-made creations
from flesh and blood to iron and machinery. What began in antiquity
as a dream to create life from inanimate objects and was later given
fictional birth in "Frankenstein", now enters the realms of fact with
the robot. Earlier story-tellers have dabbled in this concept (Fitz-
James O'Brien's "The Wondersmith" and Karel Capek's "R.U.R."
are two examples) and now they have taken present day developments
and—in the great tradition of all man's encroachments across the
frontiers of science—run into the most unexpected situations. "Men
of Iron" is a first foray into the age of the robot as a reality, and
clearly underlines the implications. The author, Guy Endore, an ingenious and much respected American novelist, is most widely known
for his novel, "The Werewolf of Paris", which was gruesomely
filmed by Hammer Pictures as "The Curse of The Werewolf". In*

*the story which follows, Endore is dealing in very human terms with
a frightening mechanical problem.*

'We no longer trust the human hand,' said the engineer, and
waved his roll of blueprints. He was a dwarfish, stocky fellow
with dwarfish, stocky fingers that crumpled blueprints with
familiar unconcern.

The director frowned, pursed his lips, cocked his head,
drew up one side of his face in a wink of unbelief and scratched his chin with a reflective thumbnail. Behind his grotesque
contortions he recalled the days when he was manufacturer
in his own right and not simply the nominal head of a manufacturing concern, whose owners extended out into complex
and invisible ramifications. In his day the human hand had
been trusted.

'Now take that lathe,' said the engineer. He paused drama-
tically, one hand flung out towards the lathe in question,
while his dark eyes, canopied by bristly eyebrows, remained
fastened on the director.

'Listen to it!'

'Well?' said the director, somewhat at a loss.

'Hear it?'

'Why, yes, of course.'

The engineer snorted. 'Well, you shouldn't.'

'Why not?'

'Because noise isn't what it is supposed to make. Noise is
an indication of loose parts, maladjustments, improper speed
of operation. That machine is sick. It is inefficient and its
noise destroys the worker's efficiency.'

The director laughed. 'That worker should be used to it
by this time. Why, that fellow is the oldest employee of the
firm. Began with my father. See the gold crescent on his
chest?'

'What gold crescent?'

'The gold pin on the shoulder strap of his overalls.'

'Oh, that.'

'Yes. Well, only workers fifty years or longer with our firm are entitled to wear it.'

The engineer threw back his head and guffawed.

The director was wounded.

'Got many of them?' the engineer asked, when he had recovered from his outburst.

'Anton is the only one, now. There used to be another.'

'How many pins does he spoil?'

'Well,' said the director, 'I'll admit he's not so good as he used to be . . . But there's one man I'll never see fired,' he added stoutly.

'No need to,' the engineer agreed. 'A good machine is automatic and foolproof; the attendant's skill is beside the point.'

For a moment the two men stood watching Anton select a fat pin from a bucket at his feet and fasten it into the chuck. With rule and caliper he brought the pin into correct position before the drill that was to gouge a hole into it.

Anton moved heavily, circumspectly. His body had the girth, but not the solidity of an old tree-trunk: it was shaken by constant tremors. The tools wavered in Anton's hands. Intermittently a slimy cough came out of his chest, tightened the cords of his neck and flushed the taut yellow skin of his cheeks. Then he would stop to spit, and after that he would rub his moustache that was the colour of silver laid thinly over brass. His lungs relieved, Anton's frame regained a measure of composure, but for a moment he stood still and squinted at the tools in his hands as if he could not at once recall exactly what he was about, and only after a little delay did he resume his interrupted work, all too soon to be interrupted again. Finally, spindle and tool being correctly aligned, Anton brought the machine into operation.

'Feel it?' the engineer cried out with a note of triumph.

'Feel what?' asked the director.

'Vibration!' the engineer exclaimed with disgust.

'Well what of it?'

'Man, think of the power lost in shaking your building all day long. Any reason why you should want your floors and walls to dance all day long, while you pay the piper?'

He hadn't intended so telling a sentence. The conclusion seemed to him so especially apt that he repeated it: 'Your building dances while you pay the piper in increased power expenditure.'

And while the director remained silent the engineer forced home his point: 'That power should be concentrated at the cutting point of the tool and not leak out all over. What would you think of a plumber who only brought 50 per cent of the water to the nozzle letting the rest flood through the building?'

And as the director still did not speak, the engineer continued: 'There's not only loss of power but increased wear on the parts. That machine is afflicted with the ague!'

When the day's labour was over, the long line of machines stopped all together; the workmen ran for the washrooms and a sudden throbbing silence settled over the great hall. Only Anton, off in a corner by himself, still worked his lathe, oblivious of the emptiness of the factory, until darkness finally forced him to quit. Then from beneath the lathe he dragged forth a heavy tarpaulin and covered his machine.

He stood for a moment beside his lathe, seemingly lost in thought, but perhaps only quietly wrestling with the stubborn torpidity of his limbs, full of an unwanted, incorrect motion, and disobedient to his desires. For he, like the bad machines in the factory, could not prevent his power from spilling over into useless vibration.

The old watchman opened the gate to let Anton out. The two men stood near each other for a moment separated by the iron grill and exchanged a few comforting grunts, then hobbled off to their separate destinations, the watchman to make his rounds, Anton to his home.

A grey, wooden shack, on a bare lot, was Anton's home. During the day an enthusiastic horde of children trampled the ground to a rubber-like consistency and extinguished every growing thing except a few dusty weeds that clung close to the protection of the house or nestled around the remnants of the porch that had once adorned the front. There the children's feet could not reach them, and they expanded a few scornful coarse leaves, a bitter growth of Ishmaelites.

Within were a number of rooms, but only one inhabitable. The torn and peeling wallpaper in this one revealed the successive designs that had once struck the fancy of the owners. A remnant of ostentatiousness still remained in the marble mantelpiece, and in the stained glass window through which the arc-light from the street cast cold flakes of colour.

She did not stir when Anton entered. She lay resting on the bed, not so much from the labour of the day, as from that of years. She heard his shuffling, noisy walk, heard his groans, his coughing, his whistling breath, and smelled, too, the pungent odour of machine oil. She was satisfied that it was he, and allowed herself to fall into a light sleep, through which she could still hear him moving around in the room and feel him when he dropped into bed beside her and settled himself against her for warmth and comfort.

The engineer was not satisfied with the addition of an automatic feeder and an automatic chuck. 'The whole business must settle itself into position automatically,' he declared, 'there's altogether too much waste with hand calibration.'

Formerly Anton had selected the pins from a bucket and fastened them correctly into the chuck. Now a hopper fed the pins one by one into a chuck that grasped them at once of itself.

As he sat in a corner, back against the wall and ate his lunch, Anton sighed. His hands fumbled the sandwich and lost the meat or the bread, while his coffee dashed stormily in his cup. His few yellow teeth, worn flat, let the food escape through the interstices. His grinders did not meet. Tired of futile efforts he dropped his bread into his cup and sucked in the resulting mush.

Then he lay resting and dreaming.

To Anton, in his dream, came the engineer and declared that he had a new automatic hopper and chuck for Anton's hands and mouth. They were of shining steel with many rods and wheels moving with assurance through a complicated pattern. And now, though the sandwich was made of pins, of hard steel pins, Anton's new chuck was equal to it. He grasped the sandwich of pins with no difficulty at all. His new steel teeth bit into the pins, ground them, chewed them and spat them forth again with vehemence. Faster and faster came the pins, and faster and faster the chuck seized them in its perfectly occluding steel dogs, played with them, toyed with them, crunched them, munched them. . . .

A heavy spell of coughing shook Anton awake. For a moment he had a sensation as though he must cough up steel pins, but though his chest was racked as if truly heavy steel pins must come forth, nothing appeared but the usual phlegm and slime.

'We must get rid of this noise and vibration before we can adjust any self-regulating device,' said the engineer. 'Now this, for example, see? It doesn't move correctly. Hear it click and scrape. That's bad.'

Anton stood by, and the engineer and his assistant went to work. From their labours there came forth a sleek mechanism that purred gently as it worked. Scarcely a creak issued from its many moving parts, and a tiny snort was all the sound one heard when the cutting edge came to grips with a pin.

'Can't hear her cough and sputter and creak now, can you?' said the engineer to the director. 'And the floor is quiet. Yes, I'm beginning to be proud of that machine, and now I think we can set up an adjustable cam here to make the whole operation automatic.'

'Every machine should be completely automatic. A machine that needs an operator,' he declared oratorically, 'is an invalid.'

In a short time the cams were affixed and now the carriage with the cutting tool travelled back and forth of itself and never failed to strike the pin at the correct angle and at the correct speed of rotation.

All Anton had to do now was to stop the machine in case of a hitch. But soon even that task was unnecessary. No hitches were ever to occur again. Electronic tubes at several points operated mechanisms designed to eject faulty pins either before they entered the hopper or else after they emerged from the lathe.

Anton stood by and watched. That was all he had to do, for the machine now performed all the operations that he had used to do. In went the unfinished pins and out they came, each one perfectly drilled. Anton's purblind eyes could scarcely follow the separate pins of the stream that flowed into the machine. Now and then a pin was pushed remorselessly out of line and plumped sadly into a bucket. Cast out! Anton stooped laboriously and retrieved the pin. 'That could have been used,' he thought.

'Krr-click, krr-click,' went the feeder, while the spindle and the drill went *zzz-sntt*, *zzzz-sntt*, *zzz-sntt*, and the belt that brought the pins from a chattering machine beyond, rolled softly over the idlers with a noise like a breeze in a sail. Already the machine had finished ten good pins while Anton was examining a single bad one.

Late in the afternoon there appeared a number of important men. They surrounded the machine, examined it and admired it.

'That's a beauty,' they declared.

Now the meeting took on a more official character. There were several short addresses. Then an imposing man took from a small leather box a golden crescent.

'The Crescent Manufacturing Company,' he said, 'takes pride and pleasure in awarding this automatic lathe a gold crescent.' A place on the side of the machine had been prepared for the affixing of this distinction.

Now the engineer was called upon to speak.

'Gentlemen,' he said fiercely, 'I understand that formerly the Crescent Company awarded its gold crescent only to workmen who had given fifty years of service to the firm. In giving a gold crescent to a machine, your President has perhaps unconsciously acknowledged a new era. . . .'

While the engineer developed his thesis, the director leaned over to his assistant and whispered, 'Did you ever hear of why the sea is salt?'

'Why the sea is salt?' whispered back the assistant. 'What do you mean?'

The director continued: 'When I was a little kid, I heard the story of "Why the sea is salt" many times, but I never thought it important until just a moment ago. It's something like this: Formerly the sea was fresh water and salt was rare and expensive. A miller received from a wizard a wonderful machine that just ground salt out of itself all day long. At first the miller thought himself the most fortunate man in the world, but soon all the villages had salt to last them for centuries and still the machine kept on grinding more salt. The miller had to move out of his house, he had to move off his acres. At last he determined that he would sink the machine in the sea and be rid of it. But the mill ground so fast that boat and miller and machine were sunk together, and down below, the mill still went on grinding and that's why the sea is salt.'

'I don't get you,' said the assistant.

Throughout the speeches, Anton had remained seated on the floor, in a dark corner, where his back rested comfortably against the wall. It had begun to darken by the time the company left, but still Anton remained where he was, for the stone floor and wall had never felt quite so restful before. Then, with a great effort, he roused his unwilling frame, hobbled over to his machine and dragged forth the tarpaulin.

Anton had paid little attention to the ceremony; it was, therefore, with surprise that he noticed the gold crescent on his machine. His weak eyes strained to pierce the twilight. He let his fingers play over the medal, and was aware of tears falling from his eyes, and could not divine the reason.

The mystery wearied Anton. His worn and trembling body sought the inviting floor. He stretched out, and sighed, and that sigh was his last.

When the daylight had completely faded, the machine began to hum softly. *Zzz-sntt, zzz-sntt*, it went, four times, and each time carefully detached a leg from the floor.

Now it rose erect and stood beside the body of Anton. Then it bent down and covered Anton with the tarpaulin. Out of the hall it stalked on sturdy legs. Its electron eyes saw distinctly through the dark, its iron limbs responded instantly to its every need. No noise racked its interior where its organs functioned smoothly and without a single tremor. To the watchman, who grunted his usual greeting without looking up, it answered never a word but strode on rapidly, confidently, through the windy streets of night—to Anton's house.

Anton's wife lay waiting, half-sleeping on the bed in the room where the arc-light came through the stained-glass window. And it seemed to her that a marvel happened: her Anton come back to her free of coughs and creaks and tremors; her Anton come to her in all the pride and folly of his youth, his breath like wind soughing through tree-tops, the muscles of his arms like steel.

CHANGELING

Ray Bradbury

(1920–   )

News reports have claimed that the moving, talking, "thinking" robot is indeed a reality—albeit behind the doors of scientific laboratories. The emergence of the computer, which in time will become the main activating power of the robot, has shown how close people are to being served in reality by the robot which has been serving them in fiction for half a century and more. Ray Bradbury and Isaac Asimov, two of the foremost writers in Science Fantasy and Science Fiction, now bring their respective talents to bear on the basic premise: Ray Bradbury, possibly the finest writer of fantasy fiction in the world today, has written various stories on the theme of robot creations, but in straightforward human terms, "Changeling" is one of his best. Its carefully built atmosphere of inevitable tragedy is masterfully handled and he gives to an age-old situation a macabre new twist.

By eight o'clock she had placed the long cigarettes and the wine crystals and the silver bucket of thin shaved ice packed around the green bottle. She stood looking at the room, each picture neat, ashtrays conveniently disposed. She plumped a lounge pillow and stepped back, her eyes squinting. Then she hurried into the bathroom and returned with the strychnine bottle, which she laid under a magazine on an endtable. She had already hidden a hammer and an icepick.

She was ready.

Seeming to know this, the phone rang. When she answered, a voice said:

'I'm coming up.'

He was in the elevator now, floating silently up the iron throat of the house, fingering his accurate little moustache, adjusting his white summer evening coat and black tie. He would be smoothing his grey-blond hair, that handsome man of fifty still able to visit handsome women of thirty-three, fresh, convivial, ready for the wine and the rest of it.

'You're a faker!' she whispered to the closed door a moment before he rapped.

'Good evening, Martha,' he said. 'Are you just going to stand there, looking?' She kissed him quietly. 'Was that a kiss?' he wondered, his blue eyes warmly amused. 'Here.' He gave her a better one.

Her eyes closed, she thought, is this different from last week, last month, last year? What makes me suspicious? Some little thing. Something she couldn't even tell, it was so minor. He had changed subtly and drastically. So drastically in fact, so completely that she had begun to stay awake at night two months ago. She had taken to riding the helicopters at three in the morning out to the beach and back to see all-night films projected on the clouds near The Point, films that had been made way back in 1955, huge memories in the ocean mist over the dark waters, with the voices drifting in like gods' voices with the tide. She was constantly tired.

'Not much response.' He held her away and surveyed her critically. 'Is anything wrong, Martha?'

'Nothing,' she said. Everything, she thought. You, she thought. Where are you tonight, Leonard? Who are you dancing with far away, or drinking with in an apartment on the other side of town, who are you being lovably polite with? For you most certainly are not here in this room, and I intend to prove it.

'What's this?' he said, looking down. 'A hammer? Have you been hanging pictures, Martha?'

'No, I'm going to hit you with it,' she said, and laughed.

'Of course,' he said, smiling. 'Well, perhaps this will make you change your mind.' He drew forth a plush case inside which was a pearl necklace.

'Oh, Leonard!' She put it on with trembling fingers and turned to him, excited. 'You are good to me.'

'It's nothing at all,' he said.

At these times, she almost forgot her suspicions. She had everything with him, didn't she? There was no sign of his losing interest, was there? Certainly not. He was just as kind and gentle and generous. He never came without something for her wrist or her finger. Why did she feel so lonely with him then? Why didn't she feel with him? Perhaps it had started with that picture in the paper two months ago. A picture of him and Alice Summers in The Club on the night of April 17th. She hadn't seen the picture until a month later and then she had spoken of it to him:

'Leonard, you didn't tell me you took Alice Summers to The Club on the night of April seventeenth.'

'Didn't I, Martha? Well, I did.'

'But wasn't that one of the nights you were here with me?'

'I don't see how it could have been. We have supper and play symphonies and drink wine until early morning.'

'I'm sure you were here with me April seventeenth, Leonard.'

'You're a little drunk, my dear. Do you keep a diary?'

'I'm not a child.'

'There you are then. No diary, no record. I was here the night before or the night after. Come on now, Martha, drink up.'

But that hadn't settled it. She had not gone to sleep that night with thinking and being positive he had been with her on April 17th. It was impossible, of course. He couldn't be in two places.

They both stood looking down at the hammer on the floor. She picked it up and put it on a table. 'Kiss me,' she said, quite suddenly, for she wanted now, more than ever, to be certain of this thing. He evaded her and said, 'First, the wine.' 'No,' she insisted, and kissed him.

There it was. The difference. The little change. There was no way to tell anyone, or even describe it. It would be like trying to describe a rainbow to a blind man. But there was a subtle chemical difference to his kiss. It was no longer the kiss of Mr. Leonard Hill. It approximated the kiss of Leonard Hill but was sufficiently different to set a subconscious wheel rolling in her. What would an analysis of the faint moisture on his lips reveal? Some bacterial lack? And as for the lips themselves, were or were they not harder, or softer, than before? Some small difference.

'All right, now the wine,' she said, and opened it. She poured his glass full. 'Oh, will you get some mats from the kitchen to set them on?' While he was gone she poured the strychnine in his glass. He returned with the mats to set the glasses on and picked up his drink.

'To us,' he said.

Good Lord, she thought, what if I'm wrong? What if this is really him? What if I'm just some wild paranoid sort of creature, really insane and not aware of it?

'To us.' She raised her glass.

He drained his at a gulp, as always. 'My God,' he said, wincing. 'That's horrible stuff. Where did you get it?'

'At Modesti's.'

'Well, don't get any more. Here, I'd better ring for more.'

'Never mind, I have more in the refrigerator.'

When she brought the new bottle in, he was sitting there, clever and alive and fresh. 'You look wonderful,' she said.

'Feel fine. You're beautiful. I think I love you more to-night than ever.'

She waited for him to fall sideways and stare the stare of the dead. 'Here we go,' he said, opening the second bottle.

When the second bottle was empty, an hour had passed. He was telling witty little stories and holding her hand and kissing her gently now and again. At last he turned to her and said, 'You seem quiet tonight, Martha? Anything wrong?'

'No,' she said.

She had seen the news item last week, the item that had finally set her worrying and planning, that had explained her loneliness in his presence. About the Marionettes. Marionettes, Incorporated. Not that they really existed, surely not. But there was a rumour. Police were investigating.

Life-size marionettes, mechanical, stringless, secretive, duplicates of real people. One might buy them for ten thousand dollars on some distant black market. One could be measured for a replica of one's self. If one grew weary of social functions, one could send the replica out to wine, to dine, to shake hands, to trade gossip with Mrs. Rinehart on your left, Mr. Simmons on your right, Miss Glenner across the table.

Think of the political tirades one might miss! Think of the bad shows one need never see. Think of the dull people one could snub without actually snubbing. And, last of all, think of the jewelled loved ones you could ignore, yet not ignore. What would a good slogan be? She Need Never

Know? Don't Tell Your Best Friends? It Walks, It Talks, It Sneezes, It Says 'Mama'?

When she thought of this she became almost hysterical. Of course it had not been proved that such things as Marionettes existed. Just a sly rumour, with enough to it to make a sensitive person crawl with horror.

'Abstracted again,' he said, interrupting her quietness. 'There you go, wandering off. What's in that pretty head of yours?'

She looked at him. It was foolish; at any moment he might convulse and die. Then she would be sorry for her jealousy.

Without thinking, she said, 'Your mouth; it tastes funny.'

'Dear me,' he said. 'I shall have to see to that, eh?'

'It's tasted funny for some time.'

For the first time he seemed concerned. 'Has it? I'm sorry. I'll see my doctor.'

'It's not that important.' She felt her heart beating quickly and she was cold. It was his mouth. After all, no matter how perfect chemists were, could they analyse and reproduce the exact taste? Hardly. Taste was individual. Taste was one thing to her, something else to another. There was where they had fallen down. She would not put up with it another minute. She walked over to the other couch, reached down and drew out the gun.

'What's that?' he said, looking at it. 'Oh my God,' he laughed. 'A gun. How dramatic.'

'I've caught on to you,' she said.

'Is there anything to catch on to?' he wanted to know, calmly, his mouth straight, his eyes twinkling.

'You've been lying to me. You haven't been here in eight weeks or more,' she said.

'Is that true? Where have I been, then?'

'With Alice Summers, I wouldn't doubt. I'll bet you're with her right now.'

'Is that possible?' he asked.

'I don't know Alice Summers, I've never met her, but I think I'll call her apartment right now.'

'Do that,' he said, looking straight at her.

'I will,' she said, moving to the phone. Her hand shook so that she could hardly dial information. While waiting for the number to come through she watched Leonard and he watched her with the eye of a psychiatrist witnessing a not-unusual phenomenon.

'You are badly off,' he said. 'My dear Martha—'

'Sit down!'

'My dear Martha,' he moved back in the couch, chuckling softly. 'What have you been reading?'

'About the Marionettes is all.'

'That poppycock? Good God, Martha, I'm ashamed of you. It's not true. I looked into it!'

'What!'

'Of course!' he cried, in delight. 'I have so many social obligations, and then my first wife came back from India as you know and demanded my time and I thought how fine it would be if I had a replica of myself made, as bait you might say, to turn my wife off my trail, to keep her busy, how nice, eh? But it was all false. Just one of those Sunday supplement fantasies, I assure you. Now put that phone down and come and have another glass of wine.'

She had stood staring at him in bewilderment during all of his pronouncement. She had almost dropped the phone, believing him, until he said the word 'wine'. Then she shook herself and said, 'Wait a minute. You can't talk me out of this! I gave you some poison a while ago, enough to kill six men. You haven't showed a sign of it. That proves something, doesn't it?'

'It proves nothing at all. It merely proves that your chemist gave you the wrong bottle, is probably more like it. I'm sorry to disappoint you, but I feel fine. Put down that phone now, Martha, and be sensible.'

She held the phone in her hand. A voice said, 'That number is A B one two two fower niyen.'

'I just want to be certain,' she said.

'All right,' he shrugged. 'But if I'm not to be trusted I'm afraid I won't come back to see you again. What you need, my dear lady, is a psychiatrist, in the worst way. You're right on the edge!'

'Hello, operator? Give me A B one two two four nine.'

'Martha, don't,' he said, sitting there, one hand out.

The phone rang and rang at the other end. Finally a voice answered. Martha listened to it for a minute and then put the phone down.

Leonard looked into her face and said, 'There. Are you satisfied?'

'Yes,' she said. Her mouth was thick. She raised the gun.

'Don't!' he screamed. He stood up.

'That was your voice on the other end,' she said. 'You were with her!'

'You're insane!' he cried. 'Oh, God, Martha, don't, it's a mistake, that was someone else, you're so overwrought you thought it sounded like me!'

She fired the gun once, twice, three times.

He fell to the floor.

She came to stand over him. She was afraid, and she began to cry. The fact that he had actually fallen at her feet had surprised her. She had imagined that a Marionette would only stand there and laugh at her, alive, immortal.

I was wrong, she thought. I am insane. This is Leonard Hill and I've killed him.

He lay with his eyes closed, his mouth moving. 'Martha,' he said. 'Why didn't you leave well enough alone. Oh, Martha.'

'I'll call a doctor,' she said.

'No, no, no.' And suddenly he began to laugh. 'You've got to know sometime. And now that you've done this, oh you fool, I may as well admit it.'

The gun fell from her fingers.

'I,' he said, choking on laughter. 'I haven't been here with you for a—for a year!'

'What?'

'A year, twelve months! Yes, Martha, twelve months!'

'You're lying!'

'Oh, you won't believe me now, will you? What's changed you in ten seconds? Do you think I'm Leonard Hill? Forget it!'

'Then that was you? At Alice Summers' apartment just now?'

'Me? No! I started with Alice a year ago, when first I left you!'

'Left me?'

'Yes, left, left, left!' he shouted, and laughed, lying there.

'I'm an old man, Martha, old and tired. The rat-race was too much for me. I thought I needed a change. So I went on to Alice and tired of her. And went on to Helen Kingsley, you remember her, don't you? And tired of her. And on to Ann Montgomery. And that didn't last. Oh, Martha, there are at least six duplicates of me, mechanical hypocrites, ticking away tonight, in all parts of the town, keeping six people happy. And do you know what I am doing, the real I?

'I'm home in bed early for the first time in thirty years, reading my little book of Montaigne's essays and enjoying it and drinking a hot glass of chocolate milk and turning out the lights at ten o'clock. I've been asleep for an hour now, and I shall sleep the sleep of the innocent until morning and arise refreshed and free.'

'Stop!' she shrieked.

'I've got to tell you,' he said. 'You've cut several of my ligaments with your bullets. I can't get up. The doctors, if they came, would find me out anyway, I'm not that perfect. Perfect enough, but not that good. Oh, Martha, I didn't want to hurt you. Believe me. I wanted only your happiness. That's why I was so careful with my planned withdrawal. I spent fifteen thousand dollars for this replica, perfect in every detail. There are variables. The saliva for one. A regrettable error. It set you off. But you must know that I loved you.'

She would fall at any moment, writhing into insanity, she thought. He had to be stopped from talking.

'And when I saw how the others loved me,' he whispered to the ceiling, eyes wide, 'I had to provide replicas for them, poor dears. They love me so. You won't tell them, will you, Martha? Promise me you won't give the show away. I'm a very tired old man, and I want only peace, a book, some milk and a lot of sleep. You won't call them up and give it away?'

'All this year, this whole year, I've been alone, alone every night,' she said, the coldness filling her. 'Talking to a mechanical horror! In love with nothingness! Alone all that time, when I could have been out with someone real!'

'I can still love you, Martha.'

'Oh God!' she cried, and seized up the hammer.

'Don't, Martha!'

She smashed his head in and beat at his chest and his thrashing arms and wild legs. She beat at the soft head until steel shone through, and sudden explosions of wire and brass coggery showered about the room with metal tinkles.

'I love you,' said the man's mouth. She struck it with the hammer and the tongue fell out. The glass eyes rolled on the carpet. She pounded at the thing until it was strewn like the remains of a child's electric train on the floor. She laughed while she was doing it.

In the kitchen she found several cardboard boxes. She loaded the cogs and wires and metal into these and sealed the tops. Ten minutes later she had summoned the houseboy from below.

'Deliver these packages to Mr. Leonard Hill, 17 Elm Drive,' she said, and tipped the boy. 'Right now, tonight. Wake him up, tell him it's a surprise package from Martha.'

'A surprise package from Martha,' said the boy.

After the door closed, she sat on the couch with the gun in her hand, turning it over and over, listening. The last thing she heard in her life was the sound of the packages being carried down the hall, the metal jingling softly, cog against cog, wire against wire, fading.

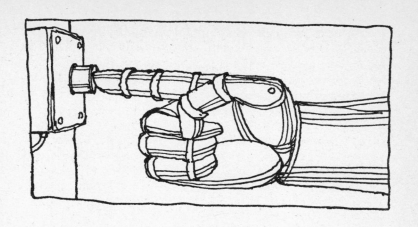

ROBOT AL-76 GOES ASTRAY

Isaac Asimov

(1920–   )

No anthology containing robots in fiction would be complete without a story by Isaac Asimov, who has proved himself the master in this particular area of Science Fiction. Whereas most other writers in the genre have almost invariably portrayed their robots as dangerous and likely to turn on their creators at any moment, Asimov saw them in quite a different light. His inspiration, he admitted, was Mary Shelley's "Frankenstein", for he saw there a sad, frustrated monster (as the authoress had intended) rather than a rampaging creature intent only on destruction. He wrote, "I consider a robot as simply another artifact. It is not a sacrilegious invasion of the domain of the Almighty, any more (or any less) than any other artifact is, and as a machine is surely designed for safety? Never, never is one of my robots going to turn stupidly on his creator for no purpose but to demonstrate, for one or more weary time, the crime and punishment of Faust." With this as his dictum, Asimov has created a whole canon of robot stories to which "Robot AL-76 Goes Astray" is as good an introduction as any. The inspiration the author found in Mary Shelley's great novel is there for the reading, but Isaac Asimov's own comments are an intriguing foretaste : "This robot is intent only on doing the work for which it is designed. It is incapable of harming men, yet it is victimised by human beings who, suffering from a 'Frankenstein' complex, insist on considering the poor machine a deadly, dangerous creature . . ."

JONATHAN Quell's eyes crinkled worriedly behind their rimless glasses as he charged through the door labelled 'General Manager'.

He slapped the folded paper in his hands upon the desk and panted, 'Look at that, boss!'

Sam Tobe juggled the cigar in his mouth from one cheek to the other, and looked. His hand went to his unshaven jaw and rasped along it. 'Hell!' he exploded. 'What are they talking about?'

'They say we sent out five AL robots,' Quell explained, quite unnecessarily.

'We sent six,' said Tobe.

'Sure, six! But they only got five at the other end. They sent out the serial numbers and AL-76 is missing.'

Tobe's chair went over backward as he heaved his thick bulk upright and went through the door as if he were on greased wheels. It was five hours after that—with the plant pulled apart from assembly rooms to vacuum chambers; with every one of the plant's two hundred employees put through the third-degree mill—that a sweating, dishevelled Tobe sent an emergency message to the central plant at Schenectady.

And at the central plant, a sudden explosion of near panic took place. For the first time in the history of the United States Robots and Mechanical Men Corporation, a robot had escaped to the outer world. It wasn't so much that the law forbade the presence of any robot on Earth outside a licensed factory of the corporation. Laws could always be squared. What was much more to the point was the statement made by one of the research mathematicians.

He said: 'That robot was created to run a Disinto on the moon. Its positronic brain was equipped for a lunar environment, and *only* a lunar environment. On Earth it's going to receive seventy-five umptillion sense impressions for which it was never prepared. There's no telling *what* its reactions will be. No telling!' And he wiped a forehead that had suddenly gone wet, with the back of his hand.

Within the hour a stratoplane had left for the Virginia plant. The instructions were simple.

'Get that robot, and get it fast!'

AL-76 was confused! In fact, confusion was the only impression his delicate positronic brain retained. It had started when he had found himself in these strange surroundings. How it had come about, he no longer knew. Everything was mixed up.

There was green underfoot, and brown shafts rose all about him with more green on top. And the sky was blue where it should have been black. The sun was all right, round and yellow and hot—but where was the powdery pumice rock underfoot; where were the huge cliff-like crater rings?

There was only the green below and the blue above. The sounds that surrounded him were all strange. It was blue and cold and wet. And when he passed people, as he did, occasionally, they were without the space suits they should have been wearing. When they saw him, they shouted and ran.

One man had levelled a gun at him and the bullet had whistled past his head—and then that man had run too.

He had no idea of how long he had been wandering before he finally stumbled upon Randolph Payne's shack two miles out in the woods from the town of Hannaford. Randolph Payne himself—a screwdriver in one hand, a pipe in the other and a battered ruin of a vacuum cleaner between his knees—squatted outside the doorway.

Payne was humming at the time, for he was a naturally

happy-go-lucky soul—when at his shack. He had a more respectable dwelling place back in Hannaford, but *that* dwelling place was pretty largely occupied by his wife, a fact which he silently but sincerely regretted. Perhaps, then, there was a sense of relief and freedom at such times as he found himself able to retire to his 'special deluxe doghouse' where he could smoke in peace and attend to his hobby of reservicing household appliances.

It wasn't much of a hobby, but sometimes someone would bring out a radio or an alarm clock and the money he would get paid for juggling its insides was the only money he ever got that didn't pass in driblets through his spouse's niggardly hands.

This vacuum cleaner, for instance, would bring in an easy six bits.

At the thought he broke into song, raised his eyes, and broke into a sweat. The song choked off, the eyes popped, and the sweat became more intense. He tried to stand up— as a preliminary to running like hell—but he couldn't get his legs to cooperate.

And then AL-76 had squatted down next to him and said, 'Say, why did all the rest of them run?'

Payne knew quite well why they all ran, but the gurgle that issued from his diaphragm didn't show it. He tried to inch away from the robot.

AL-76 continued in an aggrieved tone, 'One of them even took a shot at me. An inch lower and he would have scratched my shoulder plate.'

'M-must have b-been a nut,' stammered Payne.

'That's possible.' The robot's voice grew more confidential. 'Listen, what's wrong with everything?'

Payne looked hurriedly about. It had struck him that the robot spoke in a remarkably mild tone for one so heavily and brutally metallic in appearance. It also struck him that he had heard somewhere that robots were mentally incapable of harming human beings. He relaxed a bit.

'There's nothing wrong with anything.'

'Isn't there?' AL-76 eyed him accusingly. '*You're* all wrong. Where's your space suit?'

'I haven't got any.'

'Then why aren't you dead?'

That stopped Payne, 'Well—I don't know.'

'See!' said the robot triumphantly, 'there's something wrong with everything. Where's Mount Copernicus? Where's Lunar Station 17? And where's my Disinto? I want to get to work, I do.' He seemed perturbed, and his voice shook as he continued. 'I've been going about for hours trying to get someone to tell me where my Disinto is, but they all run away. By now I'm probably 'way behind schedule and the Sectional Executive will be as sore as blazes. This is a fine situation.'

Slowly Payne unscrambled the stew in which his brain found itself and said, 'Listen, what do they call you?'

'My serial number is AL-76.'

'All right, Al is good enough for me. Now, Al, if you're looking for Lunar Station 17, that's on the moon, see?'

AL-76 nodded his head ponderously. 'Sure. But I've been looking for it—'

'But it's on the moon. This isn't the moon.'

It was the robot's turn to become confused. He watched Payne for a speculative moment and then said slowly, 'What do you mean this isn't the moon? Of course it's the moon. Because if it isn't the moon, what is it, huh? Answer me that.'

Payne made a funny sound in his throat and breathed hard. He pointed a finger at the robot and shook it. 'Look,' he said—and then the brilliant idea of the century struck him, and he finished with a strangled 'Wow!'

AL-76 eyed him censoriously. 'That isn't an answer. I think I have a right to a civil answer if I ask a civil question.'

Payne wasn't listening. He was still marvelling at himself. Why, it was as plain as day. This robot was one built for the moon that had somehow got loose on Earth. Naturally it would be all mixed up, because its positronic brain had been geared exclusively for a lunar environment, making its earthly surroundings entirely meaningless.

And now if he could only keep the robot here—until he could get in touch with the men at the factory in Petersboro. Why, robots were worth money. The cheapest cost $50,000, he had once heard, and some of them ran into millions. Think of the reward!

Man, oh, man, *think of the reward!* And every cent for himself. Not as much as a quarter of a snifter of a plugged nickel for Mirandy. Jumpin' tootin' blazes, *no!*

He rose to his feet at last. 'Al,' he said, 'you and I are buddies! Pals! I love you like a brother.' He thrust out a hand. 'Shake!'

The robot swallowed up the offered hand in a metal paw and squeezed it gently. He didn't quite understand. 'Does that mean you'll tell me how to get to Lunar Station 17?'

Payne was a trifle disconcerted. 'N-no, not exactly. As a matter of fact, I like you so much, I want you to stay here with me awhile.'

'Oh no, I can't do that. I've got to get to work.' He shook his head. 'How would you like to be falling behind your quota hour by hour and minute by minute? I want to work. I've *got* to work.'

Payne thought sourly that there was no accounting for tastes, and said, 'All right, then. I'll explain something to you—because I can see from the looks of you that you're an intelligent person. I've had orders from your Sectional Executive, and he wants me to keep you here for a while. Till he sends for you, in fact.'

'What for?' asked AL-76 suspiciously.

'I can't say. It's secret government stuff.' Payne prayed, inwardly and fervently, that the robot would swallow this. Some robots were clever, he knew, but this looked like one of the early models.

While Payne prayed, AL-76 considered. The robot's brain,

adjusted to the handling of a Disinto on the moon, was not at its best when engaged in abstract thought, but just the same, ever since he had got lost, AL-76 had found his thought processes becoming stranger. The alien surroundings did something to him.

His next remark was almost shrewd. He said slyly, 'What's my Sectional Executive's name?'

Payne gulped and thought rapidly. 'Al,' he said in a pained fashion, 'you hurt me with this suspicion. I *can't* tell you his name. The trees have ears.'

AL-76 inspected the tree next to him stolidly and said, 'They have not.'

'I know. What I mean is that spies are all around.'

'Spies?'

'Yes. You know, *bad* people who want to destroy Lunar Station 17.'

'What for?'

'Because they're *bad*. And they want to destroy *you*, and that's why you've got to stay here for a while, so they can't find you.'

'But—but I've got to have a Disinto. I mustn't fall behind my quota.'

'You will have. You will have,' Payne promised earnestly, and just as earnestly damned the robot's one-track mind. 'They're going to send one out tomorrow. Yeah, tomorrow.' That would leave plenty of time to get the men from the factory out here and collect beautiful green heaps of hundred-dollar bills.

But AL-76 grew only the more stubborn under the distressing impingement of the strange world all about him upon his thinking mechanism.

'No,' he said, 'I've got to have a Disinto now.' Stiffly he straightened his joints, jerking erect. 'I'd better look for it some more.'

Payne swarmed after and grabbed a cold, hard elbow. 'Listen,' he squealed, 'you've got to stay—'

And something in the robot's mind clicked. All the strangeness surrounding him collected itself into one globule, exploded, and left a brain ticking with a curiously increased efficiency. He whirled on Payne. 'I tell you what. I can build a Disinto right here—and then I can work it.'

Payne paused doubtfully. 'I don't think I can build one.' He wondered if it would do any good to pretend he could.

'That's all right.' AL-76 could almost feel the positronic paths of his brain weaving into a new pattern, and experienced a strange exhilaration. 'I can build one.' He looked into Payne's deluxe doghouse and said, 'You've got all the material here that I need.'

Randolph Payne surveyed the junk with which his shack was filled: eviscerated radios, a topless refrigerator, rusty automobile engines, a broken-down gas range, several miles of frayed wire, and, taking it all together, fifty tons or thereabouts of the most heterogeneous mass of old metal as ever caused a junkman to sniff disdainfully.

'Have I?' he said weakly.

Two hours later, two things happened practically simultaneously. The first was that Sam Tobe of the Petersboro branch of the United States Robot and Mechanical Men Corporation received a visiphone call from one Randolph Payne of Hannaford. It concerned the missing robot, and Tobe, with a deep-throated snarl, broke connection halfway through and ordered all subsequent calls to be rerouted to the sixth assistant vice-president in charge of buttonholes.

This was not really unreasonable of Tobe. During the past week, although Robot AL-76 had dropped from sight completely, reports had flooded in from all over the Union as to the robot's whereabouts. As many as fourteen a day came —usually from fourteen different states.

Tobe was almighty tired of it, to say nothing of being half crazy on general principles. There was even talk of a Congressional investigation, though every reputable roboticist and mathematical physicist on Earth swore the robot was harmless.

In his state of mind, then, it is not surprising that it took three hours for the general manager to pause and consider just exactly how it was that this Randolph Payne had known that the robot was slated for Lunar Station 17, and, for that matter, how he had known that the robot's serial number was AL-76. Those details had not been given out by the company.

He kept on considering for about a minute and a half and then swung into action.

However, during the three hours between the call and the action, the second event took place. Randolph Payne, having correctly diagnosed the abrupt break in his call as being due to general scepticism on the part of the plant official, returned to his shack with a camera. They couldn't very well argue with a photograph, and he'd be hornswoggled if he'd show them the real thing before they came across with the cash.

AL-76 was busy with affairs of his own. Half of the contents of Payne's shack was littered over about two acres of ground, and in the middle of it the robot squatted and fooled around with radio tubes, hunks of iron, copper wire, and general junk. He paid no attention to Payne, who, sprawling flat on his belly, focused his camera for a beautiful shot.

And at this point it was that Lemuel Oliver Cooper turned the bend in the road and froze in his tracks as he took in the tableau. The reason for his coming in the first place was an ailing electric toaster that had developed the annoying habit of throwing out pieces of bread forcefully, but thoroughly untoasted. The reason for his *leaving* was more obvious. He had come with a slow, mildly cheerful, spring-morning saunter. He left with a speed that would have caused any college track coach to raise his eyebrows and purse his lips approvingly.

There was no appreciable slackening of speed until Cooper

hurtled into Sheriff Saunders' office, minus hat and toaster, and brought himself up hard against the wall.

Kindly hands lifted him, and for half a minute he tried speaking before he had actually calmed down to the point of breathing with, of course, no result.

They gave him whisky and fanned him and when he did speak, it came out something like this : '—monster—seven feet tall—shack all busted up—poor Rannie Payne—' and so on.

They got the story out of him gradually: how there was a huge metal monster, seven feet tall, maybe even eight or nine, out at Randolph Payne's shack; how Randolph Payne himself was on his stomach, a 'poor, bleeding, mangled corpse'; how the monster was then busily engaged in wrecking the shack out of sheer destructiveness; how it had turned on Lemuel Oliver Cooper, and how he, Cooper, had made his escape by half a hair.

Sheriff Saunders hitched his belt tighter about his portly middle and said, 'It's that there machine man that got away from the Petersboro factory. We got warning of it last Saturday. Hey, Jake, you get every man in Hannaford County that can shoot and slap a deputy's badge on him. Get them here at noon. And listen, Jake, before you do that, just drop in at the Widow Payne's place and lip her the bad news gentle-like.'

It is reported that Mirandy Payne, upon being acquainted with events, paused only to make sure that her husband's insurance policy was safe, and to make a few pithy remarks concerning her foolishness in not having had him take out double the amount, before breaking out into as prolonged and heart-wringing a wail of grief as ever became a respectable widow.

It was some hours later that Randolph Payne—unaware of his horrible mutilation and death—viewed the completed negatives of his snapshots with satisfaction. As a series of portraits of a robot at work, they left nothing to the imagination. They might have been labelled: 'Robot Gazing

Thoughtfully at Vacuum Tube,' 'Robot Splicing Two Wires,' 'Robot Wielding Screwdriver,' 'Robot Taking Refrigerator Apart with Great Violence,' and so on.

As there now remained only the routine of making the prints themselves, he stepped out from beyond the curtain of the improvised darkroom for a bit of a smoke and a chat with AL-76.

In doing so, he was blissfully unaware that the neighbouring woods were verminous with nervous farmers armed with anything from an old colonial relic of a blunderbuss to the portable machine gun carried by the sheriff himself. Nor, for that matter, had he any inkling of the fact that half a dozen roboticists, under the leadership of Sam Tobe, were smoking down the highway from Petersboro at better than a hundred and twenty miles an hour for the sole purpose of having the pleasure and honour of his acquaintance.

So while things were jittering towards a climax, Randolph Payne sighed with self-satisfaction, lighted a match upon the seat of his pants, puffed away at his pipe, and looked at AL-76 with amusement.

It had been apparent for quite some time that the robot was more than slightly lunatic. Randolph Payne was himself an expert at homemade contraptions, having built several that could not have been exposed to daylight without searing the eyeballs of all beholders; but he had never even conceived of anything approaching the monstrosity that AL-76 was concocting.

It would have made the Rube Goldbergs of the day die in convulsions of envy. It would have made Picasso (if he could have lived to witness it) quit art in the sheer knowledge that he had been hopelessly surpassed. It would have soured the milk in the udders of any cow within half a mile.

In fact, it was gruesome!

From a rusty and massive iron base that faintly resembled something Payne had once seen attached to a secondhand tractor, it rose upward in rakish, drunken swerves through a bewildering mess of wires, wheels, tubes, and nameless horrors without number, ending in a megaphone arrangement that looked decidedly sinister.

Payne had the impulse to peek in the megaphone part, but refrained. He had seen far more sensible machines explode suddenly and with violence.

He said, 'Hey, Al.'

The robot looked up. He had been lying flat on his stomach, teasing a thin sliver of metal into place. 'What do you want, Payne?'

'What is this?' He asked it in the tone of one referring to something foul and decomposing, held gingerly between two ten-foot poles.

'It's the Disinto I'm making—so I can start to work. It's an improvement on the standard model.' The robot rose, dusted his knees clankingly, and looked at it proudly.

Payne shuddered. An 'improvement'! No wonder they hid the original in caverns on the moon. Poor satellite! Poor dead satellite! He had always wanted to know what a fate worse than death was. Now he knew.

'Will it work?' he asked.

'Sure.'

'How do you know?'

'It's got to. I made it, didn't I? I only need one thing now. Got a flashlight?'

'Somewhere, I guess.' Payne vanished into the shack and returned almost immediately.

The robot unscrewed the bottom and set to work. In five minutes he had finished. He stepped back and said, 'All set. Now I get to work. You may watch if you want to.'

A pause, while Payne tried to appreciate the magnanimity of the offer. 'Is it safe?'

'A baby could handle it.'

'Oh!' Payne grinned weakly and got behind the thickest tree in the vicinity. 'Go ahead,' he said, 'I have the utmost confidence in you.'

AL-76 pointed to the nightmarish junk pile and said, 'Watch!' His hands set to work—

The embattled farmers of Hannaford County, Virginia, weaved up upon Payne's shack in a slowly tightening circle. With the blood of their heroic colonial forebears pounding in their veins—and goose flesh trickling up and down their spines—they crept from tree to tree.

Sheriff Saunders spread the word. 'Fire when I give the signal—and aim at the eyes.'

Jacob Linker—Lank Jake to his friends, and Sheriff's Deputy to himself—edged close. 'You think maybe this machine man has skedaddled?' He did not quite manage to suppress the tone of wistful hopefulness in his voice.

'Dunno,' grunted the sheriff. 'Guess not, though. We woulda come across him in the woods if he had, and we haven't.'

'But it's awful quiet, and it appears to me as if we're getting close to Payne's place.'

The reminder wasn't necessary. Sheriff Saunders had a lump in his throat so big it had to be swallowed in three instalments. 'Get back,' he ordered, 'and keep your finger on the trigger.'

They were at the rim of the clearing now, and Sheriff Saunders closed his eyes and stuck the corner of one out from behind the tree. Seeing nothing, he paused, then tried again, eyes open this time.

Results were, naturally, better.

To be exact, he saw one huge machine man, back towards him, bending over one soul-curdling, hiccupy contraption of uncertain origin and less certain purpose. The only item he missed was the quivering figure of Randolph Payne, embracing the tree next but three to the nor'-nor'west.

Sheriff Saunders stepped out into the open and raised his machine gun. The robot, still presenting a broad metal back, said in a loud voice—to person or persons unknown—

'Watch!' and as the sheriff opened his mouth to signal a general order to fire, metal fingers compressed a switch.

There exists no adequate description of what occurred afterward, in spite of the presence of seventy eyewitnesses. In the days, months, and years to come not one of those seventy ever had a word to say about the few seconds after the sheriff had opened his mouth to give the firing order. When questioned about it, they merely turned apple-green and staggered away.

It is plain from circumstantial evidence, however, that, in a general way, what did occur was this.

Sheriff Saunders opened his mouth; AL-76 pulled a switch. The Disinto worked, and seventy-five trees, two barns, three cows and the top three quarters of Duckbill Mountain whiffed into rarefied atmosphere. They became, so to speak, one with the snows of yesteryear.

Sheriff Saunders' mouth remained open for an indefinite interval thereafter, but nothing—neither firing orders nor anything else—issued therefrom. And then—

And then, there was a stirring in the air, a multiple ro-o-o-oshing sound, a series of purple streaks through the atmosphere radiating away from Randolph Payne's shack as the centre, and of the members of the posse, not a sign.

There were various guns scattered about the vicinity, including the sheriff's patented nickel-plated, extra-rapid-fire, guaranteed-no-clog, portable machine gun. There were about fifty hats, a few half-chomped cigars, and some odds and ends that had come loose in the excitement—but of actual human beings there was none.

Except for Lank Jake, not one of those human beings came within human ken for three days, and the exception in his favour came about because he was interrupted in his comet-flight by the half-dozen men from the Petersboro factory, who were charging *into* the wood at a pretty fair speed of their own.

It was Sam Tobe who stopped him, catching Lank Jake's head skilfully in the pit of his stomach. When he caught his breath, Tobe asked, 'Where's Randolph Payne's place?'

Lank Jake allowed his eyes to unglaze for just a moment. 'Brother,' he said, 'just you follow the direction I ain't going.'

And with that, miraculously, he was gone. There was a shrinking dot dodging trees on the horizon that might have been he, but Sam Tobe wouldn't have sworn to it.

That takes care of the posse; but there still remains Randolph Payne, whose reactions took something of a different form.

For Randolph Payne, the five-second interval after the pulling of the switch and the disappearance of Duckbill Mountain was a total blank. At the start he had been peering through the thick underbrush from behind the bottom of the trees; at the end he was swinging wildly from one of the topmost branches. The same impulse that had driven the posse horizontally had driven him vertically.

As to how he had covered the fifty feet from roots to top —whether he had climbed, jumped, or flown—he did not know, and he didn't give a particle of never-mind.

What he *did* know was that property had been destroyed by a robot temporarily in his possession. All visions of rewards vanished and were replaced by trembling nightmares of hostile citizenry, shrieking lynch mobs, lawsuits, murder charges, and what Mirandy Payne would say. Mostly what Mirandy Payne would say.

He was yelling wildly and hoarsely, 'Hey, you robot, you smash that thing, do you hear? Smash it good! You forget I ever had anything to do with it. You're a stranger to me, see? You don't ever say a word about it. Forget it, you hear?'

He didn't expect his orders to do any good; it was only reflex action. What he didn't know was that a robot always obeys a human order except where carrying it out involves danger to another human.

AL-76, therefore, calmly and methodically proceeded to demolish his Disinto into rubble and flinders.

Just as he was stamping the last cubic inch under foot, Sam Tobe and his contingent arrived, and Randolph Payne, sensing that the real owners of the robot had come, dropped out of the tree head-first and made for regions unknown feet-first.

He did not wait for his reward.

Austin Wilde, Robotical Engineer, turned to Sam Tobe and said, 'Did you get anything out of the robot?'

Tobe shook his head and snarled deep in his throat. 'Nothing. Not one thing. He's forgotten everything that's happened since he left the factory. He must have got *orders* to forget, or it couldn't have left him so blank. What was that pile of junk he'd been fooling with?'

'Just that. A pile of junk! But it must have been a Disinto before he smashed it, and I'd like to kill the fellow who ordered him to smash it—by slow torture, if possible. Look at this!'

They were part of the way up the slopes of what had been Duckbill Mountain—at that point, to be exact, where the top had been sheered off; and Wilde put his hand down upon the perfect flatness that cut through both soil and rock.

'*What* a Disinto,' he said. 'It took the mountain right off its base.'

'What made him build it?'

Wilde shrugged. 'I don't know. Some factor in his environment—there's no way of knowing what—reacted upon his moon-type positronic brain to produce a Disinto out of junk. It's a billion to one against our ever stumbling upon that factor again now that the robot himself has forgotten. We'll never have that Disinto.'

'Never mind. The important thing is that we have the robot.'

'The hell you say.' There was poignant regret in Wilde's

voice. 'Have you ever had anything to do with the Disintos on the moon? They eat up energy like so many electronic hogs and won't even begin to run until you've built up a potential of better than a million volts. But *this* Disinto worked differently. I went through the rubbish with a microscope, and would you like to see the only source of power of any kind that I found?'

'What was it?'

'Just this! And we'll never know how he did it.'

And Austin Wilde held up the source of power that had enabled a Disinto to chew up a mountain in half a second— *two flashlight batteries!*

BABY

Carol Emshwiller

(1935–)

As this collection began with, and was inspired by, the writing of a
woman, it is only fitting that a story by a present-day woman writer
should conclude it. This happens to be a most appropriate one, for it
takes the quest which has been the raison d'être *of all the previous*
experimentors, and considers where obsession with such things might
ultimately lead to. Carol Emshwiller, the authoress, is at the fore-
front of the new school of Science Fiction writers and has already
displayed an ingenuity and style that would be the envy of Mary
Shelley herself. Indeed she has employed Miss Shelley's original
concept of the being created hopefully to serve, and extended it to its
logical—or perhaps illogical—conclusion. Though mankind looks

forward to a less troubled world where all are fed and housed, where mechanical servants take care of the routine side of life and people are freed to enjoy themselves—is the risk too great? Is the nightmare which Carol Emshwiller paints for us too near to reality? The "monster makers" have come a long way, but the dangers are all too plainly there.

THEY called him Baby. He was six feet tall, lean, and had the look of a hungry hunting animal, but the robots called him Baby.

Someone had once written in a neat script in a tome and on a white paper the carefully chosen name, Christopher John Correy, but there was no one left who could say that this particular name on this particular paper and in this particular book was the name of the man called Baby by robots.

Until a few years ago the city had had all the food it takes to make a man full grown and to keep him sleek and healthy, but now Baby's hip bones jutted forward from a concave stomach, his ribs arched above, and the strong muscles lay just beneath the skin and showed in lined bunches when he moved.

He stood naked in the dining-room, damp bare feet on the smooth black tile. He shut his eyes tight and said in a whisper, 'Please, please and please, be meat.' Then he swallowed the saliva that came at the thought of food. He chewed on nothing and waited, hoping but not expecting. 'I said please,' he whispered.

There was no one in the room but him and he watched with fox eyes on the kitchen door until it opened and a model B maid came in. The soup plates on her tray top held only brown powder. House 76 had lost its water pipes in the last freeze of the season because the heat had gone out.

But Baby hadn't come for soup. Sometimes 76 had meat and if not meat, usually an edible dessert. Baby was hungry enough for anything at all.

The model B put a soup plate in front of each empty chair

around the table, and then it waited by the kitchen door, and Baby waited, and after a time the model B took the plates away. The next course *was* meat, or had been, but something had gone wrong and the roast was burned to a dry black lump.

The Please is fooling me, Baby thought. It wants to make me angry.

The meat was impossible to eat, but the model B cut it with knife fingers, not noticing how the black flaked off and fell to the floor. It served each plate with the dark, woody chunks and also with something unrecognizable, an over-cooked or spoiled vegetable or perhaps a mouldy salad. Then it waited again and after a while took the untouched plates away and came in with the dessert, chocolate pie with whipped cream. A dairy still came to 76 and with milk from one of the underground farms where the robots still tended cows. And the stove had timed just right this time.

Baby glanced out of the glass wall behind him. 'Overseer, Rob 10, please not be there now, please.' He shut his eyes and whispered it. Then he moved fast, reaching under model B's knives just before they came down to split the pie. Model B didn't even notice its knives cut nothing. It was a poor automatic thing on a track and it had no eye. The stove ran it, adjusting it for each task as it loaded the tray. But overseer Rob wasn't like the maid. His eye flickered red, observant, and his legs telescoped at the knees and could run faster than Baby.

Baby ran across the hall balancing the pie. The walls at the end, still working smoothly, lifted to let him out into the back yard. 76's walls were not discriminating any more. They had opened and closed for Baby for a number of years now.

'Overseer, Rob 10, please not be there now, please.'

The overseer wasn't.

Baby climbed the artificial hill at the back of the house at a crouching run, and pushed through the overgrown hedge

into the neglected yard of the house that had lost its overseer
six years ago. He flopped down on his stomach behind the
young trees and bushes. He pushed out his lips and sucked
at the whipped cream on the top of the pie, not caring about
the long scratches the hedge had made across his body.

He would not have much time, here, so close to his own
home, so he concentrated on eating rapidly and without
relish. This was something just to fill his stomach. He was
hungry now for meat or milk.

He was losing faith in Please. It didn't work as often as it
used to. And he was losing faith in Nursie too, but she could
still catch him when he was close to his home like this. In
spite of how she was now, her arms were still long enough,
and her eye still saw. She was slower, but not too slow. She
was strong, broad-bottomed with a caterpillar tread and she
could still lift him. He was only really safe from her a couple
of miles or so from his house. And even then it was usually
only a matter of time for her to find him. Now he was behind
75 and his own home was just next door.

'Baby, Baby. Come to Nursie, you scallywag.'

Baby raised his head, mouth dripping chocolate, smears
on nose and cheeks. He leaned over the pie like an animal
over a fresh kill, wary and challenging.

'Baby, come to Nursie. It's time for your nap. Don't make
Nursie hunt all over, that's a good Baby. I've milk and
cookies.'

I'd take a nap for milk and cookies, Baby thought, but
the glass is always empty now and the cookies, when there
are any, aren't fit to eat. He bent to the pie again. His teeth
scraped on the pan as he bit at the crust, tearing at it doglike.

He couldn't get away now. She would find him and catch
him, and take the pie away if he didn't finish it fast. Pies are
not for little babies, she would say.

There was silence while she circled, slowly scanning, and
he wolfed the last of the crust. At the half circle she caught
the warmth and with a wheeze, scratch, scratch, wheeze,

scratch, scratch, she came after him. She sounded slower
than she was. Baby didn't try to get away. In a moment one
of her long flexible arms reached out into the bushes and
took him about the waist gently but firmly. He yielded to
the pull, stood up and walked towards Nursie, leaning on
her soft arm. He hadn't tried to fight her for a long time now.
It had always been useless.

'There's a good boy. Here's milk and cookies, and then
we'll pop into bed for a nap.' She put the empty sip-glass
into his hand. 'Baby do it all by himself.'

'There *is* no milk for Baby here. You never have milk for
me any more.'

'Yes, it's there. I got it from the dairy box just now. The
milk-robs came, early, early, while you were still asleep, and
they brought this good milk just for Baby.'

A feeling came over him like getting into a warm bath
only the warmth flowed inside him. For a moment he could
say nothing at all, and then he said, 'Where's my milk?' in a
whisper. His arm muscles tightened and he clenched his
fists against his stomach.

There was something wrong with him lately, and it was
getting worse. Something that gnawed at him and knotted
his stomach like this. A great need, overpowering, for an
unknown thing. It drove him to far wanderings about the
city, to taking stupid risks, to fits of running after nothing
in the empty streets, to staring at the sky, sometimes to a
wild howling, and to climbing, climbing dizzily and trembling on narrow perches about the high buildings.

'Where's my milk?' He screamed it this time. 'Ask Rob 6
if there is milk there.' The overseer will tell her and *then* she
will doubt. She will no longer believe in Please nor in Central,
and because she is so sure, her doubts will be devastating.
He would see her fall on the ground and scream with horror
of her lost belief.

'Come, drink it up,' she said.

'Central is stopped! There is no Please!' he shouted.

Both soft mother-arms came out to embrace him. There
was a place, a specially built place at her breast (or what
stood for breast) to cradle a baby or pillow a young head,
but it was too low for him now even when he knelt. Still, she
pulled him to her.

'Don't worry, Baby. Don't cry. There's always milk for
Baby. As much as you want. Come along and we'll get some
more.'

'There isn't any milk.' He was calm suddenly. 'Please ask
Rob 6. I said please. Now ask Rob 6, please.'

'Such a good, polite boy. All right, we'll ask Rob 6
if you want. Yes. You said please, didn't you? Yes you
did.'

There was a time a long time ago when Baby always
answered eagerly and proudly, 'Yes, I did, didn't I,' but
now he said nothing, his face as expressionless as Nursie's
flat tray of features always was.

She took his strong hand, calloused from climbing, and
led him across his own neat lawn to his home. The front
wall panel rose to let them in as they neared.

Nursie stopped just inside, and Baby knew she was scanning for Rob 6. Maybe she was even talking to him in the
silent way they had that Baby could never hear. A long time
ago he had felt for the first time the fierce frustration of not
hearing. Even though the discovery of it had come gradually,
the understanding came all at once. It was as if he 'knew'
they were doing it long before he 'realized' it. That day a
feeling like the one he had now had washed over him in a
hot flush. They're hard and hurt-proof, and I'm soft; they're
strong with long changeable arms, and I'm weak and only
one shape; and now they talk together and I can't hear it.
My Nursie talks silently to that Rob 6.

That day of realization he had gone down to the high
buildings where the statue was, tall to the third window of
one of them, and he had climbed all the way to the top of
the white head for the first time. He scraped his thumb on

the way up. He remembered the blood smearing the fleshy part of his hand, and the drops making three red lines down his arm.

At the top he had shouted, 'I wish to be Rob 6.' He sat right on the big head with a foot on each ear, drunk with height. 'I don't want to be Baby anymore. I must be more than I am. Please, please, please, and please. Baby said please.'

He had looked at the hot summer sun and shouted, 'I say please twice to the sun in the sky,' and then he turned towards Central, 'and four times to Central.' He liked the sun best, but he knew Central was more powerful. He smeared the blood from his hand across the white statue head and shut his eyes tight. I am getting hard and strong, he thought. I have one eye here in the centre and it flickers red. He could feel his two eyes merging slowly to just above his nose. My arms are interchangeable, and if I jump I will land on rubber feet and my knees will spring, one section up into the other, and I won't be hurt. I am Rob number one thousand and twenty-six. I am changed.

And he had jumped then.

It took Nursie almost a whole day to find him. 'You naughty boy. You naughty, naughty boy, to go so far from home.' She carried him back gently and called the Rob-Doc, and Baby had lain in bed a long time after that. She had been happy with him for being a good boy all that time, but he had cried each night with pain and frustration, and he had wondered, since he couldn't be Rob 6, when he would be at least a man, whatever that was. Nursie always just said, sometime.

And now he would try to hurt her as he had hurt then, inside, and as he hurt now with an unknown need.

She started off, after the few seconds' wait at the door, pulling Baby along after her. Her broad caterpillar tread easily mounted the stone steps behind the huge carefully rustic fireplace. She crossed, in rubbery silence, the metal-tiled hallway while Baby pad-padded behind her, leaving dirty damp outlines of his feet on the spotless floor. They crossed the kitchen by the centre ramp and entered the door to the brain centre of house 74.

The room was large and filled with wires and pipes and conveyer belts, but the main control unit was small. The thing that ran everything in the house including this maze of crisscrossing wires and pipes, was bread-box size. Rob 6 stood before it, propped back on his third leg, the one he used for balance when walking and as a prop when standing still. He wore his mechanic hands and had plugged himself into one side of the control unit by a long flexible thumb.

'There is something wrong,' Rob 6 said, but it is not here. Control is fine.'

'Baby says there is no milk,' Nursie said, 'but I heard the milk-robs come this morning. Baby is fooling Nursie again. He fools and fools. And, Rob 6, Baby is getting so big. *Such* a big boy. Too big for Nursie. Or do I need to be fixed too? Will you check, Robby 6?'

'You are thirty-eight years old. You should have been replaced.'

'We make do with what we have. Yes we do.' She chanted it as if she were reciting a nursery rhyme. 'But *now*, Robby 6, *is* there milk in the dairy box for Baby?'

'I doubt it.'

'I don't understand. I don't understand at all. There is *always* milk in the dairy box at seven twenty-three.'

'Things are not going right and they are getting worse. There is something wrong with 74 now, but Control is fine. Library did not send a tape with motor repair information. I dialled and none came. And I asked and Central did not answer.'

'That's too bad, *too* bad,' Nursie chanted, and then she said, 'but if at first you don't succeed, try, try again,' and, 'Things will be better tomorrow.'

'Not without human beings.'

'They'll come back. Mommy and Daddy will come back *later*.'

'Nurse 16, you helped to bury them yourself after the enemy seeded the sickness.'

'Why Rob 6! And in front of Baby too! He understands things now, you know.'

Baby squatted down, flat-footed, on the metal-grilled floor of the control room. Rob 6 and Nursie never used chairs and neither did he since he'd outgrown his high-chair. 'He's only said it a thousand times already,' he muttered, sullen faced, carefully not looking at them.

It wasn't going to happen now either, or ever. No matter what he said or did, Nursie would be the same. She would never know anything she didn't already know now. Her eye looks at me, but she doesn't really see me at all, he thought. If I were gone or even stopped like some of the robots, she would say only, 'He's coming back *later*,' like she says over and over about Mommy and Daddy and Jeannie. She sees my shape, but not me. I am a nothing thing to her, but *she* is less than that even.

'Baby was inside Nursie then,' Nursie said. 'That was a long time ago and you were just a little scallywag.'

'You're just a nothing,' Baby said.

'Hush, dear. That's not very polite. You know, I kept you inside me a whole extra year like your Mommy and Daddy said and when you came out you were just as safe as can be, and now you're growing up to be a little gentleman just like Mommy and Daddy wanted you to be.'

Baby breathed out loudly and hunched lower over his knees. She will *not* change and she will *never* see me. 'You're both just nothings,' he said, 'and there is no Central and no Please at all.'

'What a thing to say,' Nursie said.

'Ask, then—ask Central and Library. Ask *them* why there is no milk any more.'

Rob 6 and Nursie stood silent. They're asking, Baby

thought, feeling an unbearable irritation. Rob 6, even, is asking Central and he knows it doesn't answer.

'Central doesn't answer,' Rob 6 said.

Suddenly Baby found it difficult to breathe. Squatting over his knees was too cramping and he stood up.

'Central *never* answers any more.' His voice sounded different to him, low and tense. 'Yesterday and yesterday and yesterday before that, a long time before even, it didn't answer, but you keep asking and asking.'

'It is right to ask Central first,' Rob 6 said.

'Of course it is,' Nursie said. 'You know that, yes you do. Always ask Central *first*. It will tell you what to do *next*.'

He began to tremble and he felt a hot knot swell in his stomach. Part of him seemed to stand apart and ask, what's wrong lately? Rob 6 and Nursie are not so different than they used to be.

He remembered a time when they had seemed enough in every way, observant enough, intelligent enough, loving enough, but that was a long time ago, and he had changed somehow and he was changing even more. Now he was full of unreasonable, uncontrollable angry feelings.

He kept his eyes carefully off Nursie. He felt he would burst if he looked at her empty, wide eye. 'Rob 6,' he spoke slowly, 'Central will never answer . . . *never answer* any more. What are you going to do about it?'

Rob 6 stood silent. Is he asking again, Baby wondered? Is he asking Central what will he do now that Central is out?

Suddenly it was too much. The swelling hot knot inside him burst and he was shouting. 'This is the end of it. I will not listen to any one of you any more. You don't understand anything. You have no eyes and no ears that are any more good than stopped ones.'

'Let's not have a tantrum now,' Nursie said, interrupting him. 'Why Baby needs his nap. My goodness, no wonder. It's way past the time.' She reached out to him.

Fighting wouldn't do any good. He could never hurt her, never dent her, in her mind nor in her body. He was still nothing to her even when he fought, but now he fought. He bit at the soft arms and kicked at her treads, bruising his feet, and he began to laugh an odd, sobbing laugh. The fighting was silly and the laughter shook him so that it was only weak fighting anyway. 'You can't even see me. You never have. Never, never.'

She was carrying him slowly, but easily, up the wide low stairway, and she was talking, gently soothing. 'You must learn to be a *good* boy, and not fight. You know, there's an enemy, a barbarous enemy, far away, and we, the robots, protect the city for all the peace-loving peoples of the world, for this city is more than just a place for people to live and work. It stands for a way of life. It is a haven of civilized living and we must keep it safe.'

He'd heard all this before.

Tall wide-leaved plants, rooted at the foot of the stairs, brushed at them as they rose. Baby tore off a whole branch with one violent sweep of his arm.

'No, no,' Nursie said. 'Mustn't touch.' This made Baby laugh louder and more, though he didn't know why, and the laughing hurt his stomach, but he couldn't stop.

They crossed the balcony, Nursie swaying a little with Baby's tossing weight. The door of the nursery slid open as it always did instantly for Nursie, but never for anyone else, not even Baby, though it would have opened for Mommy and Daddy.

They were there, in his bright special room, circular, windowed top to bottom, with a blue ceiling where stars winked on and off. A room specially planned by a loving mother and father for a son named Christopher John.

Nursie put him gently into his bed and shut the gate. 'You'll feel much better after your nap,' she said. '*Then* you'll be my good boy again and we'll play in the sandpile at the park if you like.'

Baby doubled up with painful laughter. Why was everything so funny now?

She left and the gay red door slid shut after her, shut to stay, until she came back.

The bed was youth-size. Baby lay, knees drawn up, laughing and holding his stomach. Gradually the laughter stopped and it was like after crying, leaving him empty and looking at his starred ceiling.

Later he put his feet tight against the bottom of the bed and braced his hands at the top. 'This is not even my bed,' he said out loud. 'It's too small.' And he pushed until the wood panel broke and his feet came through and he lay out straight. 'I'm me,' he said. 'They can't see me, but I am me, and quite big.'

He got up and stepped over the side of the bed. He went to the section of the wall with movable panels. He had broken the levers long before, on that moonlight night of the first escape when he was half the size he was now. House 76 had not registered it even then so no one came to fix it. He slid the glass panel to the side, letting the hot outside air come in. He grinned again, pulling his lips back from his teeth, a dog grin, or wolf.

He stepped out on the thin wire frame that held the patio roof. 'Please,' he said, but there was a downturning of his voice, half mockery, yet not quite sure. He ran out on the frame, tightrope style, sure-footed, jumped at the end and landed rolling in the grass beyond the grey-and-orange circle of the patio. There was no one in sight.

'Good Please?' He loped across the back, leaped the dried-up stony bed where the imitation stream used to run, pumped in a rambling circle about the back yard. He climbed the carefully random rocks at the far end and jumped a retaining wall to the footwalk below.

The sub-belt entrance, a stone lean-to at the corner park, was a 200-yard sprint. Baby ran down the slow-moving ramp into the bright white-tiled tunnel and at the bottom stepped easily from the slower belts to the fastest. But even there he kept running along the moving aisle past the line of seats.

This was not a time for sitting. Now he was going farther and faster than ever before, and never coming back. He went at an easy run, hands low, relaxed, head tipped back. He looked ahead down the long bright tunnel, empty and bare as far as he could see—but then everywhere he had ever looked had been empty and bare except for occasional robots.

He ran until, even in this cool place, the sweat dripped down from under his arms. He felt the dampness between his shoulder blades and on his upper lip and he smelled himself, a sticky, unrobot smell, bitter and sweet. After a while he tired and sprawled, knees spread wide, in one of the hard moulded chairs at the side.

A long time had passed, he knew. Usually he was impatient with the sub-belt. He had never been able to stay underground more than about an hour without coming up to take a look, but this time he had the patience to stay. The running had eased the turmoil but something still smouldered inside him and now he had a new kind of patience.

He lay back, eyes half shut, not moving, hypnotized by the long white way before him and the humming movement. Hours were nothing to him now.

It was hunger, finally, that woke him to reality again, but still he didn't go up outside. He began a series of belt-changings, branching off at random but staying on the fast lanes. His stomach growled and he knew that even leaving the belts was no insurance of a meal. He would have to hunt and sneak and hide from overseers or wild dogs. But if this was to be forever, a change for keeps, it had to be far and devious, and so he stayed.

Much later he took the slower lanes to the slowest and then to a rising ramp.

He came out on a wide-walled footwalk. The summer sun was low and red, and Baby stood, watching it. He could almost see it move past the tree tops. He whispered nothing, but he felt the feeling he used to feel when he said Please and it was important, the same feeling when Rob 6 asked Central and Central used to answer and was always right.

He stared at the sun, thinking, this will be the place, Sun. Here I will be me and robots will not tell me what to do and I won't belong to any house or any overseer.

He walked across the grassy tree-lined footwalk to the smooth grey wall. It was half again as tall as he was and had not the slightest hand hold. Baby bent his knees low, jumped from a stand, and grasped the top with both hands. He swung his left foot up, curled the toes over the top and then pulled himself up. Resting on elbows and one knee, he looked down into the garden, a richer, larger garden than he had ever seen before. He felt an exhilarating excitement for this looked really new and different.

He rolled gently over the wall and landed on hands and knees in the grass. He stood up and walked boldly down the neatly kept path that led away from the wall. He didn't hide or watch for overseers. Whatever would happen, he felt, would be different here in this different place, and he went eagerly forward to meet whatever would come.

He passed rows of thick hedges, then a group of tall, pungent-smelling pine trees. He rounded a bank of white-flowered bushes and there, before him, surrounded by cut hedges like the walls of a room, was a fountain and a statue.

The pool was edged with natural-looking rocks and on the largest rock in the centre was a figure of stone about his own size.

Baby laughed out loud, then splashed through the clear cold water and climbed up the slippery rock to stand just below the figure. He had seen others, oddly shaped like this, in parks and downtown sections sometimes: the rounded body, looking strangely lumpy top and bottom, with a thin waist in the centre. He knew the names that went with this shape were woman, girl and lady.

This figure held the head of a serpent. The long snake body crossed the waist just under one of the pointed chest-lumps. The snake's mouth was wide, and inside there was the tiny pipe where the water of the fountain came flowing.

Baby stooped and drank from the serpent's mouth, and then looked up and it seemed as if the statue's bent head and half-closed eyes looked at him with a steady gaze, and there was something there that was not like a robot. Something that made him sad.

He reached up and ran his fingers down the soft curve of the cheek, so soft-looking but so hard to the touch. He touched the nose and then his own nose. This is a little baby too, he thought, smaller than I am. He went round to the back. He laughed because the hair hung down so far from the head. He ran his hand from under the arm, inward to the waist and down over the hips and he laughed again because his own shape was right and this shape was a joke.

Then he remembered how hot it was and how cool the water below felt on his legs. It was a shallow pool. The water came only just above his knees, but he climbed down and lay full length in it, splashing and blowing and putting his head in all the way.

He sat up, wiping the water from his face with the palms of his hands, and there, in the path before him, it seemed as if the statue had come to life, coloured a rosy tan. It was all there, but different from the stone: damply curling tan-brown hair, the darker etched eyebrows, tan-brown eyes, lips lightly red and also the tips of the two round shapes at the chest.

Soft, it was, but it stood like the statue, and he, half rising on one knee, stood like a statue too. He stared a long time, not moving, afraid almost to breathe even, and the other stared back. Then he stood up slowly, so slowly, as if a strange mad dog or wild cat was before him. The only sound was the water dripping from his body, but that lasted only a few moments and again they stood and stared. Then Baby moved

again, stepping slowly forward this time. He was not afraid.
This creature was smaller than he was and looked so vulner-
able.

The creature took a step back then, and Baby took a faster
step forward. Then the thing turned and ran, but Baby
caught it easily in two leaps and they fell together, one warm
soft body against another. This contact shocked them. They
drew apart quickly, stilled again like statues, and they stared
silently. Then slowly Baby touched a finger to the creature's
chest. The wonder of the feel made him draw his hand away
again, but slowly this time. 'Soft,' he said in a whisper,
'soft and warm,' and then he touched his own chest. 'I
too.'

The other stared silently a moment and then asked suddenly, also in a whisper, 'Are you . . . human?'

Baby grasped the creature's upper arm then, shaking it
boldly but lightly back and forth. 'You feel good,' he said.
'Strange, but good.'

'I'm human,' it said then.

'So am I. I'm Baby.'

'I'm Honey.'

'I came to find a new thing and I found you.'

'They all say there are no humans left.'

'Rob 6 and Nursie are wrong and so are all the others, and
now there's you. I'm glad I ran away from them and came
here. Why is your hair so long?'

'It just is.'

'And you're shaped all wrong.'

'It's you that's wrong. This is the way I am. Like the
statue is the way to be and that's my way.'

'I know. You're woman. You look funny, but you feel
nice.' He cupped the other's chin in his palm. He ran his
fingers over the lips and then down across the neck and
lower even, to the pink, soft tip of the round shape at the
chest. She drew away. 'You tickle,' she said.

'I like human beings,' Baby said, 'better than Nursie or

Rob 6 or dogs and cats. I didn't think I would, but I do.'
'I think I do too.'

They both stiffened at the sound of a distant voice. 'Honey, Honey. Where are you? It's almost time for bed.'

They stared at each other but they didn't move to go.

The Nursie came nearer. Baby could hear the wheeze and scratch. When she rounded the corner, finally, she looked exactly like his own Nursie, but he could tell, absolutely, it wasn't Nurse 16.

She reached quickly and drew Honey away from him. 'What are you doing here?' she asked. 'This is private property.'

Without thinking, Baby gave the information he always gave, the way Nursie had taught him. 'I'm Baby number 2, family PR 1-54-238, overseer Rob 1026. I live in Forest Knolls, and I came here and found this human being.'

'How did you get in?'

'I climbed the wall.'

'Those wall guards, they just don't work any more.' She stood motionless and Baby knew she was calling some other rob. He looked at the human being again, fascinated with the curiously shaped body, drawn by its softness and vulnerability, and he waited, staring at it, and it stared too, back at him. He could see its eyes move, tracing the contours of his body. In a few minutes the overseer came.

'Trespasser,' the Nursie said. 'Male too. I do hope nothing happened. 2, PR 1-54-238, 0-1026. And we must do something about the wall guards. Poor Honey must be protected from this sort of thing.'

The robot made a quick examination. 'Nothing happened,' he said. 'There's been no trespasser for eighteen years and four months now.' He took Baby firmly, rounding each wrist with an all-purpose pincer hand and led him away.

Baby went quietly, too dazed to think. He kept his head turned back, watching the creature called Honey until they rounded a corner.

The robot took him to a rambling house, all glass and vines and stone. The wall lifted on a small corner room. The overseer pushed Baby in and the wall came down again. There was a white marble table, and large plants growing beside it from a dirt section in the floor, and there were three long low green lounge chairs. Baby lay back in one. He was filled with silent wonder. Eyes wide, he watched the twilight fade outside, lights come on in other parts of the house, and curtains close.

Later the overseer brought cold unsour milk and a plate with the meat cooked just right. Baby ate and drank squatting on the floor beside the low table, spilling gravy across it as he lifted the meat in his hands. It was the best meal he'd had in a long time, but now he didn't notice the taste or care about it.

After he ate he walked about the room like a caged animal. The lights went out in the other parts of the house. Baby pounded his fists against the glass walls and gave a shout, but the walls of the little room held the sound in tight, he knew, and he gave only one call.

He stood, nose against the glass, and after a while, in the dark, the creature came and the wall lifted for it and slid shut after it.

Baby's impatience left the moment it came in.

He touched its hand, but he did not speak and neither did the creature. Softness, warmth . . . there was something here that was the answer to everything.

What was the answer?

He pulled at the creature roughly then, and it sucked in its breath and pulled away, and he let go. What *was* the answer? It was tantalizing, close, and yet . . .

He touched the creature's hair gently, and it didn't move away this time. He felt full of gentleness and of violence too, and he held himself tight, tensing his muscles against themselves.

They sat down together on the edge of one of the lounge

chairs. They touched each other and they watched each other smile in the dim light of the rising half moon.

The answer was close . . . closer . . . and yet so far. Not to know and to be so close was worse than the howling and the running in moonlit streets. Much worse.

He grabbed the other, shaking it, squeezing the answer out with all his violent pent-up strength. Answer! But it only cried out in pain and then made a sobbing sound. And when he loosed his grip a bit because of the sounds it made, it pulled away and the panel was open and shut again before he realized it and the creature was gone.

When Rob 6 came in the early morning to take the lost boy home, the marble table was broken, the plants were trampled. The foam from inside the three lounges was strewn about the room. Baby had a scratch across his cheek, black-and-blue marks on his legs, and bloody knuckles, but he went quietly, wrist cuffed in Rob 6's two metal fingers.

At home Nursie bathed him and put him in his room. 'I wish you would try to be good,' she said. 'I wish you would just try.'

He slept heavily for a short while, then climbed out of the window and took the same sub-belt.

He tried to remember the time it took, and the changes. Once he came out at an edge of the great city where the towers of the barrier wall stretched giant pointing fingers that sent invisible currents arcing across the city to protect it from an enemy that never came any more.

At night he took the belt that led home to Forest Knolls. His eyes were slits now, his mouth a firm line. There would be no more fits of running in the empty streets, or wild howling, or climbing. Instead, this crease between the eyes.

He searched the next day, and the next, and the next . . .

The important thing, the answer to everything, was somewhere there in the vast, decaying city, an answer to the robots and to the decay, to the city and to the world and most of all to him, but it was . . . *lost.*